RELIGION, CULTURE AND POLITICS IN
THE TWENTIETH-CENTURY UNITED STATES

Columbia Series in Religion and Politics

Edited by Gaston Espinosa and Chester Gillis, this series will explore major debates and conflicts involving religion and politics in both American and transnational contexts.

Religion, Culture and Politics in the Twentieth-Century United States

MARK HULSETHER

COLUMBIA UNIVERSITY PRESS   NEW YORK

Dedicated to my students in American religion.
May you choose wisely which traditions to leave behind,
and which to hold onto and improve.

Columbia University Press
Publishers Since 1893
New York

Copyright © 2007 Mark Hulsether

First published in the United Kingdom by Edinburgh University Press

Library of Congress Cataloging-in-Publication Data
A complete CIP record is available from the Library of Congress

ISBN 978-0-231-14402-5 (cloth : alk. paper)
ISBN 978-0-231-14403-2 (pbk. : alk. paper)

∞

c 10 9 8 7 6 5 4 3 2 1
p 10 9 8 7 6 5 4 3 2 1

Contents

Introduction

On issues from A to Z, abortion to Zionism, it is impossible to understand the full contours of US political culture without attention to religion. Therefore, this book is not solely for people with a personal commitment to a religious or spiritual practice; it is for anyone who wants to understand where culture and politics in the US has been and where it is going. Our goal is an overview of the interplay among religious practices and identities, sociopolitical competition and conflict, and wider dynamics in US culture.

Two things make this study distinctive compared with other books covering similar ground. First, it is especially concise. Several excellent books are available that survey the territory of US religion in the context of US history, society, and culture.[1] However, whereas we might imagine many of these texts as fairly comprehensive atlases – thus cumbersome for some purposes – this book is more like an orientation map and a guide to a set of representative cases. It is ruthless in paring down the boundless sets of names and dates that might claim a place in a comprehensive survey. Its goal is an uncluttered introduction that can be used in conjunction with other books. Some readers may use it in courses on US religion to contextualize and weave together finer grained studies of specific issues. Others may use it to bring religious issues into dialogue with other explorations in US cultural history.

Secondly, this book focuses its argument and selects its examples in a distinctive way – to relate religion to issues of cultural recognition and sociopolitical power that are particular concerns in the fields of American Studies and cultural studies. We will not neglect theology, denominational histories, secularization, devotional practices, or other matters that are commonly stressed in books on US religion. However, compared with other books, we will give less attention to dialogues with theology and religious studies, and more attention to multiculturalism and cultural hegemony. Each of these points deserves more reflection.

I

Mapping US Religion

Let us begin with the matter of brevity, and consider its implications for how readers should approach this book. When I teach on US religion, I compare our syllabus to the itinerary of a trip. Imagine travelers who have only one week to travel from New York to Seattle. What maps do they need? They might start with a general orientation. Where are New York and Seattle? Are they logical beginning and ending points? Where do the travelers currently stand in relation to these cities? What are the key landmarks between them – and insofar as people disagree about this question, what are the disputed issues?

Once we have clarified such matters the problem shifts to choosing a route. Many students enter my classes like travelers who want to tour as comprehensively as possible. They want to taste a little bit of everything. Unfortunately, the more diligently a traveler tries to be comprehensive, the more possibilities come into view. Suppose we settle on a route that passes through all fifty states plus Quebec and Mexico City. Consider how severely this would limit the time we could spend in any one place. We might have to hire a jet and fly over the route to complete such an itinerary – and how much could we learn about any one place that way? Think for a moment about a place you know well: its component parts; its sounds and smells at different times of the year; its associations with past events. Could a traveler 'cover' the task of understanding this place by driving through and checking off its name in a logbook?

Travelers should abandon the unattainable goal of comprehensive coverage, and adopt a motto that we will use for this book – striving for maximum breadth without shallowness and maximum depth of engagement without narrowness. Each person may have a different sense of what is too shallow or too narrow. Nevertheless, we can agree to seek a route through some representative cities and landmarks. We can pause to explore them, briefly to be sure, but with more attention than a flyover allows. As we pass through various places, we can shift from an orientation map to a concise guidebook. Although maps and guidebooks supply limited information, they enable informed decisions about where to stop. Importantly, they might keep us from losing the forest for the trees while traveling through a large territory. Such are the modest yet significant goals of this book.

To understand religion adequately we must eventually move to a level of mapping that is more like living in a place for an extended period than passing briefly through. The term 'religion' can mean so many things that generalizing about it is difficult. However, one thing is safe to say. Much of what constitutes a religious group – what religion *is* for this group – is its debate about what its central practices should be today, and what they should become in the future. How should the group express its core teachings? Which behaviors command its time and energy, and which are taboo? What are its values and how do these relate to everyday events and emergent controversies? Who can speak as an authority? How is this decided?

The beating heart of any religion is its process of working out such understandings, whether in overt and self-conscious ways or informally and implicitly. We cannot feel this heartbeat through memorizing cut-and-dried propositions like 'religion X believes in doctrine Y.' In fact, the complexity and fluidity of lived religion is hard to grasp without exploring several religious groups in depth, with attention to many levels of experience inside each group, interactions with outsiders, and changes over time. People who have experienced only one kind of religion are often amazed by the differences they discover through such explorations. Likewise, people who have little personal experience with any form of religion, but who have the impression that religions are monolithic blocks of tradition, are often surprised by the complexity they encounter. All large religious traditions include internal conflicts, multiple levels of experience, and subtleties such as declared principles that contradict actual behaviors, conflicting interpretations of the 'same' ideas, and rituals that carry powerful resonance for the group but are invisible to outsiders.

It is hard to dramatize such complex textures in a short book, and our challenge increases insofar as our stress on complexity goes against the grain of much academic writing. Many scholars assume that religions are cut-and-dried cultural forms – largely unchanging (or at least conservative), probably irrational, and weakened by 'secularization' in some sense of this slippery word. (For some scholars secularization means that religions are disappearing entirely; to others it means only that religions are separate from the state but otherwise thriving; and to others it means that religions are limited to a private intrapersonal sphere.[2]) Admittedly, such scholarly assumptions do match some religions we will meet on our trip. It is true that many religious people are conservative and that church and state are largely separate. Yet in many cases these assumptions are misleading – especially the ideas that religions are disappearing, unchanging, or always conservative and privatized. We must proceed case by case, starting from a premise that religions are internally complex and entangled with wider sociopolitical issues.

The assumption that religion is irrational must also be tested case by case. True, some religions make claims that are not backed by evidence that a secularist would accept; for example, many fundamentalists base their teachings about the origins of the world on a literal reading of Genesis. However, many self-professed religious people, especially from liberal traditions, interpret their religious practices and build their arguments (whether about science or other issues) using the same analytical categories and standards of evidence as secularists. Even in cases where religious claims contradict secular ones, religious people may try to persuade secularists that their beliefs – their forms of 'cultural difference' to invoke the academic buzzword – deserve as much respect as differences based on race, ethnicity, or sexuality. This does not deny that, as we move from case to case, we may encounter religious ideas that are unpersuasive or downright dangerous. The point is that we cannot make blanket judgments about this matter before concrete investigations.

Although we do not have the space to explore even one religious group in depth, we can prepare for such exploration by introducing a range of interesting groups and modeling ways to frame questions about them. In this sense, the book is a sort of reconnaissance map for travelers who may later return to a few sites that spark their interest after getting the lay of the land.

So far we have talked as if there is only one *kind* of map of religions. If so, the main question for planning our route would be how much time to spend zooming in and out of particular sections. However, travelers can choose from many *types* of maps: road maps, topographic maps, maps of roadside attractions or regional music scenes, and so on. One type might ignore roads and focus on geological features that cut across national boundaries. Another might chart historical change to dramatize how today's roads and cities emerged.

Just as travelers expect 'normal' maps to focus on roads, some readers may expect this book to chart denominations like Baptists and Catholics, categorized according to their doctrines. No doubt this is important. However, we also need to map patterns that cut across denominational lines, such as interactions of religion and media, stances toward secularization, and distinctions based on race, gender, and generation. We must chart not only leaders (priests, imams, rabbis, etc.) but also ordinary people who do not always take their cues from such leaders. Often the most important aspect of a religious group is not its doctrine, but a practice such as meditation, hymn singing, sweat-lodge ceremonies, potluck suppers, casting spells, fasting, or volunteering in soup kitchens.[3] And before we can determine which of a group's activities are the most important ones to treat in our guidebook, we may need to think carefully about how to identify the group in the first place. Consider that a doctrinal dispute might lead two nearly identical Baptist churches to condemn each other to hell. Are these two groups or one? These same Baptists may join with Mormons and Muslims in a religious-political cause. Are they one group or three? What groups deserve attention on a one-week trip? We must juggle maps that dramatize many such issues. All these maps are accurate, but which are the most useful? This depends on the questions we want to answer.

Let us consider the strengths and limitations of three maps that are especially useful for gaining an overview of the landscape our trip will cover. First, imagine a geographic map created by assigning a color to each major denomination – blue for Baptists, red for Catholics, and so on – and color-coding every county in the nation to show the largest denomination in that county.[4] With this map one can see at a glance that the Southeast is a Bible Belt of Baptist blue, the region around Utah is gray for Mormons, the Southwest is red due to Latino/a Catholics, and the upper Midwest is home to a green group – Lutherans of German and Scandinavian ancestry. We might also notice more subtle things. Why is there so much red in New England, the land of the Puritans? This reflects Catholic immigration since the nineteenth century. In fact, if we search for a Protestant establishment on this map – measured by the descendants of the former Puritan and Anglican establishments, the Episcopal Church and the United Church of Christ – we will be hard-pressed to see it anywhere. Perhaps if the map were based on the religious make-up of elite country clubs, the story would be different!

Although this map is an excellent place to start, it has limits. Not only does it render Episcopalians invisible, it does the same to many others, from Muslims and Hindus who now outnumber Episcopalians, through dozens of Christian groups, to a huge range of groups such as Jews, neo-pagans, Native Americans, and secularists. To learn about the mix of groups, we need a pie chart that can show more than one religion in any given place. A rough and ready version for the US as a whole is easy to visualize because it starts with a fifty per cent slice for white Protestants and twenty-five per cent slice for Catholics. The remaining twenty-five per cent is divided more or less evenly among African American Protestants, secularists, and a catchall category for all other groups.

The size of the secularist slice is a matter of contention, because it waxes and wanes depending on how we measure 'religiousness.' Where should we set a threshold where religiosity gives way to secularity? The above numbers are based on self-reports to pollsters. Such polls consistently show religious commitment high enough to surprise people from more secularized countries such as Britain and France: ninety per cent report belief in God or a higher power and forty per cent claim regular attendance at church (or mosque, synagogue, etc.).[5] But how much commitment do such numbers reflect? More than eighty per cent tell pollsters that they consider the Bible divinely inspired – thirty-three per cent claim it is literally true – but less than half can name even one of the four gospels, its central chapters about Jesus. Given that fundamentalists even attack bishops of large Christian denominations as 'secular humanists,' how should we categorize someone who tells a pollster she is Catholic but has not attended church in the last ten years?

Depending on our approach to such questions, we might bump the secularist slice into the fifteen to twenty-five per cent range and shave a few percentage points from other slices. And this is only the beginning of complexities that make it fruitless to press for high precision in such charts. Should we classify Mormons in the Christian category (as they insist) or as a separate religion (as many Christians prefer)? Where do we place people who practice both Catholicism and Afro-Cuban Santería? Should we count agnostics with Jewish parents as Jewish or secular? In any case, however we slice the pie, the overall picture it shows is clear: high levels of religious affiliation, strong Christian majorities, and a wide range of other groups throughout the country.

Suppose, however, that we want to explore disagreements about sex among Catholics who appear lumped together in the same slice of a pie chart. Suppose we hope to compare their patterns of disagreement to those among Mormons – a solid gray region in the geographic map – and the leading Protestant groups. Such a problem becomes increasingly complex as we draw a pie chart in greater detail. So far we have only noted that white Protestants represent fifty per cent of the pie and mentioned four denominations: Baptists, Lutherans, Episcopalians, and the United Church of Christ. We have not yet mentioned two of the largest Protestant groups, Methodists and Pentecostals, nor dozens of smaller ones – not to mention hundreds of subdivisions and name changes caused by mergers and schisms. We could easily slice a denominational pie chart into mind-numbing detail, with diminishing returns setting in rapidly because so many slices have family resemblances. One solution is to sort Protestants into three clusters: two slices of fifteen to twenty per cent each for fundamentalist and moderate denominations, and a ten to fifteen per cent slice for liberal ones. However, when issues cut across denominational lines – as do conflicts about sex – even such simple lines get in the way.

In earlier years the lines between denominations represented sharper differences than they do today. This was especially true when they coincided with lines of class, ethnicity, or language along with religion – for example, when Italian Catholics or German Lutherans lived in self-contained immigrant communities. For a time Mormons even tried to build their own autonomous state! Today, conservatives from large denominations like the Methodists or Catholics often feel that they have more in common with each other, across denominational lines, than they do with liberals in their own denominations. Whereas liberal Methodist parents before the 1960s might have strenuously opposed their child marrying a Catholic, today they might be relieved if their child marries a liberal Catholic rather than a fundamentalist Methodist.

A culture war map helps us visualize such changes. Imagine a continuum stretching from extreme religious-political liberals on the left to extreme conservatives on the right. Then take each slice from our pie chart and redraw it as a horizontal bar that ranges along this continuum. Charted this way, most denominations encompass a wide internal spectrum, although in some cases such as the Southern Baptists the bar stretches from center-left to far right, while in others like the United Church of Christ it stretches from center-right to far left. Most large denominations range across the entire spectrum. Moreover, polarization along the spectrum has increased. A culture war map highlights people who cluster near the ends of this spectrum – for example, conservative Methodists, Catholics, and Jews – and dramatizes why they may get along better with each other than with people in the liberal wing of their own traditions.[6]

Although this map is useful for understanding religious changes, it too has limitations. It takes attention away from centrists who resist being drafted into a war between liberals and conservatives. It can also distort our thinking about conflicts over race and sex, even though sex is a hot button issue on the culture war spectrum. This map encourages us to think about one coalition of liberals (including both males and females, blacks and whites) battling one coalition of conservatives (also of mixed races and genders). Many battles in real life are not structured this way. At times we may need a map that focuses our attention on what most women (whether conservative or liberal) have in common compared with men or what most blacks have in common compared with whites. African-American religion seems somewhat 'homeless' on this map because black Christians and Muslims are frequently liberal on issues of race and class but conservative on issues of doctrine and sexuality. Thus, these three maps by no means exhaust our options; they simply begin to orient us.

Because the trip we are about to begin covers so much territory in a short time, we will need to shift among different views of the landscape. As you read, try to discern which maps are most helpful for addressing the questions you bring to the trip. This book is not designed as a unitary 'master map' to use without such flexibility and discernment. True, it is a guidebook for a brief tour, but it also seeks to prepare readers for deeper explorations during return trips to places we will visit. It is an invitation to critical thinking about multiple ways to interpret the landscape, more than it is like a paint-by-number kit for reproducing one recommended view.

Thus, it is an orientation not only in the sense of a selective overview, but also because it encourages readers to get oriented – to step back and compare views of the landscape, in order to discern the best tools for addressing their priority concerns.

Religion in American Studies and Cultural Studies

Recall that our goal is not simply to pare down our subject for an uncluttered orientation, with the implications we have been discussing. We will also use this selectivity to underline a specific point: how religion is part of struggles for cultural hegemony that are at the center of discussions in American Studies and cultural studies.

American Studies is a scholarly field that studies North America (typically the US in particular) in an interdisciplinary way. When this field crystallized during the 1940s, it largely blended studies of history and literature, and its scholars often discussed which aspects of US national culture (considered as a totality) were distinctive compared with Europe. Over time, the field became cautious about making sweeping generalizations about US identity; rather it highlighted differences within the US such as racial conflict and/or issues that cut across national borders such as empire. Scholars scaled back their contrasts between the US and Europe and beefed up their comparisons between colonial or neo-colonial powers on one side (including both the US and Europe) versus their former colonies on the other. During this process, the field's interdisciplinary mix added more scholars from beyond literature and history, such as ethnographers, sociologists, and specialists in ethnic and gender studies.[7]

Cultural studies – that is, the movement that goes by this name, as opposed to all scholars who study any kind of culture – is harder to pin down because it is even more interdisciplinary than American Studies, and because a mind-boggling range of topics falls under the rubric of culture. Although there is no clear line dividing cultural studies from other fields, the field does have certain distinctive preoccupations. Like American Studies it bridges disciplines, with strong input from sociology, literature, and media studies. Broadly speaking, what the field studies is how culture as symbolic communication relates to the exercise of power. Its scholars not only analyze classic texts such as Shakespeare's plays; they also explore popular music, television, and everyday practices like sports and shopping. How do such topics relate to power? Does film X dovetail with the dominance of some group? Can activity Y change the dynamics of power? The idea is not that culture always mirrors dominant power relations; rather scholars assume that specific cultural texts and practices have multiple layers of meaning and are part of a larger jockeying for power.[8]

We can trace the origins of cultural studies to post-World War II British scholars such as Raymond Williams, E. P. Thompson, and Stuart Hall. Questions they asked about Britain – how everyday experiences of working people related both to 'high culture' and to trends like industrialization and the rise of mass media – also proved relevant to other societies. For example, one can start from Thompson's analysis of how Methodism influenced British working-class politics, and extend similar questions to US Methodists. One can compare Hall's analysis of Thatcherism in Britain to a study of Reaganism in the US. Through such explorations, a network of scholars identified with cultural studies spread around the world. Each branch of the network borrows from and/or rebels against the British founders in distinctive ways. For our purposes, the key point is that the US branch converged with American Studies.

Because scholars in the overlapping fields of American Studies and cultural studies analyze a huge range of issues from many disciplinary angles, it is hard to bring different parts of these fields into dialogue. What can a sociologist who studies French body art say to a scholar of Emily Dickinson poems? However, both fields often use the concept of cultural hegemony – a term which roughly refers to dominant patterns of behavior considered 'normal' – in a way that allows them to connect their far-flung interests. If we can analyze both a French tattoo and a Dickinson poem in relation to hegemony, we have a vocabulary to discuss whether these cultural expressions have anything to say to each other. It may turn out that they do not. But suppose that we can interpret both the tattoo and the poem as responses to dominant (hegemonic) assumptions about 'normal' feminine behavior. Perhaps we are talking about a Wiccan tattoo on a US college woman. Perhaps she obtained it while studying in Paris to rebel against her Baptist mother who sees Dickinson as a role model. Exploring this case might be fascinating. A shared language of hegemony enables us to bring these women into dialogue and to weave together insights about them from sociology and literary studies.

Since hegemony is a key category for this book, let us consider it more carefully.[9] Even though 'hegemonic' is a longish word for 'normal,' it helps us to remember that what counts for normal should not be taken for granted. Hegemony refers to a situation in which a pattern of thought or behavior (a hegemonic pattern) is taken for granted as common sense, and this works to the power advantage of one group (the hegemonic one) and the disadvantage of others. Consider what would happen if a college student tried to assign a book report to her room-mate. But it seems normal for teachers to assign reports; this reflects their hegemony in the classroom. Underdogs (whether they are students, ethnic minorities, poor people, etc.) have little hope of changing hegemonic patterns – patterns they may not even think about – unless they become aware of them, critique them, and develop alternatives. To be sure, counter-hegemonic alternatives in the realm of culture cannot create social change by themselves. Raw coercion might block such efforts; for example, the military could crush a counter-hegemonic movement that enjoys wide support. Nevertheless, cultural hegemony remains a major form of power. Building it is essential for anyone who seeks to lead through consent rather than coercion, and the ability to critique it is essential for anyone who seeks change.

We must beware of two pitfalls when using hegemony analysis. One is that some writers use terms like 'military hegemony' to describe raw force, whereas we will use the word 'hegemony' as shorthand for cultural hegemony, that is, for the exercise of power through consent without coercion. Another pitfall is the temptation to look for a monolithic structure called 'the hegemony.' True, there may be a common sense in a sports club that the coach makes the rules, an expectation in a classroom that the teacher sets the agenda, and an assumption in a fundamentalist church that families need husbands as heads over wives. Thus, a coach/teacher/husband would clearly enjoy hegemony over a player/student/wife. However, teachers may be wives, coaches may be students, and so on. Whereas classic forms of hegemony theory sometimes focused on only one kind of power (based on economic class), we will treat many kinds of power and identity – including class, race, gender, sexuality, and, of course, religion – as multiple forms of hegemony existing in complex layers. Although these layers be mutually reinforcing, most people are neither straight white male millionaires nor homeless Haitian lesbians. They fall between such extremes.

This means that we must clarify what forms of hegemony are most significant on a case-by-case basis. Imagine a rich executive who feels like an underdog because he is left-handed and shy in a world where right-handed extroverted people are hegemonic. When he competes head-to-head with extroverted right-handed executives, it might make sense for him to feel disadvantaged, but in other contexts this reflects a lack of perspective. He is taking his privilege for granted as 'normal' and exaggerating the drawbacks of being shy. This hypothetical executive helps us think about real cases in which religious conservatives feel like underdogs oppressed by secularists – even as they stand within the historical momentum of Protestant hegemony, are allies of Republicans who control the government, and promote the interests of rich white men. Granted, some claims to underdog status based on conservative religion make more sense than claims based on left-handedness. Nevertheless, we will meet religious people who, like our left-handed executive, take their privilege for granted and exaggerate their grievances.

Building hegemony is a matter of everyday persuasion and coalition building. Since it is based on underdogs internalizing 'normal' assumptions rather than bowing to coercion, successful elites must persuade underdogs that they are addressing their concerns. Such arguments may be convincing, since not all forms of hegemony are bad. For example, I try to persuade my students that my leadership is in their interest. However, someone is sure to note that my judgment about this matter is suspect since I am the teacher. This is precisely the sort of question that hegemony analysis promotes; effective teachers must either be able to answer such questions or prevent them from arising in the first place.

If classrooms need teachers, do families need male heads over wives? In an attempt to make such a case, conservatives might appeal to real concerns of women. They might stress the fragility of families: high rates of divorce and abuse; job insecurity and overwork; and economic trends that undermine communities. Yet such arguments may or may not persuade women that the best way to address such concerns is to increase male power and define the 'traditional family' (that is, the modern patriarchal nuclear family) in a way that excludes other kinds of families. Shifting to another form of hegemony, must our economy 'normally' be structured as it is? Must decisions about what is produced and how it is divided be decided by people with money, on the principle that they should invest it wherever they can make the most additional money − irrespective of whether this meets human needs or destroys the environment? Do the rich deserve to be rich? If you are poor is it probably your own fault? Once again the issue hinges on persuasion. Hegemony analysis is not about critique abstracted from cases; it is about developing a habit of asking under what conditions underdogs should accept dominant forms of common sense, and when they should redefine common sense. The concept of hegemony will help us focus on how religions interact with such questions.

One goal of this book is to contribute to a higher profile for religion in American Studies and cultural studies. Although specialists on religion have long been part of American Studies, religion deserves greater attention in the field, especially among scholars who study recent years. Despite many exceptions to this rule, the field often treats religion as a marginal factor that appears − if at all − near the end of lists beginning with race, class, gender, and empire. Cultural studies is even less likely to focus on religion. By using the concept of hegemony, we can move the study of religion closer to central conversations in these fields. Recall how analyzing a Wiccan tattoo and a Dickinson poem in terms of hegemony helped us to bring these issues into dialogue. The same principle extends to religious topics. Suppose that the mother of our tattooed Wiccan reads evangelical self-help books; we could add an expert on such books to our conversation. We could extend this analysis in many directions, for example, relating the case to scholarship about Muslim women's dress or the portrayal of witches on television.

One reason for scholars' lukewarm interest in religion is their tendency to assume that religion is normally an obstacle to counter-hegemonic struggle. According to this stereotype, religion is a static form of conservative hegemony rooted in the past. Of course, many religions do take such forms; for example, they may teach that conservative tradition must be maintained indefinitely because it reflects the eternal will of God. However, literature, law, and music can also take conservative forms, presenting themselves as normative traditions expressing timeless truths. This does not lead cultural studies to give up on the idea of counter-hegemonic art or better laws! Just as some forms of literature and law are innovative and counter-hegemonic, the same is true of religion. Decisions about what religions do today and should do tomorrow – whether in the realm of thought, ritual, or activism – are part of wider struggles to build and contest hegemony. This book assumes that religious sub-cultures are not special cases (read: conservative and irrational by definition) but require the same nuanced and multilayered study that scholars would use for any other cultural practice.

To advocate a higher profile for religion in American cultural studies is not to say that religion is always the most important factor. In certain contexts it is marginal to politics; some media discourses are oblivious to it. However, even in such cases, interesting questions arise. Why do so many citizens practice religion even under such conditions? Why does a sharp distinction between privatized religion and other parts of life seem like common sense – and since we have defined hegemony as a form of common sense that normalizes a power imbalance, who benefits from this common sense? What cultural work does religion accomplish from case to case? By exploring such questions, this book seeks to improve the quality of discussion about religion in cultural studies and American Studies.

Strategies for Dealing with Religious Diversity

We have discussed our two main goals – a brief orientation to US religion, integrated into conversations in American Studies – but one more preliminary matter remains to clarify. What do we mean by the term 'religion' in the phrase 'mapping US religion'? When we search for it, what are we looking for exactly? How can we tell if someone is not religious enough to belong in our itinerary? The answers are not always clear. Consider that people perform rituals of devotion for Elvis Presley and UFOs, sometimes ironically but sometimes with impressive zeal.

They speak of playing sports religiously. Cold War propaganda claimed that Communism was a secular religion, albeit 'godless.' Fundamentalists assert both that secularists practice a 'religion of humanism' and that members of liberal churches are not truly religious.

Suppose we agree not to consider anyone to be religious – at least for this book – unless they belong to an established institution that interacts with some god, mysterious presence, or higher power. This might help us focus. However, many New Agers lack institutional commitments yet have deep spiritual interests. Classic forms of Buddhism are atheistic. Some liberal Christians disavow belief in traditional theism; they may not believe in a God 'out there' although they teach in seminaries. We cannot work from a definition of religion that excludes all these people. However, if we include the above people – Buddhists, New Agers, humanists, Elvis devotees, and Red Sox fans – where do we stop? Should we follow the advice of certain scholars in religious studies who, in an effort to find an impartial definition, suggest that anything that is deeply valued or centers a person's worldview should be understood as a religion, even if this is something like consumerism? This has advantages, but if we define religion so broadly, is there anything that is *not* religious? Is anything more religious than anything else? Also, if someone attends a Baptist church but doesn't value the experience deeply, would this definition require us to say that attending church was not an experience with religion?[10]

In the light of such questions, it is not easy to decide what to cover in this book. Scholars have a tradition for keeping such problems under control: centering narratives on major Protestant churches while exploring how these churches interact with 'outsiders.' Scholars even have a tradition of poking fun at this procedure by quoting Parson Thwackum from the novel, *Tom Jones*: 'When I mention religion, I mean the Christian religion; and not only the Christian religion but the Protestant religion, and not only the Protestant religion but the Church of England.'[11] The point is not to go to Thwackum's extreme – they use him as a cautionary example – but to solve the problem of being paralyzed by religious diversity by centering the narrative on traditionally dominant groups. One might do this more subtly than Thwackum and less grudgingly than conservatives who see only a few true religions amid an endless supply of heresies and idolatries. That is, one might give respect to 'alternative religions' (extending to UFO devotees), 'semi-religious' practices (extending to consumerism), and so on. The point is to use the leading self-described religious institutions as the center of gravity in an overall narrative and as a baseline for selecting and analyzing outsiders. William Hutchison's book, *Religious Pluralism in America*, is a sophisticated version of this approach.[12] He comments that some scholars are so intent on mapping the diversity of Wiccans, Elvis worshippers, and the rest that they remind him of people who survey US politics without attending to Democrats and Republicans. In contrast, he centers his narrative on the Protestant establishment – denominations like the Methodists, Presbyterians, and Baptists – and its response to Catholic and Jewish immigration. In Hutchison's model, Protestant insiders began from a baseline of hegemony in the early 1800s, but had to adjust to a series of shocks to this system. He posits a time lag between first confronting diversity, then moving through three stages of response to it. In the first stage, pluralism simply meant tolerating alternatives to the status quo without legal persecution. In the second, grudging toleration changed to active inclusion or assimilation; people spoke of the US as a melting pot. Eventually a third stage emerged – pluralism as full participation in society without any sense of being a second-class citizen. At each stage Hutchison is aware of limits to pluralism. For example, Native Americans and Mormons did not enjoy toleration during his first stage, and full participation for gays and lesbians remains controversial today. Nevertheless, as long as we are alert to such limits, Hutchison offers a framework for thinking about many forms of religious diversity – both long-standing forms and recent flowerings – in the context of a core narrative that charts the interplay between outsider groups and a hegemonic center.

Recent scholars have stressed the limits of such models and moved toward a more open-ended pluralistic model that expands the range of issues to consider.[13] They began by shifting emphasis from Protestants to a triple establishment of Protestants, Catholics, and Jews. Then they went on to showcase the interplay of Buddhists, Muslims, Santeros, spiritualists, and dozens of others. In the process they greatly expanded the themes, regions, and religious forms analyzed in scholarly maps, for example, by shifting attention from Puritan theologians to popular healing rituals in New Mexico. Fewer scholars write synthetic books as opposed to targeted studies that treat groups like Hasidic Jews or Ghost Dancers in their own terms. Such explorations are essential. Yet are they sufficient? Can we map US religion without periodization schemes and patterns of organization stronger than giving equal attention to all comers? Does an aspiration to map religious diversity fully bring us back, full circle, to the impossible goal of touring every state plus Canada and Mexico in a week? Charles Lippy's overview of twentieth-century religion dramatizes these questions.[14] According to Lippy, at the dawn of the twentieth century it was still possible to presuppose Protestant hegemony, but by the end of the century this was no longer true. Lippy is aware that pluralism was already significant in 1900 due to ethnic diversity, the separation of church and state, and denominationalism. Nevertheless, he argues that pluralism 'came of age' through immigration, a relative decline in Protestant power, and the rising importance of religious dissent and individualism. Within this framework, Lippy treats a richer range of topics than Hutchison. This is a significant gain, but it has a downside: his organizing term, pluralism, experiences a sort of gridlock as a framework for analysis. Lippy treats the paradigmatic example of pluralism – harmonious relations among Protestants, Catholics, and Jews in white suburbia. He extends this paradigm of peaceful co-existence to Asian and Middle Eastern immigrants. Ranging further, still under the rubric of pluralism, he introduces the black church under slavery, the clash of Christian and Native American traditions, women's ordination, declining attendance at Catholic mass, the rise of Jewish neoconservatives, schisms over gay rights, bitter conflicts about whether abortion is murder, and an individualism so extreme that 'there were in theory as many forms of spirituality as there were Americans.' How far can the term 'pluralism' stretch before it breaks? For our purposes, we need to pare down Lippy's cast of characters and distinguish patterns among the differences that he lumps together as pluralism: widespread versus rare expressions of religion; religions that are freely chosen versus violently imposed; celebrations of diversity versus grudging admissions that diversity exists; bottom-up struggles for equal rights versus top-down pressure to assimilate; and profound personal spiritualities versus mere secular individualism.

In general, we need an approach that can dramatize diversity while at the same time identifying centers of power and underlining conflict. We have noted the dominant position of Christians, especially white Protestants. We must be alert to their power as we chart their contacts with other people, for example, encounters of Puritans or Spanish priests with Native Americans and enslaved Africans. Likewise, we must consider the internal power dynamics of various groups, for example, between

Baptist men and women. No doubt exploring such issues includes appreciating pluralism. For example, Puritan and Native American rituals both deserve respect on their own terms, and at times their interplay resulted in a harmonious blending of insight. Nevertheless, pluralism is not always the best interpretive paradigm. The relationship between a Bible-quoting slave master and an enslaved woman who never learned to read *includes* pluralism, but words such as racism, rape, and conquest – terms that call more attention to hegemony and less to a celebratory style of multiculturalism – are indispensable.

In a book of this kind, any approach to selection and definition is inevitably messy. Our strategy falls midway between Parson Thwackum's narrowness and the unattainable goal of giving all groups equal time. Rather than adopt a definition of religion that makes it hard to discover anything that is not religious, we will focus on groups and practices that are either self-described as religious (for example, churches and things associated with them) or widely discussed as religious (for example, Native American ceremonies and ritual aspects of US nationalism). We will spend more time on larger and more powerful groups. However, we will range widely and try not to stack the deck toward any single definition of religion. Rather we will try to enact a lesson of hegemony analysis – that if we start from a common-sense definition, we should be alert to the ways that this definition relates to power. As befits a work of synthesis and interpretation based on recent scholarship, we will give equal weight to stressing religious diversity and analyzing dominant religions as parts of hegemonic formations.

Chapter 1 introduces key players and themes in US religious history from the pre-conquest period to the late nineteenth century; we might think of it as fast-forwarding to the point at which our main tour begins. Two major sections follow this chapter. The first (Chapters 2 to 4) treats religion in the late nineteenth and early twentieth centuries, and the second (Chapters 5 to 7) extends this discussion to the present. Each section opens with an overview of key players and dynamics during its period (Chapters 2 and 5) then zooms into more detail on selected case studies. The middle parts of each section (Chapters 3 and 6) explore cases of religion interacting with sociopolitical conflict. The final parts (Chapters 4 and 7) explore cases of religion relating to cultural change.

Notes

1 In my endnotes, as in the main text, I have tried to be ruthlessly selective rather than comprehensive. Except when citing sources of direct quotations or referencing specific authors, I have selected only a few books that represent my top recommendations for further exploration. Surveys of US religion include Edwin Gaustad and Leigh Schmidt, *The Religious History of America* (revised edn) (San Francisco: HarperSanFrancisco, 2004) and Philip Goff and Paul Harvey, eds, *Themes in Religion and American Culture* (Chapel Hill: University of North Carolina Press, 2004). Readers include David Hackett, ed., *Religion and American Culture: a Reader* (2nd edn) (New York: Routledge, 2003) and Peter Williams, ed., *Perspectives on American Religion and Culture: a Reader* (Oxford: Blackwell Publishers, 1999). See also Charles Lippy and Peter Williams, eds, *Encyclopedia of the American Religious Experience* (New York: Scribners, 1988) and Gary Laderman and Luis León, eds, *Religion and American Cultures: an Encyclopedia of Traditions, Diversity, and Popular Expression* (Santa Barbara: ABC-CLIO, 2003).

2 José Casanova, *Public Religions in the Modern World* (Chicago: University of Chicago Press, 1994). See also R. Stephen Warner, 'Work in progress toward a new paradigm for the sociological study of religion in the United States', *American Journal of Sociology* vol. 98, no. 5 (1993), 1004–93.

3 Colleen McDannell, ed., *Religion of the United States in Practice*, 2 vols (Princeton: Princeton University Press, 2001).

4 I have in mind a famous map in Edwin Gaustad, *Historical Atlas of American Religion* (New York: Harpers, 1962); it is updated in Gaustad and Philip Barlow, *New Historical Atlas of Religion in America* (New York: Oxford University Press, 2000). A compact atlas is Bret Carroll, *Routledge Historical Atlas of Religion in America* (New York: Routledge, 2000).

5 George Gallup and Michael Lindsay, *Surveying the Religious Landscape: Trends in U.S. Beliefs* (New York: Morehouse Publishing, 2000); Wade Clark Roof and William McKinney, *American Mainline Religion: Its Changing Shape and Future* (New Brunswick: Rutgers University Press, 1987); Nancy Ammerman, *Pillars of Faith: American Congregations and Their Partners* (Berkeley: University of California Press, 2005). For an overview of data on religion and politics see Robert Booth Fowler, Allen Hertzle and Laura Olson, *Religion and Politics in America: Faith, Culture and Strategic Choices* (2nd edn) (Boulder: Westview Press, 1999).

6 Robert Wuthnow, *The Restructuring of American Religion: Society and Faith Since World War II* (Princeton: Princeton University Press, 1988).

7 Lucy Maddox, ed., *Locating American Studies: the Evolution of a Discipline* (Baltimore: Johns Hopkins University Press, 1998); George Lipsitz, *American Studies in a Moment of Danger* (Minneapolis: University of Minnesota Press, 2001); John Hartley, Roberta Pearson, and Eva Vieth, eds, *American Cultural Studies: a Reader* (New York: Oxford University Press, 2000).

8 Simon During, ed., *The Cultural Studies Reader* (2nd edn) (New York: Routledge, 1999); John Storey, ed., *What Is Cultural Studies? A Reader* (New York: Arnold Press, 1996); Paul Gilroy, Lawrence Grossberg, and Angela McRobbie, eds, *Without Guarantees: In Honour of Stuart Hall* (New York: Verso, 2000).

9 Entry points to the discussion of hegemony are Stuart Hall, 'Gramsci's relevance for the study of race and ethnicity,' *Journal of Communication Inquiry* vol. 10 , no.

2 (1986), 5–27 and Bruce Grelle, 'Hegemony and the "universalization" of moral ideas: Gramsci's importance for religious ethics', *Soundings* vol. 68, nos 3–4 (1995), 519–40.

10 On defining religion see William Paden, *Interpreting the Sacred* (Boston: Beacon, 1992); Malory Nye, *Religion: the Basics* (New York: Routledge, 2003); and John Hinnells, ed., *Routledge Companion to the Study of Religion* (New York: Routledge, 2005).

11 Henry Fielding, *Tom Jones* (Oxford World Classics edn) (New York: Oxford University Press, 1996), 109.

12 William Hutchison, *Religious Pluralism in America: The Contentious History of a Founding Ideal* (New Haven: Yale University Press, 2003).

13 Good places to enter this debate are Thomas Tweed, ed., *Retelling US Religious History* (Berkeley: University of California Press, 1996) and Laderman and León, *Religion and American Cultures*.

14 Charles Lippy, *Pluralism Comes of Age: American Religious Culture in the Twentieth Century* (Armonk: M. E. Sharpe, 2000).

CHAPTER I

Key Players and Themes in US Religion before the Twentieth Century

We have been preparing for a tour of twentieth-century religion, culture, and politics – a tour as selective as a seven-day trip from New York to Seattle. It will be difficult to cover such a large territory in the chapters that follow. However, our task in the current chapter is even more challenging. It is to do as much as we can, in the scope of a few pages, to set the historical context for our trip. Many lengthy books have been written on this subject – after all, human history in the Americas began thousands of years ago – and we cannot substitute for them here. However, we can introduce some key groups and trends to bear in mind if we want to understand the story we will join around the turn of the twentieth century.

Native Americans Meet Europeans

Given the small numbers of Native American people today, it is easy to underestimate how extensively Europeans depended on knowledge about living on the land that natives built up over thousands of years, and how much of American history between 1500 and 1900 was constituted by the interplay – through both co-operation and conflict – of red and white.[1] Major American civilizations rose and fell before Europeans arrived, and some of these were as complex as civilizations in Europe at the same time. Large-scale contact with Europeans dates from the voyages and colonization schemes of Christopher Columbus 500 years ago – although these were not the earliest contacts, since Scandinavians earlier settled in Newfoundland and explored the Great Lakes region. Africans and Polynesians probably also reached the Americas. In any case, the so-called 'discovery of America' did not occur until ninety-five per cent of human history in the Americas had passed. In parts of the US there was limited contact for another three centuries, so that whites did not become the majority until ninety-nine per cent of this history had passed.

Most scholars believe that the first Native American people migrated to the Americas from Asia over the Siberian land bridge. In contrast, native accounts of their origins often stress how their ancestors emerged from underground with the help of supernatural beings – in effect, they were born from the earth of the Americas. People who do not accept such teachings as scientific facts might still reflect on how these myths underline the deep roots of native people in the land compared with European latecomers.

It is misleading to assume that the communities encountered by British settlers represented typical native societies. Suppose we imagine (although this did not really happen) that Iroquois explorers had reached a remote part of Norway in the Middle Ages after its population was decimated by the bubonic plague, and had concluded that this 'empty' place told them all that they needed to know about Europe. Shouldn't they have visited London or Rome? We risk a similar mistake if we assume that the observations of European colonists report on 'timeless' native ways. Europeans carried germs for which natives had little resistance, and epidemics preceded colonizers to many regions. Most of these infections were not intentional – although at times colonizers used tactics like distributing 'gifts' of blankets infected with smallpox germs, and there was a cumulative impact if epidemics arrived at the same time as slavery and/or the loss of land. (If a prisoner in a slave labor camp dies of tuberculosis, we do not blame the death solely on tuberculosis germs, and we should not make a similar mistake when thinking about the conquest of America.) In any case, epidemics caused a shocking demographic collapse that eventually killed up to ninety per cent of the people.

To avoid the mistakes of our hypothetical Iroquois explorers, let us focus on the clash between the Spanish conquistador Hernando Cortez and the Aztec empire – the 'London' or 'Rome' of the Americas since it was the dominant power among an evolving set of complex Meso-America societies including Olmecs, Mayans, and many more. Societies somewhat comparable to the Aztecs, although on a smaller scale, had earlier risen and fallen in the Mississippi valley. Like the Meso-Americans, these Mississippean people built cities centered on pyramids and ruled by a priestly-administrative elite. Trade routes allowed them to share ideas and technologies. However, by the time of European contact the largest cities north of Mexico – for example, Cakohia near the place where the Mississippi, Missouri, and Ohio rivers meet – had been abandoned. Native societies reorganized in a network of villages, linked by confederations and trading systems but relatively decentralized and self-sufficient.

It is nearly impossible to identify a 'typical' native society. They were as small as hunting bands of a few extended families, and as large as the leading cities in the world at the time. They encompassed huge differences in foods, lifestyles, kinship systems, degrees of hierarchy, and emphasis on military values. They used hundreds of languages, some with differences as large as those between Russian, Swahili, and Chinese. Just as the Norwegians that we imagined being discovered by Iroquois have long histories with many stages – for example, a period as pagan Viking adventurers and another as Christians under Nazi occupation – something similar is true of native groups. Consider the Lakota Sioux – a group that whites often imagine as 'normal' Indians, living in tipis and using horses to hunt buffalo. Lakotas only hunted buffalo on horseback for one century of their history. They did not acquire horses until the late 1700s, after horses had escaped from Spanish settlements and spread throughout the plains, enriching tribes that acquired them and threatening other tribes with extinction. Before this time most Lakotas lived further east; they moved to the plains after losing territorial wars with Ojibwe people who enjoyed stronger alliances with fur-traders. By the late 1800s whites had slaughtered most of the buffalo and forced the Lakota onto reservations. Yet, like present day Scandinavians who are no longer Viking raiders, the Lakota are still alive even though buffalo hunts are part of the past.[2]

A few generalizations tend to hold for Native American religion before 1900, and most of them still hold today. First, it is hard to draw clear lines between religious aspects of native cultures and their general ways of life. Although certain ceremonies and aspects of nature are recognized as especially powerful or sacred in a way that corresponds loosely to the Western category 'religious,' such things are not seen as separate from the ordinary so much as on a continuum with it. Secondly, although Meso-Americans developed literacy, native cultures in the US did not do so until well after European contact. Unlike Christian or Islamic cultures in which texts like the Bible or the Qur'an are central to religious life and the teaching of youth, native cultures stressed oral tradition. The goal of education was to learn such traditions and acquire life skills. Thirdly, despite large differences from place to place, gender relations were often more balanced and less hierarchical compared with the Europeans, with more scope for women's political power, matrifocal families, female ritual leaders, and veneration of both gods and goddesses.

Fourthly, tribes existed in a less antagonistic relationship with the rest of the natural world, compared with Europeans who considered themselves above nature and stressed subduing it for their ends. Native people were more likely to understand themselves as part of a web of nature and to live in ecologically sustainable ways – although we must not romanticize this point, since natives did take from nature and sometimes damaged ecosystems severely. Native myths and rituals stressed maintaining relationships of respect and balance within their communities and local ecologies. People offered prayers to corn mothers, thunder beings, and animal spirits; they practiced seasonal ritual cycles linked to hunting and agriculture. This present-minded, cyclically-oriented, and locally-grounded focus of religious energy contrasts sharply with a modern Western mindset based on visions of universal progress. The contrast is especially strong if 'progress' demands traumatic imbalances such as uprooting people from communities and ravaging the environment.

Every native society eventually suffered military conquest by a European power, resulting in the loss of most land and self-determination.[3] Some cultures disappeared entirely. The Spanish typically displaced native elites and exploited the native population through slavery or other forms of forced labor, while the British stole land and pushed native people out of the way. The French in the Mississippi valley and Great Lakes region were somewhat less disruptive – often *métis* (or blended native-French) communities grew up around Catholic missions and trading posts – but the French too transformed and exploited native communities through the fur trade and the forms of dependency that accompanied it. Russians in the Pacific Northwest blended the Spanish and French models.

By the late 1800s colonization was nearly complete, and the British model was winning out in most of Canada and the US (which by this time had seized half of Mexico). The last military confrontation between the US Army and Native Americans occurred at Wounded Knee, South Dakota in 1890. Memories of these wars of conquest were still fresh – and, of course, bitterly painful and demoralizing from the native perspective – as the twentieth century opened.

It is misleading, however, to start from the extreme military-political imbalance in 1900 and project it backward even 100 years, much less to the 1600s. Native warriors could have expelled or absorbed the first wave of European colonists. However, there was room for all; the kernel of truth in self-serving ideologies about empty land is that resources were abundant, partly because of the epidemics noted above. Moreover, there were motives for co-operative exchange and coalition building. Both groups had ideas and technologies of interest to the other. Settlers needed native expertise about what plants and animals they could eat – eventually crops developed by natives including corn, potatoes, tobacco, and tomatoes become staples in Europe – and about surviving on the land. By no means was the settlers' quality of life self-evidently better; many 'white Indians' joined native communities through capture or running away and had no desire to be rescued.

From a native perspective, European metal tools for cooking, hunting, and war gave major advantages to groups that developed the trade or kinship relations to acquire them. Access to horses was even more valuable. Often these advantages were more important in the context of competition with rival native groups than with whites. Particularly at first, few Indians worried about their grandchildren waking up a hundred years later to discover that whites had stolen their land and enslaved them. Native groups did not make a united front to push the first wave of colonists back into the sea because it seemed more important to keep *each other* in check; often they wanted settlers as allies in complex diplomatic relations involving multiple native and European nations. Thus, for example, native enemies of the Aztecs co-operated with Cortez. Creek diplomats played British, French, and Anglo-American colonists against each other to negotiate better terms of trade and maintain their power vis-à-vis native rivals. Of course, natives eventually realized that they were becoming dependent on European goods and that a wave of conquest was sweeping over them, but often this took a long time to develop.

Therefore, between first contact and the late stages of conquest, there were periods of rough parity in power and respect, sometimes lasting for generations. Scholars call this the 'middle ground' and stress its creative aspects.[4] It involved complex negotiations in which the Europeans were not always the most powerful players. Such interplay was not only about jockeying for control of land; it was also about intercultural exchange. Europeans traveled on Indian roads, traded with natives, and sometimes married them. Natives adopted European technologies and often became

Christian. Europeans struck deals for access to hunting grounds and orchards. During at least half of the time between Columbus' arrival and the turn of the twentieth century, especially during the 1600s and early 1700s, it is more accurate to say that American history was constituted by cultural-political exchanges with natives – often involving forced labor and war, but sometimes a creative middle ground – than to imagine that Europeans simply showed up and displaced older ways of life.

However, the middle ground had collapsed almost everywhere by 1900. In every region some native people eventually turned to armed resistance when the power balance tilted too far. Examples include the war of Metacom (or King Philip) against Puritans in 1675, the Pueblo Revolt in New Mexico from 1680 to 1692, Pontiac's campaign in the Great Lakes region in the 1760s, and struggles from the Ohio valley to Florida in the early 1800s. Battles with Sioux on the northern plains and Apache in the Southwest continued after the Civil War. Prophets who called their people back to traditional ways often led the resistance; frequently this divided communities into bitter factions, as some followed prophetic visions and others rejected them. We should not imagine that all these resistance efforts were doomed, as dramatized by the success of the Pueblo Revolt. However, native warriors increasingly went down to defeat.[5]

Thus, in 1900 whites stood on Indian land and moved within the momentum of centuries of interaction with Indians, but native people themselves were militarily defeated and decimated by disease. Whites took children from their parents and raised them in boarding schools where they were indoctrinated into Christianity and forbidden to speak their own languages. Missionaries ran many of these schools; indeed from 1870 to 1882, missionaries were literally given control of the government's Indian Office (the forerunner of today's Bureau of Indian Affairs) largely to promote this policy. Whites also imposed a policy called allotment that broke up tribal communities and sold off tribal land in individual parcels. In theory this taught natives to 'progress' toward US individualism; in practice it mainly opened the door for whites to acquire native land through tactics that were tantamount to theft.[6] Native people continued to fight for cultural survival, and as we will discuss in Chapter 7, their struggles gained significant momentum by the second half of the twentieth century. For the moment, however, most whites considered native people a part of the past.

From Red and White to Red, White, and Black

Viewed from the perspective of centuries rather than millennia of experience, the foundation on which Americans stood in 1900 was created more by the history of red–white–black relations than red–white relations alone. Almost immediately after Columbus reached the Caribbean, he began to import African slaves to replace natives who were dying from epidemics or mounting resistance. Before the 1800s – that is, for 300 of the 500 years since Columbus arrived – more people crossed the Atlantic from Africa than from Europe. In much of the Americas, especially the Caribbean and coastal parts of South America, Africans became the majority population. In this regard South Carolina was the most typical of the thirteen colonies that formed the US, even though it is sometimes seen as unusual because it had a black majority after 1700. Overall, blacks accounted for a third of the population in Britain's American colonies if we include Barbados (which was larger than Massachusetts and Virginia combined in 1660) and Jamaica (larger than New York in 1760). A settler society like Massachusetts, with thirty-five times more whites than blacks, was the unusual one in an Americas-wide perspective.[7]

Forced labor has been common throughout world history; African slave-traders were an integral part of the Atlantic slave business and slavery also existed in Native American societies. However, the emerging American system was based on plantations of sugar, tobacco, cotton, and other goods that were integrated into an international market, and this led to intense exploitation of labor on an unprecedented scale. For example, slavery among the Cherokees had earlier taken place on a small scale, sometimes as a prelude to a captive's assimilation into the community. Many escaped African-Americans were integrated into tribal societies. Over time Cherokee slavery was drawn into the world system. Cherokee elites owned plantations similar to Anglo-American ones, and some Native Americans made money catching runaway slaves and selling them back into the market. What happened on a small scale with such native entrepreneurs took place on a massive scale in Africa.[8]

To understand the dynamics of African-American religion, we must grasp the slave system's brutality, both physical and cultural. The middle passage was harrowing; high percentages of people died en route to the Americas while packed into the dark and unspeakably unhealthful holds of ships. Once at international slave markets, captives from the same regions of Africa were separated so that their languages and customs would be hard to maintain, and families were often divided. Many masters raped enslaved women. Most slaves were forbidden to read and write, and various practices humiliated them and dramatized their second-class status. The system was maintained with whippings, murders, ruthless pursuit of escaped slaves, and intense repression of revolts.

At the same time, enslaved people were not passive victims without resources to persist and in limited ways thrive as a community. Let us recall that the social order in today's America is also maintained quite violently – in this case through the discipline of the market and prison system – but even the poorest citizens survive within these constraints, not without some happiness. So it was under slavery. People did not experience rape, torture, or seeing their children auctioned every day; with luck it might happen rarely. Enslaved workers had some scope to negotiate about working conditions. If pressed too hard they could slow down, sabotage equipment, or steal food. Cooks could poison their masters. Although slave work was grueling and exploitative – among its bitterest legacies is that blacks created much of the society's wealth, only to see it inherited by descendants of their oppressors – it did have seasonal rhythms. Under the circumstances slave communities developed which were surprising healthy and resilient.

At times, bonds of affection developed across racial lines, for example, between white children and slaves who cared for them or between masters and their personal attendants or sexual consorts. (Thomas Jefferson's long-running affair with his slave Sally Hemings is a famous example.) This dynamic has been distorted through the stereotype of the nurturing black 'Mammy,' which has trivialized black women and romanticized slavery in films like *Gone With the Wind*. Nevertheless, some mutual influences between the races were positive and creative. Moreover, enslaved people learned that masters often saw themselves as paternalistic caretakers of their property, with a moral-religious responsibility to civilize slaves and care for them like children. If they chose, slaves could appeal to such paternalism to win better living conditions in places where resistance seemed impossible. Such strategies have been controversial because they undermined support for more radical rebellion and risked internalizing a 'slave mentality' which accepts paternalistic hegemony. Scholars debate about the impact of black conversion to Christianity in this context.[9]

Before discussing how religion related to this situation, let us reflect on the concept of race. Slave systems in world history have not always cared about the variations in skin tone that signal 'race' as we commonly understand it, but in the Americas the lines between masters and slaves were racialized in ways that reverberated through the society long after slavery ended. In the early years of British colonization, enslaved Africans and indentured servants from Europe were not treated in markedly different ways. However, elites decided that indentured Europeans could work for a specific period and then move to a free status – the first step on a road that later led to citizenship and voting rights – while Africans would be locked in permanent servitude. Skin color became a marker of difference, along with other physical and cultural signals that today allow suntanned 'white' suburbanites to have darker skin tones than many 'black' people without observers confusing their 'color' status. Race was used to divide and conquer the work force. Poor Europeans aligned themselves with elite Europeans in an emerging category of 'whiteness,' when they might otherwise have formed stronger alliances with poor Africans. Creating and enforcing hierarchies based on race, with its many cultural and institutional ramifications, became a foundational aspect of US society that continues to the present.[10]

Despite laws and cultural norms that forced people into separate and unequal racial categories, the red, white, and black populations of the US mixed to a greater degree than many people realize. Consider the genealogical line dramatized in the 1970s television series, *Roots*, between writer Alex Haley and his enslaved Gambian ancestor, Kunte Kinte. In six previous generations, Haley had 267 ancestors in addition to Kunte Kinte – and almost a third were Cherokee, English, or Irish. One study found that fifty per cent of black students in South Carolina had a grandparent with Native American blood, and the numbers in Mississippi were higher. Such evidence reflects the fact that some 'disappearing' natives did not die; rather they were enslaved and blended into the 'black' populace. (Africans could also be absorbed by native societies; seventy-five per cent of the gene pool of one culturally intact tribe in Belize can be traced to Africa.) [11]

African-American religion is an especially important example of cultural mixing – a key locus for the interplay between European hegemony, African tradition, and counter-hegemonic struggle. It is difficult to generalize about the religions that Africans brought to the Americas. Up to a quarter of the captives were Muslim. Most of the others practiced traditional forms of West African religion. These religions were typically polytheistic, and they paid considerable attention to the veneration of ancestors. Like Native American religions, African religions did not distinguish sharply between religious and non-religious parts of their culture. Often they emphasized drumming, dancing, divination, and spirit possession.

Slave masters worked with greater or lesser diligence to stamp out these religions. Openly organizing slave mosques was out of the question; thus, even when educated Muslim slaves were able to maintain traditions such as daily prayer, Islamic practice did not survive across generations in an organized way. Ceremonial drumming was outlawed, alongside most other unsupervised meetings. One scholar sees the result as a 'spiritual holocaust' that nearly stamped out African religions in the emerging US outside of a few pockets such as New Orleans.[12]

This result was not inevitable. In some places – more often in Latin America than the British colonies and more often on large plantations with complex slave quarters than smaller ones where blacks and whites were in closer contact – ceremonies were passed intact to new generations, with relatively minor adaptations for language and/or blending influences from different parts of Africa. Such religions continue to thrive as Santería and Vodou in the Caribbean and Candomblé in Brazil. In regions where masters periodically replenished their slave quarters with new arrivals from Africa, it was easier to maintain traditions than in places (including most of the emerging US) where the slave population was self-sustaining.

Colonies run by Roman Catholics were more conducive than Protestant colonies to a blending of traditions that extended African religions. In Catholic colonies where everyone residing in a parish was a church member, slaves often received perfunctory baptisms that they would not have received in a Protestant system. However, often this meant little in terms of learning doctrines or participating in Christian rituals. Africans and Native Americans both embraced Christianity more readily, insofar as they could continue worshipping traditional deities by addressing these deities with a dual set of names – one as Catholic saints and another extending traditional understandings. Church-sanctioned societies called confraternities became key institutions that carried forward selected African practices. Spanish and French Catholics were far more open to such practices than British Protestants, given that a key concern of Puritans was stamping out the veneration of saints.[13]

In the US, what survived were not fully developed traditions like Haitian Vodou, but fragmented aspects of African traditions – sensibilities toward ancestors, folk tales, styles of music and dance, and a system of charms, healing practices, and magic called conjure. Just as specific African words were lost but much of the underlying pattern of thinking – the 'African grammar' so to speak – was passed on, something similar was true of African religion. This is easy to see in the cases of music and the so-called superstitious practices of conjure. Even when ceremonial drumming was outlawed, African rhythms, tunes, vocal styles, and call-and-response sensibilities continued. Even without fully articulated traditional communities, African folk tales continued to be retold and people still consulted conjurers for charms, curses, and healing.[14]

For slaves in the US, the main result of this process was the creation of a distinctive form of Christianity, heavily inflected by African influences and the concerns of enslaved people about how religion relates to power and hegemony.[15] (Later we will discuss twentieth-century efforts to rebuild non-Christian forms of African religion in dialogue with immigrants from the Caribbean and the Muslim world.) However, the process of Christianization was surprisingly slow, considering that conversion was a key ideological rationale for slavery. Blacks had obvious reasons for maintaining their traditions and refusing to worship a God in whose name they had been enslaved – a God who was imagined as white. However, whites were also standoffish toward converting blacks, since this blurred lines of racial separation. Moreover, whites had inherited a common-sense assumption that Christians could not be enslaved. This was the law in Virginia in the early 1600s, and although such laws were easily rewritten, the common sense informing them lingered on. Whites felt that Christianization might make slaves harder to discipline, and they did not want to worship with blacks or even imagine an afterlife where the races were equal. Conversion risked the awkward scenario of baptizing slaves, only to inform them that they could not read the Bible since it was illegal for them to read at all.

In this context, missionary efforts made limited headway. In the British colonies, an arm of the Anglican Church began preaching to slaves in 1701, but it gained few converts to its staid and cerebral style of religion. In the mid- to late 1700s, missionaries from then radical Protestant sects like the Baptists, Moravians, and Methodists risked pariah status by leading inter-racial worship, addressing black converts as brothers and sisters in Christ, and condemning slavery. These preachers faced such strong opposition from other whites – including social ostracism and physical violence – that their growth was limited before the 1800s. Not until white southern evangelicals stopped criticizing slavery and convinced themselves that spiritual equality in the eyes of God carried no implication of sociopolitical equality did they gain many white converts. Eventually, in reaction to attacks by abolitionists, they stopped teaching that slavery was a necessary evil and began to describe it as a positive Christian good.

Nevertheless in the evangelicalism which emerged in a series of revivals known as the Great Awakenings – often led by Baptists and Methodists – blacks found a form of Christianity that they were willing to embrace, as long as they could do so on their own terms. Evangelicals worshipped in an emotionally expressive style that was open to the incorporation of African musical sensibilities, dance, and ecstatic behavior somewhat reminiscent of African spirit possession. Moreover, evangelical institutions (especially Baptist) stressed bottom-up leadership and local autonomy, with few educational barriers to leadership. This allowed ordinary rural folk to address their priority concerns through their sermons and church activities. Thus, in the early 1800s, 200 years after slavery came to Virginia, US blacks finally began to embrace Christianity on a large scale.

Before slavery ended, much of black Christianity developed as an invisible institution. Southern whites did not allow blacks to meet alone; sanctioned worship involved blacks sitting in the back of white churches or white clergy preaching to slaves. However, blacks preferred an African-inflected music style, a type of dance-like worship called shouting, and an emotionally charged form of chanted preaching. They interpreted the social implications of Christianity differently from most whites; they focused on themes of suffering, stressed compassion and justice for the poor, and rejected a dualism between spiritual and sociopolitical equality. Whites highlighted Biblical texts like 'Slaves, obey your masters' (Ephesians 6:5) and stories about biblical heroes who gained slaves as a reward for their virtue. Blacks sang spirituals such as 'Didn't My Lord Deliver Daniel?' based on a Bible story about God protecting a prisoner thrown into a lion's den. Whites interpreted the story of the Exodus from Egypt to the Promised Land either as an apolitical teaching about individual souls seeking God or as an allegory about Puritans fleeing religious persecution in Europe for an American promised land. Blacks interpreted America not as a promised land but as an Egypt to flee. If blacks wished to hear such preaching and sing their own songs, they had to do so in secret, so they often met at night in brush arbors in remote parts of their plantations.

Free blacks in cities like Philadelphia and Charleston could afford to be less secretive. Independent black Baptist and Methodist churches began to organize in the late 1700s and early 1800s, about the same time that the invisible institution was developing in the South. Churches became key centers for the African-American community. Because black participation in business, the military, and the professions was highly limited, black clergy came to play key roles as community leaders. This role continued after the Civil War as blacks faced ongoing racism and poverty, both in southern agricultural regions that maintained a system of segregation and tenant farming that provided little improvement over slavery, as well as among the growing group of blacks who migrated to cities like Atlanta or Chicago. After emancipation, southern black churches moved from invisibility toward formal organization on a large scale. Because Baptists are so decentralized, they were slower to create a national organization than black Methodists, who organized the African Methodist Episcopal Church (AME) and African Methodist Episcopal Church Zion (AMEZ) in 1816 and 1821. In 1895 the National Baptist Convention emerged as the largest black denomination.

Key Players in European-American Religion during the Colonial Era

Europeans increasingly dominated the interplay of red, white, and black that constituted American history from 1500 to 1900.[16] In many places, settlers created small-scale transplanted European societies, where African-Americans and Native Americans had limited day-to-day presence, the population was fairly homogeneous, and there was an established church. This was especially true in New England. As we have seen, in Catholic regions and the South there was more cultural mixing, but Europeans typically dominated. The middle colonies had European majorities, but considerable ethnic and religious diversity: the Dutch and British vied for control of New York, which also was home to Swedes, French, and Sephardic Jews; Protestants and Catholics co-existed uneasily in Maryland; Pennsylvania welcomed Quakers, Presbyterians, and German sectarians; Maryland had a slave economy; New York had many slaves and was home to the Iroquois Confederacy; and some of the leading free black churches were based in Pennsylvania. In the long term, colonies that welcomed pluralism (such as Pennsylvania) or accepted it because diversity overwhelmed efforts to police uniformity (such as New York) became models for the US as a whole. However, at first this by no means seemed inevitable, and it took a long time to develop. Massachusetts had an established church for more than half its history, until 1833, and most southern colonies had them until the 1780s.

Most colonists were at least nominal Christians. Unlike polytheists, Christians believe in a single creator God who takes three forms known as the Trinity: the Creator of the universe; the spirit of God present in the world; and Jesus Christ, the founder of Christianity who began as a Jewish prophet and teacher, was killed by the Roman Empire, and later came to be understood by such names as Savior and Son of God. Unlike religions based on oral traditions, Christians stress written sources (especially the Bible) and literacy. When Protestants put the Bible in the hands of grassroots Christians in the early modern era, this led to significant change. It transformed the everyday experience of religion for ordinary people, and it shifted power within Christianity because it allowed laypeople to interpret the Bible for themselves. A vivid example of the conflicts that could arise is the African-American reading of Exodus as a warrant to rebel against slavery; one southern elite commented that anyone who wanted slaves to read the entire Bible 'belonged in a room in the Lunatic Asylum.'[17]

All Christians emphasize doing the will of God as revealed through Jesus's teachings about compassion and justice, seeking forgiveness for human imperfection and wrongdoing, and participating in rituals called sacraments, including baptism (through which one joins the church) and holy communion (in which Christians eat together and remember a key moment in Jesus's life). Roman Catholics practice additional sacraments (confession, confirmation, marriage, anointing the sick, and ordination) and have an elaborate hierarchy headed by bishops and the Pope in Rome; they trace this back to the earliest years of the Church. We might think of Catholicism as the trunk of Western Christianity and Protestantism as a major branch off this trunk. Protestants repudiated the authority of bishops, stopped venerating saints, de-emphasized and/ or reinterpreted many of the sacraments, and closed monasteries and convents. According to Protestants, these things had become so corrupt that they interfered with the teaching of Jesus and the direct relationships needed between God and believers.

Since Protestants lack the unified structure that allows Catholic diversity to flourish as movements and niches within an overarching church, and since Protestants encouraged believers to interpret the Bible for themselves, Protestantism splintered into hundreds of denominations. We can sort out its key families – Anglicans, its Lutheran-Calvinist mainstream, and the Radical Reformation – based on how sharply they broke with Catholicism and shifted authority toward the grassroots. Anglicanism, or the Church of England, made the smallest changes. It began when King Henry VIII declared the independence of the English Church from the Pope, but otherwise changed little of the worship, theology, or authority structure based on bishops. One result was that later stages of the British Reformation proceeded as a revolt against Anglican bishops in addition to Catholic ones. Anglicans came to the Americas as an arm of the British government; after the American Revolution they reorganized as the Episcopal Church.

Lutherans, named after the monk Martin Luther who sparked the German Reformation, stressed the teaching of salvation through God's grace alone. Lutherans became dominant in Germany and Scandinavia; they came to the Americas with immigrants from these places. Calvinists, named after the Genevan minister John Calvin, shared Luther's key ideas but put more stress on God's sovereign power and made more radical changes in Catholic liturgies. Calvinists led the efforts to radicalize the English Reformation and thrived in many parts of northern Europe; they came to the Americas as English Puritans, Scots–Irish Presbyterians, French Huguenots, and German and Dutch Reformed Churches.

Whereas Lutherans and Calvinists made their peace with Protestant rulers and organized state churches (at times Calvinists experimented with theocracies), Radical Reformers saw such arrangements as too compromised. They favored selective (or sectarian) churches that gathered serious disciples distinct from mainstream society. These groups are also called Anabaptists because they considered Catholic baptisms invalid and re-baptized their converts. Persecution forced them to the margins of society in separatist communities, often pacifist, which came to the Americas as Mennonites, Amish, and similar groups.

The main concerns of Luther and Calvin were theological rather than political. They felt that Catholics obscured essential teachings about God's grace and sovereignty by relying on priests, saints, and sacraments as intermediaries between individuals and God. No human works could bring sinners closer to God, since (as Calvin put it) human nature is 'totally depraved.' However, shifts in theology had political implications. Ever since Christianity became the official religion of the Roman Empire, European governments and clergy had been deeply entwined. There was no sharp distinction between tithes and taxes, and bishops were part of the aristocracy, which meant that questioning bishops was also rebellion against the aristocracy. Elites feared that chaos would result if all members of their societies were not subject to the same religious–political laws. Thus, the Reformation was also about political shifts and alliances. Protestant–Catholic conflict was linked to the long-term rise of modern nation states and the middle classes; both gained power at the expense of feudal aristocracies who spoke for a unified Christendom. Largely due to such considerations, the Reformation sparked a series of wars.

Moreover, the Reformation and the conquest of the Americas began at the same time. Luther published his manifesto called *The Ninety-five Theses* in the same year (1517) that Cortez began his campaign against the Aztecs. In both Catholic and Protestant countries a key rationale for conquest was the goal of expanding the reach of Christianity; debates about what forms of slavery were justifiable were argued using evidence from the Bible and canon law. Religious wars in Europe translated into wars for empire in the Americas. Just as we cautioned against lumping together rival groups like the Cherokees and Creeks as a single bloc against white encroachment, we must not lose sight of the bitter differences among European colonizers.

Let us consider the four key players on the Euro-American religious scene during the colonial era: Roman Catholics; Anglicans; Puritans; and the unchurched. Beyond the thirteen colonies that formed the US – that is, in a huge territory including Latin America, Canada, California, and the Mississippi Valley – Catholicism was the major European religion.[18] Priests were part of the political apparatus of the Spanish and Portuguese empires. In the northern parts of colonial Mexico such as California and Texas, as well as Spanish settlements in Florida, clerics established a line of mission settlements, often utilizing forced labor. They founded a key settlement on the Rio Grande at Santa Fe, New Mexico in 1598, a full century after Columbus but still earlier than the first British colonies in Virginia and Massachusetts. A 1680 revolt of Pueblo Indians expelled the Spaniards, although they returned twelve years later.

In the upper Midwest and Canada the main Catholic presence was through French missionaries loosely associated with the fur trade. As noted above, the French were less likely than the British or Spanish to steal land or enslave natives, at least in regions that became part of the US, however, in Quebec their settlements did displace native people. The most lucrative French colony, Haiti, was based on plantation slave labor, at least until the Haitians successfully rebelled in 1791 – a fateful event for the US since the war caused an influx of refugees to New Orleans and allowed Jefferson to acquire French-claimed territory cheaply in the Louisiana Purchase of 1803. The US gained a largely Catholic region with a blend of French, Spanish, and Afro-Caribbean cultures.

Only a handful of Catholics lived in the British colonies. The Catholic aristocrat George Calvert founded Maryland in 1634, and for a time he sponsored Catholic worship led by Jesuit priests. However, anti-Catholic rioting and a Protestant political takeover put Catholics on the defensive and limited their religious practice to private homes. In general Maryland's religious institutions were weak after 1650, and it was not until the 1840s, with an influx of Irish immigrants and the US seizure of the northern half of Mexico, that Catholicism became a major player in the US at large. We will pick up this story later.

The two obvious key players in the British colonies were the Anglican and Puritan established churches of the southern colonies and New England.[19] Anglicans came as an arm of the English government and/or the companies it chartered, beginning in Virginia in 1607. They were supported by taxes and in theory everyone in their colonies was born into an Anglican parish. Prominent laity organized in boards called vestries played a key role in running parishes. However, recruiting a high-quality cadre of clergy to the wilds of the New World proved difficult; many rural southerners had tenuous connections to churches. Two additional factors eroded Anglicanism's long-term influence: evangelicalism proved more attractive to rank-and-file southerners than the Anglicans' cerebral and formal style, and most Anglican clergy sided with the losing British side during the American Revolution. Nevertheless, the Anglicans, reorganized as Episcopalians after the revolution, continued to enjoy many advantages and to recruit elites to their churches.

More passionate about religion were the Puritans, including the Pilgrims who arrived at Plymouth, Massachusetts in 1620 and a larger group that founded Massachusetts Bay Colony in the 1630s. These were strong Calvinists whose name signals their desire to purify Anglicanism, which they considered little better than Catholicism. In Britain the law eventually made space for the peaceful co-existence of Anglicans and Calvinist dissenters, including both Presbyterians (who vested power in regional bodies called presbyteries) and Congregationalists (who gave autonomous power to local congregations). However, in the early 1600s the Puritans (who organized as Congregationalists and split between one group which sought to reform Anglicanism and another which wanted to separate from it) were highly dissatisfied with, and persecuted by, British authorities. Puritans sought a colony to shape according to their sense of God's will. They spoke of their covenant with God to create 'a city on a hill' – a Biblical allusion that also evokes the idea of being 'the light of the world' (Matthew 5:14). In effect, they saw themselves as junior partners in a vanguard experiment to establish God's will on earth.

The Puritan quest for religious freedom imposed sharp limits on the freedom of non-Puritans. Quaker missionaries and accused witches were executed, while Pequot Indians were killed, enslaved, or confined to 'praying towns.' A pious Puritan woman named Anne Hutchison was exiled for questioning the authority of male clerics. Blasphemy and adultery were capital crimes, and people were required to attend worship services that lasted for hours. Puritan colonies were not theocracies in the sense that clerics ruled directly, but magistrates were expected to enforce Puritan policies and only church members could vote.

To join an Anglican parish, one simply had to be presented for infant baptism. In contrast, to join a Puritan church, one had to give persuasive testimony to existing church members that one was among God's elect. Recall how all Calvinists, including Puritans, taught that it was futile to seek salvation through human works; this included choosing to be saved. Puritans felt that the decision to forgive sin was entirely in the hands of a sovereign God and that the human soul was so corrupt that striving for election was like spinning a car's wheels in the mud, miring one deeper in sin. Imagine a defendant in court who is a million dollars in debt and working at a minimum wage job; if he tells a judge that he will pay his debt by working harder, he simply reveals that he does not understand his predicament. His only hope is for someone to forgive his debt. According to Puritans, God's grace toward sinners is like such forgiveness. Misguided efforts to focus on good works would only dig sinners into deeper holes, like Catholic 'priestcraft.' Thus, joining a Puritan church was not a matter of choice or recruitment, but of declaring one's confidence that one had been elected by God.

Sociologist Max Weber later suggested in *The Protestant Ethic and the Spirit of Capitalism* that the anxieties created by this theology – the need for confidence about election even though no one could be sure about it – drove Calvinists to work harder than other people. Moreover, because they criticized distracting trappings of wealth and eliminated special vocations of priests and nuns, their hard work was channeled into the everyday world – above all, into building wealth and (in the Puritan case) colonizing the New World. In effect, worldly success came to be seen as a religious vocation and a rough-and-ready indication of whether one was saved – even though this was not their theologians' intention. Weber believed that later stages of Euro-American capitalism retained a quasi-religious version of this 'Protestant work ethic' without the overt theology. This in turn helped to explain why the nations that emerged as leaders of the modern world system were often Calvinist. In effect, the Puritans' psychological anxiety, stress on literacy, and sense of mission (recall their vision of building a city on a hill) fit together with aspects of modernity such as visions of progress, individualism, and the rise of science. The point is not that Calvinism caused modernity or vice versa, but that the two grew up together and were mutually reinforcing. Many scholars believe that a broad Puritan sense of collective mission has been a lasting component of US culture, despite the fact that the original Puritan churches were already struggling by the late 1600s as New England changed from the land of pious Puritan pilgrims to the land of individualistic Yankee merchants.[20]

In light of the Puritan legacy, we could easily overestimate the pervasiveness of religion in colonial America. In fact, the fourth key player alongside Catholics, Anglicans, and Puritans was the largest of all: the unchurched. Only ten to fifteen per cent of people in the British colonies in 1776 were church members, compared with more than fifty per cent in the twentieth century.[21] True, church membership was more demanding in the past, especially for Puritans; increased membership does not prove increased commitment. Nevertheless, significant levels of disinterest in Christianity have been ongoing. Recall how rural folk had little contact with clergy in much of the South; this was also true on the frontiers of westward expansion for years to come. Although immigrants were sometimes the most pious members of the European communities they left behind – as was true of Puritans – often they were the *least* pious: young people; unattached males; restless adventurers; the ambitious and disaffected; people fleeing the draft. Even in New England after the first couple of generations, most people did not join churches. One scholar notes that Puritans were required to attend lengthy Sunday services, but numerous attendees were 'horse-shed Christians' who spent much of the day hanging around in the horse sheds socializing.[22] By 1692, when Salem, Massachusetts prosecuted its famous witch trials, only fifteen per cent of taxpayers were church members in many New England towns.

For both horse-shed Christians and the unchurched – and, indeed, for church members as well – folk religious practices held great importance. We have noted the prevalence of conjure among Africans, and similar practices were widespread among whites: healing charms; stories about devils; popular magic; so-called superstitions; and so on. Ancient astrological theories and European traditions mingled with African and Native American ideas. Even Puritan clerics were fascinated by miraculous signs, divination, and witches; for the unchurched such interests were near the center of everyday religious practice.

Expanding the Cast of Key Players

From the mid-1700s to the mid-1800s, three more groups emerged as key players: evangelical revivalists; Deists who stressed harmonizing religion and Enlightenment reason; and a set of religious innovators who stretched the boundaries of Christianity or moved beyond them.

Evangelicals gained their following by recruiting the unchurched on a large scale – church membership had doubled to twenty-five per cent by 1860 – and creating schisms and spin-offs from established churches. Beginning with two waves of revivalism in the years around 1740 and the early 1800s – the First and Second Great Awakenings – revivalism became a permanent fixture on the landscape; evangelicals soon won a place alongside Episcopalians and Puritans in the religious establishment.[23] Evangelicals appealed to working people, and – as in earlier stages of Protestant history – this translated into a sort of counter-cultural rebellion as dissenters refused to defer to authority in expected ways. Their structures of institutional power were bottom-up as opposed to top-down; the contrast between Anglicans and Baptists was especially striking. Far more than Puritans, they appealed to the exercise of human will and the importance of emotion. Many of them repudiated Calvinist theology by exhorting people to make a conscious choice to be saved and by stressing good works. Preachers raised emotions to a fever pitch in frontier camp meetings that mingled ecstatic forms of African-American religion and white evangelical styles. Listeners responded by fainting or shouting. Even when evangelical worship was less raucous, it tugged at the emotions through sentimental music and preaching that instilled the fear of hell. All this was focused toward the trademark goal of evangelicalism: leading sinners to make a personal decision to accept Jesus as savior, also known as being 'born again.'

Although revivalists emerged from a full spectrum of Protestantism

– Anglicans, Lutherans, Calvinists, and Anabaptists – Methodists and Baptists made the greatest gains. Methodism began as an offshoot of Anglicanism; it was a renewal movement that sought a more profound piety and more effective outreach to working people. Eventually it broke away to become a separate denomination. Because of these origins, Methodists had bishops and a strong central organization. This helped them plant new churches through a system of circuit riding, in which preachers traveled by horseback over large territories on the frontier. Schisms somewhat like the one between Anglicans and Methodists were common. Presbyterians split between conservatives and a revivalist 'New Light' faction. Lutheran Pietists battled Lutherans who maintained a stress on liturgies and historic confessions. People broke from Congregationalism to start Baptist churches. Wherever evangelicals perceived elite clergy becoming complacent, intellectualized, or corrupted by establishment status, schisms followed.

Since Baptists have (until recently) prided themselves on local autonomy and freedom from central authority, they are a paradigmatic example of the decentralized and schismatic quality of evangelicals. Although they built seminaries like other groups, any farmer-preacher with a Bible and a call to ministry could start a church. They divided theologically, with Free Will Baptists embracing emergent teachings about emotions and the human will while other Baptists maintained Calvinist teachings. They divided between newer frontier churches and older, more elite, 'Tidewater' churches. They split over centralized structures, such as boards for co-ordinating missionary work (Missionary Baptists supported them and Primitive Baptists opposed them), and whether to join the Southern Baptist Convention when it developed as a structure to link southern congregations. We have noted how Baptists divided racially; later we will discuss how they split over modernism. Baptists do agree on a few things such as the need for baptism by full immersion under water, not as an infant but only after consciously professing one's faith; they also share songs and traditions. Nevertheless, there are dozens of kinds of Baptists. Moreover, what is true inside the Baptist family is also true in wider evangelical world – Baptists represent only one family (albeit the largest) among dozens of others.

Later we will discuss other trees in the evangelical forest, but for now it is best to think of evangelicals (Methodists, Baptists, and others) as one broad movement and contrast it with two other key players – Deists and a cluster of alternative religions outside the mainstream. During the late

1700s many leaders of the emerging nation – including Thomas Jefferson, Benjamin Franklin, and George Washington – harmonized religion with emergent forms of Enlightenment reason.[24] They embraced Deism, a religion closer to what we would today call humanism than to evangelicalism. Deists stressed the importance of moral laws and a divine creator – what the Declaration of Independence called 'the Laws of Nature and Nature's God.' Sometimes they remained half-hearted church members, and Deist politicians tried not to antagonize evangelicals too much. However, when Deists spoke of moral laws they meant the same natural laws that anyone – such as the ancient Greeks – could discover through reason. These had little to do with Biblical revelations, although Deists argued that the core ethical teachings of Jesus agreed with natural law, at least if his teachings were disentangled from supernaturalist corruptions added by the clergy. The Deist creator was like a watchmaker who builds a watch, winds it up, and leaves it to run on its own. God was not present in the world, especially to perform miracles or answer prayers. Human moral and mental capacities were sufficient.

Although few people embraced Deism to the exclusion of other religions, Deist ideas became widely influential. As we will see, its underlying goal of rethinking religion in light of reason remained important for years to come. A movement called Unitarianism, which emerged largely from New England Congregationalism, extended the Deist emphasis on moral issues and its rejection of aspects of religion that were inconsistent with humanistic values. Unitarianism's name signals its rejection of orthodox Trinitarian theology, especially the doctrine that Jesus was supernatural. Although its following was small, it was influential in elite circles around Harvard University, and it formed a bridge between liberal religious thinkers in the Revolutionary Era and at the turn of the twentieth century.

Deists stressed freedom of conscience, and their push for laws that are not biased toward any single religion became part of the nation's foundational legal structure. The Constitution lacks even vague language about 'Nature's God,' much less commitments to an established church or a Christian nation. Except for a sentence prohibiting religious tests for public office, it is silent about religion. Virginia led the way in passing laws that stripped established churches (in this case Anglican ones) of tax support and official status, while guaranteeing individuals the freedom to practice dissenting religions, or no religion at all, without penalty. Jefferson spearheaded this effort, in alliance with Baptists who agreed with few of his religious ideas except his opposition to Anglicans. Virginia's law became a model for the First Amendment to the US Constitution: 'Congress shall make no law respecting an establishment of religion; nor prohibit the free exercise thereof.' Since this amendment prevented Congress both from creating a national church and from interfering with established churches in specific states, some state churches survived for several more decades, but only in a defensive posture.[25]

We should not overestimate the religious freedom in the emerging nation. It was mainly freedom for varieties of white Christianity – often only white male-led Protestantism – as opposed to multiculturalism as currently understood. Native Americans and enslaved blacks reaped few benefits, although the First Amendment did give free black churches somewhat more room to maneuver. Benefits for women and non-Protestants were circumscribed. Moreover, this is a time to recall Hutchison's framework, discussed in the Introduction, for mapping stages in the evolution of pluralism. At first it meant mere toleration of dissent, as opposed to positive inclusion or full participation, even for sects like Baptists and Shakers who most benefited from the First Amendment. The more a group flaunted accepted behaviors as well as teaching unorthodox ideas, the less toleration it enjoyed.

Nevertheless, we should not forget how radical the US commitment to religious freedom was in its day. From a European perspective, it was a vanguard experiment that had never been tried as state policy before. Many people feared that it would lead to moral anarchy. In retrospect we know that religions thrived when they were cut free of entanglements with the state. They became markedly more popular when the corruptions of politics became a smaller part of religious life and people's resentments of political bosses were less likely to translate into resentment of religious leaders. However, at the outset the experiment seemed bold and risky. Even today some people resist its implications.

Because the state's official neutrality toward religion created a relatively level playing field for religious entrepreneurs, many new religious experiments flourished in the 1800s.[26] Although most were small, as a group we might consider these innovations as a final key player on the religious scene. Especially interesting were the many experiments with new religious communities. Some were utopian communities formed by Unitarians or secular reformers. Others were radical offshoots of evangelicalism under idiosyncratic prophets. Still others stressed innovations in health. In the long run, the most successful was the Church of Jesus Christ of Latter-day Saints, or Mormonism, which was founded in 1830 by Joseph Smith. By the 1850s it had built a self-sufficient nation called Deseret (later the state of Utah). Mormons saw themselves reviving the religion of the Hebrew patriarchs – including plural marriage, economic co-operation, and theocratic rule – based on new revelations to Smith in scriptures called the *Book of Mormon*.

As we will discuss more fully below, to understand any religion we must consider its impact on women and how it reinforces or challenges hegemonies related to gender.[27] This is especially true of alternative religious experiments during the 1800s. If women felt a calling to preach at this time, they had to exercise it beyond mainstream Christianity. One example is Ann Lee's founding of the Shakers, a communal movement that gained its name from its ecstatic style of worship. Shakers taught that the divine principle was both masculine and feminine and that Ann Lee was equal to Christ. Another example is Mary Baker Eddy's 1879 founding of Christian Science, a method of mental healing with an associated metaphysic linked to an unorthodox reading of the Bible.

If people wanted to experiment with new configurations of the 'normal' bourgeois family, they also tended to move toward alternative religions. For example, Ann Lee had suffered greatly in childbirth (this was not unusual as high percentages of women died while giving birth in this era). She taught that sexual lust was the original sin; the Shaker community she founded practiced celibacy, with sex roles that were distinct but with a strong sense of gender equality compared to 'normal' society. In another religious experiment, the Oneida Community founded by John Humphrey Noyes, community members were bound together in 'complex marriage.' This included sex with multiple spouses and a higher degree of gender equality compared with conventional marriage, although Noyes did exercise a degree of patriarchal control. Not all experiments with alternative family structures increased women's power, however. Most scholars interpret Mormon polygamy as more patriarchal than mainstream society, although Mormon economic communalism and the co-operation between wives in polygamous families may have appealed to some women.[28]

An especially interesting religion to analyze from the perspective of gender is Spiritualism, which centered on séances in which spirit mediums passed on messages from the dead, somewhat like today's psychics and channelers. Deceased family members, especially children who died young, were popular communicants but other spirits also appeared, including Native American ones. Spiritualism was widespread in the mid-1800s; most middle class families included people who experimented with it, and séances were even held in the White House. In Spiritualism, unlike most other religions of this era, the most powerful leaders were female. One scholar argues that mediums who gave lectures in trance were the first major group of US women permitted to speak in public. Spiritualism was a two-edged sword for women's empowerment, since women became mediums partly because people considered their essential nature to be more passive and receptive than men's; they were not themselves seen as speaking. Nevertheless, the work of mediums helped prepare for later forms of women's leadership. There was a large overlap between Spiritualists, the first generation of women's rights activists, and Quaker social reformers (Quakers were another religion friendly to women since they had no clergy and taught that every person had his/her own inner light). Spiritualists championed reforms related to issues including divorce, marital rape, health, and women's dress. For them, seeking alternatives to Christianity and to hegemonic gender roles went hand-in-hand.[29]

We could easily extend a list of alternative religions, just as we could range beyond our list of key players in the religious landscape. We could, of course, explore each group we have mentioned in more depth, as well as chart interactions among these groups in many situations. For example, westward expansion and the Civil War were both major sociopolitical dramas in which religious actors of many kinds – red, white, and black, male and female, northern and southern, mainstream and alternative – played important roles. Consider the ideology of Manifest Destiny that promoted conquest of territory between the Appalachians and the Pacific. It drew on ideals reminiscent of the Puritans, the desire of evangelicals to convert native people, and Enlightenment confidence about spreading civilization.[30] We cannot tell its story without attention to missionaries, frontier churches, and native resistance movements led by new prophets – and, of course, the native and mestizo communities that had already been established in the West for generations before the Anglos arrived.

Likewise religion, both black and white, loomed large in debates about slavery and southern identity. Northerners and Southerners both insisted that God was on their side in the Civil War. Most national Protestant denominations split along North–South lines. Abolitionism and religious reform were deeply entwined, and Harriet Beecher Stowe's

1852 religious anti-slavery novel, *Uncle Tom's Cabin*, was the best-selling book of the nineteenth century; when President Lincoln met Stowe, he said, 'So this is the little lady who caused this great war.'[31] At the turn of the twentieth century, memories of the war remained vivid in the minds of aging soldiers who had fought on both sides. The northern victors added 'The Battle Hymn of the Republic' to a short list of songs evoking US national identity. With its chorus, 'Glory, Glory, Hallelujah, God's Truth is Marching On' its Biblical resonances were unmistakable. In the South a cultural sensibility emerged that scholars call 'The Religion of the Lost Cause.' It combined idealistic nostalgia for antebellum society, rituals of respect for slain Confederate soldiers, ongoing resentment of Yankee aggression, and biblical motifs of suffering and vindication. Together these themes gave a religious cast to what whites called southern identity.[32]

Naturally, the black understanding of southern identity was different; blacks were, of course, more likely to notice the Ku Klux Klan (KKK), the semi-secret militia that served as the armed wing of white southern society. The KKK began after the Civil War as one of many male-only secret societies that flourished throughout the country. It overlapped with, and was somewhat akin to, Masonic lodges in that it taught esoteric rituals and had an elaborate hierarchy. Klansmen were famous for burning wooden crosses as warnings to their enemies and organizing processions in which they dressed in hooded outfits, somewhat like ghosts. Whereas most lodges were relatively apolitical, the KKK served as a militia and vigilante group that resisted the northern armies that occupied the South after the war, as well as politicians who co-operated with them. Although officially secret, in some places the KKK functioned as a quasi-public shadow government. It was notorious for terrorizing blacks and their white sympathizers, often by lynching people or burning homes and churches. It perceived itself as a self-defense organization upholding southern Christian traditions.

Westward expansion and the Civil War and its aftermath are just two among many themes that we would need to explore more fully if our goal were a comprehensive analysis. Rather than expanding on this point, however, let us draw this chapter to a close. Recall that our goal was not to survey all aspects of religion before 1900, but rather to move quickly to the years when our main discussion begins, introducing key names and themes along the way. If we bear in mind the interplay of the players we have introduced – Native Americans, African-Americans, four

European groups in colonial America (Catholics, Anglicans, Puritans, the unchurched), and three emergent players (evangelicals, Deists, and alternatives to all of the above) – we will be in a good position to consider new developments at the turn of the twentieth century.

Notes

1 This chapter, like those that follow, draws on three decades of reading, such that citing all sources is both impossible and incompatible with our goal of brevity. If a source relates to my treatment of a topic in multiple chapters, I have tried to cite it only once, and when faced with a choice between citing sources more useful to students or sources that could make me less vulnerable to academic attack, I have tried to err on the side of students. Orientations to Native American culture and religion include Joel Martin, *The Land Looks After Us: a History of Native American Religion* (New York: Oxford University Press, 2001); Lawrence Sullivan, *Native American Religions: Selections from the* Encyclopedia of Religion (New York: Macmillan, 1989) and Calvin Martin, ed., *The American Indian and the Problem of History* (New York: Oxford University Press, 1987).

2 On Lakotas see Raymond DeMallie and Douglas Parks, eds, *Sioux Indian Religion: Tradition and Innovation* (Norman: University of Oklahoma Press, 1987); on changes in plains cultures see Pekka Hamalainen, 'The rise and fall of plains Indian horse cultures,' *Journal of American History* vol. 90, no. 3 (2003), 833–62.

3 David Stannard, *American Holocaust: the Conquest of the New World* (New York: Oxford University Press, 1992); James Axtell, *The Invasion Within: the Contest of Cultures in Colonial North America* (New York: Oxford University Press, 1985).

4 Richard White, *The Middle Ground: Indians, Empires, and Republics in the Great Lakes Region, 1650–1815* (New York, Cambridge University Press, 1991) and Ramón Gutiérrez, *When Jesus Came, the Corn Mothers Went Away: Marriage, Sexuality and Power in New Mexico, 1500–1846* (Stanford: Stanford University Press, 1991).

5 Joel Martin, 'Before and beyond the Sioux Ghost Dance: Native American prophetic movements and the study of religion,' *Journal of the American Academy of Religion* vol. 59 (1991), 677–702.

6 On missions see Axtell, *Invasion Within* and George Tinker, *Missionary Conquest: the Gospel and Native American Cultural Genocide* (Minneapolis: Fortress Press, 1993).

7 David Wills, 'The decade ahead in scholarship,' *Religion and American Culture* vol. 3, no. 1 (1993), 15–22. Broad studies on black history and religion include Albert Raboteau, *Canaan Land: a Religious History of African Americans* (New York: Oxford University Press, 2001), Sidney Mintz and Richard Price, *Birth of African American Culture* (Boston: Beacon, 1992) and Timothy Fulop and Albert Raboteau, eds, *African-American Religion: Interpretive Essays in History and Culture* (New York: Routledge, 1997).

8 Theda Perdue, *Slavery and the Evolution of Cherokee Society, 1540–1866* (Knoxville: University of Tennessee Press, 1979).

9 A classic study stressing paternalistic aspects of slave religion is Eugene Genovese, *Roll, Jordan, Roll: the World the Slaves Made* (New York: Random House, 1972); a classic response is Lawrence Levine, *Black Culture and Black Consciousness* (New York: Oxford University Press, 1977).

10 Barbara Jean Fields, 'Slavery, race, and ideology in the United States,' *New Left*

Review no. 181 (1990), 95–118; Jack Forbes, 'The manipulation of race, caste and identity: classifying Afro-American, Native Americans and red–black people,' *Journal of Ethnic Studies* no. 17 (1990), 1–51. The system was less binary in places with more free blacks and/or where native people were the main labor force. Consider the terms 'mestizo' (referring to a blend of European, Native, and a smaller amount of African influences) and 'mulatto' (a blend of European, African, and a smaller amount of Native influences). It is striking how often mestizo identity is valorized as the foundation of Mexican culture (despite some indigenous people and descendants of Spaniards who hold out for purity) compared with the reluctance to embrace mulatto identity in the US. There are strong traditions of white resistance not solely to inter-racial sex, but also to 'culturally mulatto' practices like minstrelsy and rock and roll.

11   David Moore, 'Routes: Alex Haley's *Roots* and the rhetoric of genealogy,' *Transition* no. 64 (1995), 4–21; Forbes, 'Manipulation of race, caste and identity.'

12   Jon Butler, *Awash in a Sea of Faith: Christianizing the American People* (Cambridge, MA: Harvard University Press, 1990).

13   Joseph Murphy, *Santería: African Spirits in America* (Boston: Beacon, 1993) and Murphy, *Working the Spirit: Ceremonies of the African Diaspora* (Boston: Beacon, 1994).

14   Joseph Holloway, ed., *Africanisms in American Culture* (Bloomington: Indiana University Press, 1990).

15   On black Christians see, in addition to books already cited, C. Eric Lincoln and Lawrence Mamiya, *The Black Church in the African American Experience* (Durham: Duke University Press, 1990) and Albert Raboteau, *Slave Religion: the 'Invisible Institution' in the Antebellum South* (New York: Oxford, 1978).

16   There is a huge literature on every group treated in this section; see the bibliographies in Lippy and Williams, *Encyclopedia of the American Religious Experience*. For overviews, see Butler, *Religion in Colonial America* (New York: Oxford University Press, 2000) and Sydney Ahlstrom, *A Religious History of the American People* (New Haven: Yale University Press, 1972).

17   Cited in Charles Joyner, *Down By the Riverside: a South Carolina Slave Community* (Urbana: University of Illinois Press, 1985), 158.

18   On the Southwest, see Gutiérrez, *When Jesus Came, the Corn Mothers Went Away*. For general citations, see the notes on Catholics in Chapter 2.

19   A good place to enter the literature on Puritans is the work of David Hall including *Worlds of Wonder, Days of Judgment: Popular Religious Belief in Early New England* (New York: Knopf, 1989) and his edited collections including *Puritans in the New World: a Critical Anthology* (Princeton: Princeton University Press, 2004). On Anglicans see David Holmes, 'Anglican tradition in colonial Virginia,' in Williams, *Perspectives on American Religion and Culture*, 66–79.

20   Max Weber, *The Protestant Ethic and the Spirit of Capitalism* (Los Angeles: Roxbury, 1996); Daniel Walker Howe, 'The impact of Puritanism on American culture,' in Williams and Lippy, *Encyclopedia of the American Religious Experience*, 1057 ff.

21   On numerical trends, see Roger Finke and Rodney Stark, *The Churching of America, 1776–1990: Winners and Losers in our Religious Economy* (New Brunswick: Rutgers University Press, 1992).

22   Hall, *Worlds of Wonder*.

23   Nathan Hatch, *The Democratization of American Christianity* (New Haven: Yale

University Press, 1989), Christine Heyrman, *Southern Cross: the Beginnings of the Bible Belt* (Chapel Hill: University of North Carolina Press, 1998); Leonard Sweet, ed., *The Evangelical Tradition in America* (Macon: Mercer University Press, 1984).

24 Edwin Gaustad, *Neither King Nor Prelate: Religion and the New Nation* (Grand Rapids: Eerdmans, 1993); Henry May, *The Enlightenment in America* (New York: Oxford University Press, 1976).

25 R. Laurence Moore and Isaac Kramnick, *The Godless Constitution: the Case Against Religious Correctness* (New York: Norton, 1995).

26 Stephen Stein, *Alternative American Religions* (New York: Oxford University Press, 2000); R. Laurence Moore, *Religious Outsiders and the Making of Americans* (New York: Oxford University Press, 1987).

27 Ann Braude, *Women and American Religion* (New York: Oxford University Press, 2000); see also articles by Braude and Ann Taves in Tweed, *Re-Telling American Religious History* and Susan Juster and Lisa McFarland, eds, *A Mighty Baptism: Race, Gender, and the Creation of American Protestantism* (Ithaca: Cornel University Press, 1996).

28 Lawrence Foster, *Religion and Sexuality: the Shakers, the Mormons, and the Oneida Community* (Urbana: University of Illinois Press, 1984).

29 Ann Braude, *Radical Spirits: Spiritualism and Women's Rights in Nineteenth Century America* (2nd edn) (Bloomington: Indiana University Press, 2001).

30 Classic work in American Studies on these themes includes Richard Drinnon, *Facing West: the Metaphysics of Indian-Hating and Empire Building* (New York: Schocken Books, 1990) and Ronald Takaki, *Iron Cages: Race and Culture in Nineteenth Century America* (2nd edn) (New York: Oxford University Press, 1990).

31 Cited in Braude, *Women and American Religion*, 59.

32 Randall Miller, Harry Stout, and Charles Reagan Wilson, eds, *Religion and the Civil War* (New York: Oxford University Press, 1998); Charles Reagan Wilson, *Baptized in Blood: The Religion of the Lost Cause, 1865–1920* (Athens: University of Georgia Press, 1980).

CHAPTER 2

Changes in the Religious Landscape in the Early Twentieth Century

We have seen that by the turn of the twentieth century, the landscape of US religion included a rich mix of traditions. There was a flowering of diversity within a sort of free market for religious entrepreneurs created by a state that was officially neutral on religious questions. There were efforts to recast religious traditions in ways consistent with Enlightenment reason. There was conflict based on racism, struggles to end slavery, and imperial conquest. There was also a Protestant establishment, including evangelicals and the remnants of earlier established churches. Although Protestant elites had lost many legal privileges, they still enjoyed considerable cultural hegemony at least among the middle and upper classes, and they actively proselytized throughout society.

During the early twentieth century the key players already introduced, plus additional players not yet mentioned, faced far-reaching cultural changes. Consider a few things that most citizens now take for granted which were introduced in the first half of the century: automobiles; women's suffrage; movies; Social Security; access to reasonably reliable contraceptives; electric refrigerators; jazz; the right to organize labor unions without government harassment; radios; professional football; and a forty-hour working week. It was not until 1920 that half of US citizens lived in cities. Not until mid-century did middle class Protestants think of Catholics and Jews as part of mainstream society; Italian-Americans or American Jews with Russian grandparents faced questions about whether they belonged, somewhat like Iraqi-Americans and American Hindus with grandparents in Calcutta do today. In important ways, people during these years were creating a world like our own for the first time. At the same time, US culture early in the twentieth century remained very different from our own. It lacked televisions, computers, the internet, interstate highways, atomic bombs, black voting rights in the South, suburban sprawl, women's access to safe abortions and professional careers, sizeable Asian immigration, visible gay and lesbian communities, cars made in Japan, hip-hop music, fears of global warming, or wide access to universities for the middle class.

In the next two sections, we will slow down and unpack some of the complexity that resulted as our key players interacted with evolving trends. Each section has three chapters, beginning with one that clarifies religious demographics and flags major historical developments at a high level of generality. Each section then follows with two chapters that zoom in to treat selected cases in more detail, concentrating on sociopolitical issues in the middle chapter of each section and cultural issues in its concluding chapter. There will be a sense of circling through related material more than once, somewhat like holding up a cut gem and examining its facets from different angles. Sometimes we will be looking at a different part of the gem; other times what is interesting is the shifting play of light on the same part of the gem.

New Key Players on the Landscape: Jews and Roman Catholics

By 1900, Jews had emerged as a key player alongside the groups introduced above, largely on the strength of nineteenth-century immigration.[1] A handful of Jews had been present at least since 1654 when a small group arrived in New Amsterdam (later New York) and successfully lobbied to stay over the objections of its governor. Their arrival was part of the fallout from a Christian campaign to expel Muslims from Spain in the 1400s, a campaign of Catholic expansion that the colonization schemes of Columbus extended. The fortunes of Spanish Jews took a sharp turn for the worse after this struggle. Jews were exiled, pressured to convert, and hounded by the Spanish Inquisition. The 1654 immigrants were refugees from this persecution, having escaped to Holland, moved to a Dutch settlement in Brazil, and then fled when Spain took over this settlement. Sephardic Jews – that is, Jews of Spanish ancestry – had different customs and a higher social status than Ashkenazi Jews from central Europe who joined them in the Americas. However, because the community was so tiny – in 1776 its total size in the British colonies was less than a tenth of one per cent of the population – Sephardim and Ashkenazim had to co-operate to maintain synagogues and hire specialized workers to do such things as butcher meat in approved ways, serve as cantors to lead worship, and perform the initiation ritual of circumcision. Wealthy lay trustees dominated the community's life because the first rabbis (teacher/scholars who served as Jewish authorities) did not arrive until the 1840s. If people needed legal judgments they wrote to rabbis in Europe. Most Jews worked as merchants, as they had done in Europe where they were forbidden to own land. Over several generations in the colonies, they blended into the emerging business classes.

After 1820, immigration from Germany increased, and Jews were soon building synagogues and establishing themselves as merchants throughout the country, often working their way up from jobs as traveling peddlers. From 1776 to 1880 the population increased a hundredfold to 250,000. Still this was well under one per cent of the population. The numbers swelled between 1880 and 1920, when impoverished Jews from small towns in Poland and Russia suffered intense persecution. Perhaps a third of all east European Jews emigrated. By 1925 there were 4.5 million Jews in the US, representing more than three per cent of the population and a far higher per centage of the nation's most influential city, New York, where most of the new immigrants and nearly half of all US Jews lived. Other places where Jewish influence was stronger than we might expect from their slice of the demographic pie (now in the two per cent range) include Hollywood, which took off as the center of the film industry in the 1920s under Jewish leadership, certain businesses including the garment trades and banking, and professions such as law and university teaching. Although most Jews, especially the immigrants of 1880–1920, arrived extremely impoverished, the community as a whole prospered so much that by the Cold War era many people found it natural to talk about the country's three main religions – Protestant, Catholic, and Jewish – as roughly equal in cultural weight.

However, in 1900 the community was either very small (insofar as we are discussing relatively prosperous Jews) or extremely poor and centered on self-contained ethnic neighborhoods in a few cities (insofar as Jews had significant demographic weight). It was not until the children and grandchildren of the immigrants of 1880–1920 moved out of inner city ghettos into the suburbs and professions on a large scale – joining Jews from long-established families – that the community entered the mainstream. This happened throughout the twentieth century, although not without resistance from Anglo-Protestants. Jews suffered various kinds of social and economic discrimination and there were more than enough anti-Semitic politicians to be worrisome.

The first wave of German immigrants embraced Reform Judaism, a movement somewhat analogous to Deism and Unitarianism in its stress on reason, ethics, and using Enlightenment criteria to evaluate which traditions to retain and which to leave behind. Reform Judaism implied change in how the community was structured and religion itself was understood. Jews had existed as a community dispersed around the Mediterranean and Europe ever since the Romans destroyed their Jerusalem temple in AD 70; rabbis had become community leaders and guardians of tradition. Although the community was multifaceted – in Europe the Yiddish language and the stories and songs associated with it were especially important – much community life centered on studying Jewish holy texts, the Torah and the Talmud, and observing the laws set down in them. Torah refers to the first five books of the Hebrew Bible – what Christians call the Old Testament – and by extension to a larger set of laws and sensibilities for structuring an observant life. The Talmud is a set of commentaries on Torah by rabbis. Consider how the US Constitution is continually being reinterpreted for new situations through a body of legal precedents and innovations. Somewhat similarly, Jews study and debate the Torah and its Talmudic interpretations.

Until recently women were excluded from this study – in fact, Orthodox Jewish men still say a daily prayer thanking God that they were not born as women, so that they can study the Torah. However, all Jewish men, not just a few rabbis, were ideally supposed to dedicate themselves to this study. In practice there is a range of commitment to this ideal. Nevertheless, among all the world's religions, Judaism is among those most focused on literacy – a focus that helps to explain the success of Jews in the US educational system compared with Native Americans and many Christian groups. It also makes Judaism highly 'portable' compared with religions centered on particular regional landscapes, since it can move wherever Jewish communities can study Torah and follow its laws. Because European Christians typically forced Jews to live in self-contained ghettos – and because these communities often suffered persecution and/or exile – an internally rich and outwardly defensive Jewish culture grew up around this religious center.

By the early 1800s in Germany, and almost from the beginning in the Americas, Jews faced an unaccustomed choice between blending into the wider society and continuing to live in close-knit communities built around a distinctive culture. How should Jews respond to Enlightenment experiments with religious freedom, in which governments assumed that many religions could coexist, largely as matters of private belief, but that the public realm of work and politics could be religiously neutral? Reform Jews made the controversial decision to privatize their religion, focus on abstract ethical teachings as opposed to a set of customs and rituals that shape an entire way of life, and change (hopefully improve) many aspects of their life that were in tension with the hegemonic society. Led by rabbis such as Isaac Meyer Wise of Cincinnati and institutions he helped to create such as the Hebrew Union College, Reform synagogues moved further and faster than other Jews down the road of creating a Judaism that felt at home in modernity. For example, they argued that following the elaborate dietary laws prescribed by Torah (also known as keeping kosher) and separating the sexes during worship (women often sat in a balcony behind a screen) were not required for faithful Jews in the modern world. Such practices no longer seemed sensible, much less mandatory, when weighed against the Jewish value of celebrating the human capacity to critique and improve outmoded traditions. Reform Jews noted that core truths of the Torah had been expressed in many cultural-legal forms over the years; they argued that progress required holding onto these kernels of wisdom but leaving behind the husk of traditionalism in order to build appropriate Jewish practice for the modern era.

Most Reform Jews stopped keeping kosher – in a famous case, the Hebrew Union College scandalized conservatives by serving shellfish, a food traditionally considered unclean, at a commencement banquet – and their synagogues used 'family pews' so that men and women could participate together. This was just one way in which worship moved toward what was called decorum, which generally meant that attending synagogue was becoming more like middle-class Protestant worship: more solemn and emotionally subdued, with vernacular instead of Hebrew language, and increased women's participation. Rabbis came to act more like Protestant clergy, as opposed to their traditional roles as scholars. They were expected to give talks somewhat like Protestant sermons, manage synagogues and raise money for various projects, and generally please a clientele that presupposed the voluntarism that shaped US religion – that is, people could decide for themselves whether or not to co-operate with a rabbi's plans. The goal was to blend mainstream US and Jewish identities into a seamless whole. However, one long-term consequence was a sense that there could be something like 'religious Jewishness' – the private practice of Judaism – distinguishable from being Jewish as a total culture and way of life. (A later movement called Reconstructionism sought to soften this distinction by valorizing a broader sense of 'positive historical Judaism,' within an approach that presupposed Reform Judaism's adjustments to modernity as opposed to reviving orthodox observance.)

East European Jews who immigrated between 1880 and 1920 had little interest in a Reform version of Jewish identity. They lived in a different socioeconomic and linguistic world from assimilated German-Americans. Either they wanted to be Orthodox, or they wanted to be part of a general Jewish community – living in Jewish neighborhoods, eating Jewish foods, speaking Yiddish, and so on – without studying the Torah or investing significant time at any synagogue at all. In general the third of east European Jews who came to the US represented the least pious third of the community, since Old World rabbis discouraged emigration, fearing that America was unclean and irreligious. Orthodox rabbis were scarce, and a sizable number of immigrants were indifferent or hostile to synagogues. Nevertheless, most immigrants were fairly observant; typically groups of men from the same region in Europe organized a set of small and decentralized synagogues in urban storefronts. Families observed the Sabbath and other traditional practices as they could.[2]

The story was different for these immigrants' children and grandchildren. Among Jews, like many other ethnic groups, there was a pattern in which first generation immigrants attempted to transplant Old World practices as fully as possible, but their children ran as far away from these traditions as they could. Later, what the second generation had tried to forget, the third generation tried to remember – but in a revised form, less as a total way of life and more as a personal choice of selected practices which made less dense and authoritative claims on their lives. The form of Jewish religion that benefited most from this pattern was Conservative Judaism (Orthodox Judaism remains vital down to the present, but as a minority option).

By the mid-twentieth-century, Conservatives had become the largest Jewish religious group because their suburban synagogues captured the most second and third generation immigrants. Conservative congregations, as well as Reform congregations which were close behind them in numbers, often built large synagogue centers that served as community centers as well as spaces for worship and studying the Torah – not merely humble *shuls*, or places for prayer, but often '*shuls* with pools.' The weekly rhythm of such congregations became a thinner suburban version of the more vibrant communal life of inner-city neighborhoods. Many rabbis complained that attending worship was one of the lower priorities of congregation members, except on holidays such as Yom

Kippur or when youth celebrated their coming-of-age ceremonies called *bar mitzvahs* (and by mid-century also *bat mitzvahs* for girls). In general, Jews attend weekly worship at significantly lower rates than Christians.

Conservative Judaism represents a compromise position between Reform and Orthodoxy. Compared with Reform it is more reluctant to change traditions in the name of progress and enlightenment. It attempts to remain observant unless it sees compelling reasons to change. Thus, while Reform rabbis boldly Americanized, the president of the Conservatives' leading school, the Jewish Theological Seminary, wrote that 'there is nothing in American citizenship which is incompatible with our observing the dietary laws, our sanctifying the Sabbath ... or our perpetuating any other law essential to the preservation of Judaism ... In this great, glorious, and free country we Jews need not sacrifice a single iota of our Torah.'[3] Nevertheless, most Conservative Jews moved from inner-city neighborhoods to the suburbs during the middle years of the century and lived relatively assimilated middle-class lives. Although they were slower than Reform Jews to adopt family seating, permit people to drive to synagogues on the Sabbath (the strictly observant only walk because of the many prohibitions on Sabbath activities), or allow women to read from scrolls of Torah during worship, by mid-century Conservatives had adopted all these practices. Later, Reform Jews would be the first to ordain a female rabbi, in 1972, while the Jewish Theological Seminary did not accept female rabbinical students until 1983 (Orthodox Jews still do not ordain women). Often Conservatives expected their rabbis to keep kosher, and they themselves made some efforts to observe dietary laws, but they did not follow these laws strictly, especially when they ate at restaurants or socialized with Gentiles.

A fourth Jewish movement that is deeply inflected by religion (if not a religious tendency in its own right) cuts across the Reform, Conservative, Orthodox, and secular camps. This is Zionism, or Jewish nationalism – support for an autonomous homeland where Jews could form their own state free of persecution by Gentiles. Zionism began to build momentum in the 1890s under the leadership of Theodore Herzl. He lobbied the British government for land in Palestine – which became part of the British Empire after World War I – and pioneering Zionists began to build settlements there. At first most US Jews were lukewarm or hostile toward Zionism. Reform Jews stressed universal values over nationalist commitments, and if asked to identify with a state they opted for the US. 'We are unalterably opposed to political Zionism,' they declared. 'America is our Zion.'[4] Jewish socialists also stressed universal values – in this case the international solidarity of workers – and they saw Zionism as wrongheaded and divisive. Many Orthodox Jews felt that Zionism cheapened messianic hopes that should be left in God's hands when they reduced them to everyday politics; for example, Herzl preferred to base his state in Palestine, but was willing to negotiate with the British for part of Uganda if necessary.

Nevertheless, the idea of a safe and autonomous homeland was attractive, and envisioning Jewish control of the historic city of Jerusalem resonated with Biblical texts about the return of the Messiah. Zionism picked up significant support in the 1930s when only a handful of Jewish refugees from Nazism were allowed to enter the US. Then, during and after World War II, the tide shifted and Zionism gained strong majority support as people learned of the magnitude of Hitler's effort to exterminate all European Jews in death camps. Jews sent monetary donations to Israel after its 1948 founding and often traveled there. They created many groups that are Zionist either in the narrow sense of supporting Israel, or the broader sense of pursuing a model of autonomous Jewish organization and self-defense. For example, the largest Jewish women's group, Hadassah, is Zionist; it was first organized to aid Jews in Palestine early in the century. Jews successfully lobbied the US government for strong pro-Israeli policies, joined by conservative Christians who saw Israel fulfilling Biblical prophecies. Relatively few US Jews have seriously considered moving to Israel, and in recent years they have increasingly questioned whether Israeli policies toward the Palestinians are morally defensible and/or in the best interests of Jews. Nevertheless, participation in a broadly Zionist movement became part of the identity of most US Jews, at least as a broad cultural sensibility.

Although no immigrant religion increased in cultural and demographic weight more than Jews, Roman Catholics were the immigrants who made the greatest overall impact between the mid-1800s and mid-1900s because of the huge numbers of people involved.[5] We have seen that, even though Catholicism was the most influential European religion in the Americas throughout the colonial era, it was marginal in the British colonies before the early 1800s. This changed dramatically by the 1840s, when the staple crop of potatoes failed in the predominantly Catholic country of Ireland, and millions of Irish came to the US. They joined considerable numbers of Irish who had already arrived, as well as another large group of German Catholics who had settled in rural communities in the Midwest.

Considered as proportion of the population at the time (as opposed to raw numbers, which grew in later years) this was the largest immigration wave in US history, and its impact was compounded by two religious factors. First, since the Irish were the first large group of US Catholics and were strongly committed to building churches, they came to dominate the leadership ranks of the US Catholic hierarchy down to the present. Secondly, these immigrants entered a country where the hegemonic groups were intensely anti-Catholic. Protestants literally defined their religion in opposition to Catholics. Well into the twentieth century, when speaking of a 'Christian America' they meant 'Protestant America'; they nursed bitter memories of Protestant–Catholic wars and the persecution of Protestants by Catholic rulers. Deists, the top defenders of religious freedom among US elites, were even more hostile to Catholic bishops than they were to the Protestant religious establishment. They saw 'Old World' Catholic institutions as the antithesis of progress and democracy and feared that Catholic influence was undermining the democratic virtue of the US. All this was in addition to sociopolitical competition and the Irish impact on the labor market, which also loomed large.[6]

Equally significant for US Catholicism was the Anglo conquest of the Southwest. In the early 1800s Anglo-Protestants began to settle in the northern Mexican territory of Texas and in 1835 they engineered a rebellion that first declared Texas an independent republic, and later brought it into the US as a slave state. Then, during 1846–8, the US went to war with Mexico, primarily to seize its territories between California in the west and Colorado in the east. (There was talk about annexing the entire country, but the same cultural fears that made Anglos worry about absorbing the Irish population also made them worry about absorbing the centers of Mexican population.)

In all these places, longstanding Spanish and Native American communities came under Anglo rule, with considerable violence and expropriation of resources. Wherever there had been Spanish mission settlements, the aggrieved communities were Catholic. Some of the most complex interactions took place when gold was discovered in northern California in 1848. A huge tide of miners and associated fortune-seekers moved to California from China, the eastern US, and South America, joining Native Americans and Spanish *Californios* who had lived there for centuries. The Irish were prominent among the newcomers, and Irish Catholics assumed strong religious leadership. They built on the Spanish missionary presence and competed intensely with Protestant missionaries. Chinese immigration was curtailed in the 1880s, and Protestant and Catholics became dual pillars of the California religious establishment.[7]

Thus, Catholicism rapidly emerged as one of the nation's most powerful churches. By 1850 it claimed more members than any other denomination. This was an apples and oranges comparison since it was based on counting all Irish as Catholics, whereas the Methodists in second place counted only church members. (Baptists did not even count children as members until after they were baptized as young adults.) In any event, by the early decades of the twentieth century there was no ambiguity – due to massive immigration of industrial workers from places like Italy and Poland, Catholics were by far the largest denomination, nearing the twenty-five per cent demographic slice they have roughly maintained to the present.

US Catholics were largely – although not exclusively, especially in the Mexican-American and German-American cases – urban and working class. Although in theory Catholicism was a universal faith for which cultural differences did not matter – each local parish was supposed to offer the same essential teachings/practices and include all people who lived within its territory – in fact, parishes usually catered to specific ethnic groups. Often conflict developed between Irish clergy and Catholics from other ethnic backgrounds. German–Irish tensions were the most intense in the early years, but Italian–Irish and Polish–Irish frictions later reached similar levels; related conflict between Latino/a and Euro-American Catholics continues today. Catholic ethnic groups had major differences in languages, ritual practices, holidays, respect for clergy, attitudes toward alcohol, and other matters. Nevertheless, Catholics shared a focus on weekly attendance at mass, a liturgy in which all Catholics heard the same Latin words and took part in the same celebration of Holy Communion. Catholics were also united in a religious sensibility that placed less emphasis on preaching and individual conversion compared with Protestants; rather it emphasized sacraments, sensual aspects of worship such as incense and pictures of saints, devotional practices such as lighting votive candles and praying the rosary, and a communal sense of shared participation in an overarching tradition that had lasted for centuries.[8]

Frequently churches stood at the center of immigrant community life, interwoven with groups such as unions, lodges, saloons, and political machines in ways that varied from place to place. Immigrants who faced hostility from the dominant culture often desired their own hospitals, orphanages, and other social organizations, especially if their first language was not English. In this context priests and church-related organizations often led efforts to establish such institutions. Bishops worried that educating children in public schools was incompatible with passing on a Catholic faith, given these schools' Protestant teachings and overt goal of assimilating immigrants into a melting pot. Although at first some bishops tried to work with Protestants toward religiously neutral public schools, the majority of bishops voted to reject this strategy. In 1884 they decreed that every parish in the country should sponsor its own school. Education became a central focus of energy for US Catholics. It was the most important job of nuns, whose low-paid work as teachers made the system possible, and the major way that children learned how to be Catholic.

Despite their shared commitment to resist assimilation into a Protestant-flavored melting pot by building autonomous schools, hospitals, and other institutions, Catholic bishops divided between an Americanist tendency led by Cardinal James Gibbons and a more conservative group led by Archbishop Michael Corrigan. The Americanists were somewhat analogous to Reform Jews in their openness to adapting traditions to hegemonic US religious practices – although the differences are also instructive.[9] Americanists bitterly disagreed with traditionalists about strategies for Catholic success: how much compromise and dialogue with Protestants was desirable and/or inevitable? Whereas the Americanists saw themselves responding creatively to positive aspects of US society, traditionalists saw Americanists throwing out the baby with the bathwater because they had been seduced by false ideologies of American progress. They felt that Americanist bishops were becoming too comfortable as junior partners in circles of power and losing touch with their parishioners.

At first Americanists seemed to be winning their battle for control of the US hierarchy, but by the turn of the century they were on the defensive because the leaders of world Catholicism had sided with their opponents. As we will see, positions similar to the Americanists' eventually triumphed. However, before the 1960s Americanists aroused suspicion in the upper ranks of the church hierarchy for what the Vatican feared was excessive accommodation with modernity (even today

Rome's opinions matter because it holds the power to appoint bishops, but Rome had even more leverage before 1908 because the US church still had missionary status). The Vatican felt that US bishops were not fighting hard enough against religious pluralism – an unfortunate situation since (in the Vatican's view) there was only one true Church, which should be recognized by the state. Rome worried about bishops who sought compromises with public schools and/or co-operated with labor unions in which Catholics made common cause with Protestants and socialists. The Vatican also opposed scholarly efforts to harmonize Catholic doctrine with modern ideas or engage in dialogues with other religions on a basis of equal respect. In truth, such scholarship did not advance very far in Catholic circles until later years – but this was largely because Rome forbade such explorations in Catholic schools. In the 1890s, Pope Leo XIII issued pronouncements known as encyclicals that condemned Americanists and called for a church that 'enjoyed the favor of the laws and the patronage of the public authority.'[10] In 1907 Pope Pius X followed with a sweeping condemnation of modernism. Similar decrees by Protestant authorities would simply have caused schisms, but Catholics were centralized enough to enforce policies in their schools and to make most bishops toe the line. At least by Protestant standards, Catholics were remarkably disciplined and unified.

We need to remember, however, that Protestant standards of unity do not set a high bar. Catholic practice on the ground was diverse – especially if we focus on what laity actually did as opposed to what bishops thought they should do. Many clergy saw Rome's condemnation of the Americanists as a damaging blunder; they continued to work for more liberal policies in the spaces available to them, which were by no means trivial, since, once appointed, bishops had considerable autonomy. Moreover, Catholics stress the principle of subsidiarity, which means that decisions should be made at the lowest feasible level of organization. For example, parish priests decide on local matters unless bishops need to intervene, bishops run their dioceses unless cardinals need to intervene, and so on. This plus the immense complexity of Catholic organizational structures – with dioceses, Vatican offices, many orders of priests and nuns, civic groups, conferences, schools, devotional societies, and activist groups co-existing with cross-cutting and overlapping authority – means that Catholics are far less monolithic in practice, compared with both the official policies of its leaders and the fears of its critics. Also, upcoming generations of Catholic laity moved toward the

US mainstream in patterns somewhat like those that we have already noted among Jews – whether or not the Vatican approved. Catholics did not climb the ladder of middle-class success as quickly or consistently as Jews. However, by the mid-twentieth century white Catholics were entering the mainstream as professionals, business leaders, and workers in the nation's most desirable blue-collar jobs.[11] Even before 1900, in many cities with large Catholic populations (including former Puritan strongholds like Boston) Catholics were more than just one key religious player; they were becoming the dominant player.

Emergent Developments in the Protestant Mainstream

Well before 1900, the top evangelical groups (especially Baptists and Methodists) and the heirs to the old Protestant establishment – Episcopalians, Congregationalist descendants of the Puritans, and Presbyterians (the main Calvinist denomination in the middle colonies) – had made an uneasy peace with each other, the better to advance their shared ideals against Deists, Catholics, and alternative religions. Taken together, these Protestants functioned as a religious establishment. Although this was not a formal legal establishment, Protestant influence became more pervasive in the nineteenth century than it had been during the colonial era. Public schools featured Bible readings and Protestant prayers, churches were tax exempt, laws enforced the Christian practice of closing businesses on Sundays, most universities were church related with clergy as presidents, Congress had chaplains, clergy administered Indian reservations, and politicians filled their speeches with words like 'Christian Nation' and 'God bless America.'[12]

Protestant ideals based on faith and revelation blended, at least in the popular mind, with Enlightenment ideals that emphasized progress and reason. People assumed that things stressed by Deists, such as democracy and freedom, advanced hand-in-hand with things stressed by evangelicals, such as mission and morality. Already in the revolutionary era, while Deists spearheaded the independence movement using ideologies of natural rights guaranteed by Nature's God, Protestant preachers had followed close behind, preaching what scholars call civil millennialism. In other words, they perceived the new nation as representing progress toward fulfilling God's will in history, and they spoke about this progress in relation to the millennium, a thousand-year period of peace mentioned in Biblical texts about the end of time. Sermons often assumed that the new republic could play a vanguard role in God's plan for the future of humankind, thus fulfilling Puritan dreams of building a city on the hill. Dramatizing this sensibility, the committee that designed the Great Seal of the US considered using an image of the Exodus; eventually they settled on the slogans, *Annuit Coeptis* (God smiles on our undertaking) and *Novus Ordo Saeclorum* (a new order of the ages).[13]

Such ideas continued during the era of Manifest Destiny. Conquest that appears in retrospect to American Studies scholars – and certainly appeared to Native Americans and Latino/as at the time – as a sordid and bloody exercise of imperialist greed, appeared from the perspective of whites (especially Protestants, but joined on this issue by many Catholics and Jews) as, on balance, a virtuous and divinely mandated extension of progress, democracy, and religious civilization. Protestants built a dense network of organizations known as the Benevolent Empire to promote their values and push for social reforms. In the absence of an official state religion this network was voluntary, but it had a quasi-established flavor. Some of its interlocking organizations were sponsored by single denominations; others were co-operative or independent. Missionary societies supported work both on the US frontier and in places like India and China. Organizations such as the Young Men's Christian Association (YMCA) and the settlement house movement sought to uphold a sense of Protestant identity in emerging cities and to help immigrants address the challenges they faced. Other groups published Bibles, tracts, periodicals, and pulp fiction that promoted Christian values. Some of these causes were mainly part of efforts to proselytize and were relatively apolitical, although they did strengthen Protestant cultural hegemony. However, other parts of the Benevolent Empire promoted controversial political causes like abolishing slavery, winning women's right to vote, and outlawing alcohol. As we will see, in the twentieth century Progressive reform, labor conflicts, and war became major preoccupations of this network.

A movement for church unity, or ecumenism, developed partly out of Protestant co-operation on such causes ('life and work' issues) and partly from a search for common ground on theology and structures of denominational authority ('faith and order' issues). By 1908 a Federal Council of Churches linked many of the top Protestant denominations, and in 1950 this expanded into the National Council of Churches (NCC). Related processes spearheaded by missionary leaders led to a World Council of Churches (WCC), which represents something like a Protestant version of the United Nations. By the 1950s these councils, along with several denominational bureaucracies and social service agencies, were headquartered in a New York office building nicknamed the God Box.

Let us consider the so-called seven sisters that were the largest Protestant groups as the century opened. The largest family was Methodism; it included black and white branches that had split around 1800, as well as northern and southern branches of white Methodism that had split over the Civil War. (In 1939 most white Methodists patched up their differences and formed the precursor of today's United Methodist Church.) Some of the strongest activist agencies were Methodist. Baptists were in second place as a group – although as we have seen, their family was deeply divided. Relatively liberal northern Baptists (known as American Baptists after 1907) represented them among the seven sisters, while the larger Southern Baptist Convention (SBC), and many smaller groups stayed aloof from the establishment. (The SBC passed the Methodists to become the largest Protestant denomination by the late twentieth century.) In third place were Presbyterians, who had grown from their base as elite churches in colonies such as New Jersey and Pennsylvania to become the largest Calvinist denomination. Presbyterians maintained high educational standards for their clergy and a more centralized organizational structure than most evangelicals; they attracted relatively affluent and urban members.[14]

Next in line was Lutheranism, the tradition of most Scandinavians and many Germans. Lutherans were nearly as prone to schism as Baptists, with organizational divides reflecting dozens of differences based on ethnicity (Swedes versus Norwegians versus Germans versus others), doctrine (more versus less pietistic), region (East versus Midwest), and time of immigration (earlier and more assimilated versus later and more 'ethnic'). However, Lutherans were coalescing into a three-party system by the first half of the century. One cluster included most Norwegians and was more Midwestern. Another included most Swedes and was stronger in eastern cities; it was somewhat less pietistic and its leaders were better connected in establishment circles. Germans were important in both branches. If we compare stances toward assimilation among Lutherans to the stances of Jewish immigrants, both these Lutheran clusters were most analogous to Conservative Judaism. Early in the century Lutherans included many second and third generation immigrants, and although their overall instincts were traditional they were open to changes such as shifting from Swedish to English liturgies, blending selected aspects of Anglo-American revivalism with traditional liturgies, and embracing middle-class values. By 1988 these two groups merged to form the Evangelical Lutheran Church in America. A third group, the Lutheran Church Missouri Synod, took a stance more analogous to Orthodox Jews. It clung to the German language and a sectarian ethnic-religious identity based on strict readings of Lutheran doctrine. Like Catholicism it built its own school system because it mistrusted public schools. In the twentieth century, most Missouri Synod Lutherans assimilated into the middle class while retaining their strict doctrines; thus insofar as they are like Orthodox Jews, the relevant comparison is mainstream orthodox practice rather than ultra-orthodox Hasidic communities. Scholars often mapped the Missouri Synod with the fundamentalist Christian right, although its theology and liturgical style remained distinctive.

As the twentieth century opened, Lutherans were the least visible of the seven groups in the establishment, despite the efforts of some of their leaders. In many places, especially the rural Midwest, Lutheran churches were more like Catholic parishes catering to ethnic enclaves than downtown Presbyterian churches. Although Lutherans (along with Reformed immigrants from Holland and Germany) faced less resistance to cultural acceptance than any other group of non-Anglo immigrants, this resistance was not trivial for impoverished rural people whose first language was not English. Like Catholics, Lutheran immigrants often built their communities around churches. By mid-century most Lutherans were entering the urban middle class or were reasonably prosperous farmers, and scholars typically mapped most Lutherans, except the Missouri Synod, in the Protestant mainstream. They played an increasingly significant role, due in part to a demographic weight that is now larger than Presbyterians.[15]

Before discussing the fifth of our seven sisters, let us briefly note the sixth and seventh, the Congregationalists (heirs to the parts of the Puritan establishment that did not become Unitarian) and Episcopalians. Both steadily lost market share to evangelicals – not just since the 1960s as common wisdom has it, but since 1800 at the latest. Nevertheless, their historical momentum and elite membership meant that they remained important, especially in prestigious seminaries and ecumenical organizations. Episcopalians have been the nation's wealthiest religious group throughout most of US history – although Jews now equal it on this front – and nearly half of all US Presidents have been either Episcopalian or Presbyterian. (The family of George W. Bush is predominantly

Episcopalian; although Bush is formally a Methodist, the church he most often attends is a liberal Episcopal one.) Alongside the theological differences among Protestant churches, class differences are equally important; southerners used to joke that 'A Methodist is a Baptist who wears shoes; a Presbyterian is a Methodist who has gone to college; an Episcopalian is a Presbyterian who lives off his investments.'[16] Although by 1900 the leading congregations in all these denominations were solidly middle-class, levels of affluence and distinctions between old and new wealth remained important.

To place the fifth sister, the Disciples of Christ, we need to introduce two additional branches on the 'tree' of the wider evangelical movement. We will call these the 'Of Christ' and 'Of God' families because many sub-groups in each family end the names of their churches with these words.[17] (Not all denominational names ending with these words match the families, but enough do so to serve as a rule of thumb.) The 'Of Christ' family was a strong force alongside Baptists and Methodists in Southern and Midwestern revivalism in the 1800s. Its leaders were dismayed by denominational divisiveness and sought to restore the purity and unity of Christianity by returning to original or 'primitive' Biblical precedents. Thus, they are also known as Restorationists, and their ideas influenced not only their own churches but also kindred groups like Primitive Baptists. At first they simply went by the name 'Christians,' and throughout their history they have been leaders in the push for church unity. Nevertheless, they eventually formed their own denomination. This denomination later split between the more liberal and northern-based Disciples of Christ – the fifth of our seven sisters – and the more conservative and southern-based Churches of Christ.

At the turn of the century the 'Of God' family was far more likely to be ignored or disparaged as 'Holy Rollers' than to be mentioned as part of the establishment; it attracted economically disadvantaged people and many considered it strange and exotic. Nevertheless, it was gaining strength and by the end of the century it had grown into one of the leading players on the religious landscape. Like Baptists the 'Of God's' have a bewildering number of sub-groups, but they cluster in two camps. The older camp, the Holiness Movement, began in the mid-1800s. It was largely an offshoot of Methodism but also drew other people who desired a renewal of piety. It includes denominations like the Church of the Nazarene, the Salvation Army, and several simply named 'Church of God.'

Recall that many evangelicals rejected Calvinist teachings about human depravity and the futility of good works. Holiness churches radicalized this critique, with varying theological emphases. Some remained within a broad Reformed tradition but aimed for deeper piety and spiritual empowerment, while others swung the theological pendulum to the opposite extreme from Calvinism, so that their goal was not merely salvation in which one's debt of sin is forgiven despite ongoing guilt. Rather, salvation was only a first step, after which believers could advance to a second step of becoming perfectly 'sanctified,' or holy. Holiness groups spoke of a foursquare gospel. The first side of the square, being 'born again,' did not distinguish them from other evangelicals, but there were three more sides. One was expecting an imminent return of Christ to end history. Two more tapped into the supernatural blessings (or charismatic gifts) of divine healing and receiving a Holy Ghost Baptism that perfected and empowered them.[18]

Whereas nineteenth-century evangelicals often joined the middle class and smoothed off their rough edges of emotionalism and radicalism, Holiness believers continued to nurture counter-cultural sensibilities, organize camp meetings, and press for revival. One of the most radical Holiness groups (a tiny but still revealing minority) interprets the Biblical text 'They shall take up serpents and if they drink any deadly thing it will not hurt them' (Mark 16:18) not as a metaphor of God's protection or even a conditional promise like 'if you are bitten by a serpent you will not die.' Rather, they read it as a literal command from God to handle poisonous snakes. Through obeying this command they have created a form of worship that dramatizes the precariousness of life and the depth of their faith in the most visceral way imaginable, with an impressive sense of community and purpose.[19] (If, as some sociologists theorize, churches thrive if they do not allow 'free-riders' to join them without making a serious commitment, serpent-handling churches should be the fastest growing religion in the world!) Most Holiness people interpreted sanctification in less extreme ways: working hard; cultivating virtues like witnessing and charity; studying the Bible; and avoiding behaviors such as dancing, attending movies, and (for women) wearing clothes deemed inappropriate such as pants or sexy outfits. In any case a drive toward radical obedience and a sanctified life remained.

The second sub-group in the 'Of God' family, Pentecostalism, began around the turn of the century as an offshoot of the Holiness movement that drew especially deeply on African-American ecstatic worship and focused special attention on the charismatic gift of speaking in tongues.

The Bible speaks about Jesus's disciples receiving the ability to speak in unknown foreign languages, or tongues, on the day of Pentecost, shortly after his execution and resurrection. To tap this ability in the present, Pentecostal worship cultivated the build-up of ecstatic emotion that we have discussed as a feature of evangelical revivalism. Prayer, music, and preaching often focused on bringing worshippers to the point of ecstatically speaking unknown words. Amid the ways that groups in the 'Of God' family blend and diverge – a complex issue because Holiness churches often evolved into Pentecostal ones or were absorbed by them – an emphasis on tongues is what most distinguishes Pentecostals.

Most tongue-speaking seems to be a learned behavior of letting down one's emotional guard – what psychologists call 'disassociating' – and uttering syllables with no objective meaning. However, it is unclear whether this is all that ever happens in tongue-speaking and what psychic depths and/or dialogues with realities beyond the psyche are unlocked through the experience. (One could ask similar questions about ritual healing, whether by Pentecostals or healers in other traditions; although some cases seem to involve self-suggestion or fakery, the relations between psychic processes and healing are so poorly understood that sweeping pronouncements about this matter are hazardous.) Many people clearly craved this sort of experience; whether it trivialized or deepened one's spiritual life remained contentious.

Pentecostals blend what one scholar calls primitive and pragmatic impulses.[20] Primitivism refers to a radical commitment to follow God's spirit wherever it leads, even if this means handling snakes, letting women preach, being jailed for pacifism, or generally forsaking the world. Some Pentecostals traveled to foreign lands without language training, expecting to be able to preach in tongues when they arrived, although this experiment was abandoned with no firm evidence that it ever worked. Pragmatism refers to the ambition, improvisational spirit, and savvy to build institutions by any means necessary – even if this requires disregarding ethical and doctrinal standards expected by others. In this sense Pentecostals have been quite 'worldly' despite their primitivism. The combination of both impulses in the same people helped Pentecostals build churches, radio stations, Bible schools, and other institutions faster than virtually any other denomination. Starting from nothing at the turn of the twentieth century, by the end of the century they had become one of the leading US denominational families and even a world religion.

Pentecostals extended the blending of African and European influences begun by earlier African-American Christians; to some extent, tongue speaking represents a Christianization of practices similar to African spirit possession. We could go overboard with such thinking, because it is clear that the roots of Pentecostalism are not solely African-American. Holiness churches, dispensationalist teaching, and European revivalism were key influences, and white Pentecostals often claim that a white preacher named Charles Parham started the movement on New Year's Day in 1901. Nevertheless, southern revivals had brought together black and white for decades before Parham. At key revivals that formed the backdrop for Pentecostalism, blacks were present who had experienced Afro-Caribbean practices in which devotees go into trances and allow spirits to possess their bodies and speak through them. By far the most important event for launching the Pentecostal movement, the 1906–9 Azusa Street Revival in Los Angeles, was led by a black preacher, William Seymour. Thus, tongue speaking and other Pentecostal practices can be interpreted, at least in part, as a 'blackenization' of evangelicalism. (We should be clear, however, that this line of interpretation is foreign to the mindset of most Pentecostals; they see themselves responding to God and recovering practices from Biblical times, not from Africa.)[21]

During the first two decades of the twentieth century, Pentecostalism was among the more racially integrated social spaces in the whole country. Some southern Pentecostal churches remained integrated for years even during the depths of Jim Crow segregation, with ministers like Seymour serving as mentors for white Holiness clergy. This was by no means a trivial matter even though it was short-lived. However, Pentecostalism largely failed to sustain itself as an inter-racial movement; it split into predominantly black denominations (notably the Church of God in Christ) and predominantly white ones such as the Assemblies of God.

Three Final Groups, plus Multiple Maps for Multiple Interactions of our Key Players

We must be careful not to extend our lists too long in an effort to be comprehensive, until we are like travelers who become obsessed with seeing just one more site, and then another, until all their companions are burned out and exhausted. Nevertheless, before we reflect on how to map interactions among our key players – the founding cast of characters introduced in Chapter 1 plus Jewish and Catholic immigrants and emergent Protestant groups like Lutherans and Pentecostals – three additional groups beyond the mainstream require brief mention. Although they are not key players on all national maps, they are major forces in certain cultural niches, and far too important to neglect entirely.

One such group is Orthodox Christianity, a tradition as rich as Roman Catholicism, with roots reaching back to the beginnings of Christianity in eastern Europe and southwest Asia. Compared with other forms of Christianity, it has an especially profound and elaborate liturgical life and visual culture. When thinking about the sin from which Christianity saves people, Orthodox believers put less stress on breaking a sinner's pride and forgiving willful wrongdoing, and more stress on overcoming ignorance and gaining spiritual wisdom. Orthodox churches split with Rome in 1054, long before the Reformation, and came to exist as a set of loosely associated, often competitive, national churches. An especially powerful bishop called a patriarch, who ideally works as an arm of the state, leads each church. Historically, Orthodox churches have had even less distance from political-administrative power than have Roman Catholics, and the patriarch of Constantinople (later Istanbul) has exercised special power. Orthodox Christians came to the US from places like Russia, Serbia, Syria, Armenia, and Romania during the same decades as east European Catholics and Jews. There are Orthodox variations on many of the same questions about immigration, ethnicity, and assimilation faced by Roman Catholics and Jews.[22]

Amid a kaleidoscope of Orthodox groups in the US, the Russian and Greek Churches are the most influential. The Russians have a longer history in the Americas, beginning in Alaska in the 1700s.[23] Its missionaries baptized perhaps a sixth of Alaska's native people and mediated between native converts and Russian traders who were more interested in exploiting the natives than converting them. By the early 1900s the church had moved its headquarters to New York and emerged as an umbrella organization for Orthodox immigrants from many places. However, because of traditional entanglements between this church and the Russian state, its politics became murky after the Russian Revolution of 1917 – schisms resulted as churches representing non-Russian groups declared independence and disputes about who were the legitimate Russian Orthodox leaders wound up in the US courts. Nevertheless, the top Russian group, the Orthodox Church of America, remains one of the two leading Orthodox groups in the US, along with the larger

Greek Orthodox Church, which had two million members by the 1990s. In the National and World Councils of Churches, the rich history of Orthodox Christians and their ability to mediate between Protestants and Roman Catholics make them important in ecumenical dialogues. However, Orthodox leaders have acted at times as brakes on innovation, especially efforts toward gender equality, because of their male leadership and traditionalism.

A group introduced in Chapter 1, the Mormons, experienced striking growth and change from the late nineteenth century to the present. In the mid-1800s Mormons built a series of settlements that were embroiled in conflict with non-Mormon neighbors. After an Illinois mob murdered their founder, Joseph Smith, the main branch of Mormons moved to a territory near the Great Salt Lake, where they displaced Shoshone and Ute Indians (smaller Mormon groups broke away at this time). By the time of the Civil War, both the theocratic Mormon state and the territory of Utah claimed this land, and for four decades there were dual governments jockeying for power. Since the US Army easily won the military confrontation, the main negotiations were about the terms under which Utah could enter the Union as a state. At this time the press was fascinated by Mormon polygamy. Although this practice was modeled on the Bible – in general, Mormons emerged from the same matrix as Restorationists who tried to rebuild Christianity on Biblical precedents – many people saw plural marriage as an anti-woman outrage and interpreted it along similar lines as the popular image of Oriental harems. Others used polygamy as an opportunity to talk publicly about sex in a context in which the subject was largely taboo.

Mormon family law became a test case for how much deviance from 'normal' religious practice would be tolerated. Although polygamy was outlawed in 1862, many Mormons ignored the law – perhaps a quarter of their families had multiple wives – and in 1879 the issue came to a head in the Supreme Court's first case based on the Constitution's free exercise clause. In *Reynolds* v. *US*, the court ruled that the Constitution guaranteed the freedom of a Mormon elder (George Reynolds) to his 'opinions' about doctrine, but not his freedom to engage in *behaviors* 'in violation of social duties or subversive of good order.'[24] This included polygamy, even though Reynolds testified that he would be damned if he did not practice it. (The court's distinction – freedom of religious opinion but criminalization of religious behavior – set a precedent for many subsequent cases.) Eventually the US took the reins of power in Utah, where it seized Mormon economic resources and refused to give them back unless Mormons renounced polygamy and capitulated to the US legal system, in which case they could get their property back and become a state. In the 1890s this deal was done. In some ways it represented a defeat for Mormons, but since they dominated Utah's demographics and economy they were able to put a strong stamp on the regional culture. Mormon traditionalists still practice polygamy in a semi-underground way.

Starting from this baseline of conflict with the mainstream, twentieth century Mormons became a paradigmatic example of embracing hegemonic US values. They gave up not only polygamy but most of their economic communalism (although vestiges remain in their discipline of giving and their social service system). Far from maintaining cultural-economic radicalism, Mormons tilted toward conservatism, and after 1960 they stressed the centralization of church institutions on a model reminiscent of large corporations. They lobbied to be considered as just one among other Protestant groups – even though some scholars see them more like a separate religion alongside Christians and Jews – and called by their full name, the Church of Jesus Christ of Latter-day Saints (LDS). They stressed their commonalities with other Protestants despite many distinctive teachings and temple practices, including avoiding alcohol and caffeine, wearing special undergarments, teaching that God has a material body and humans evolve into Gods, vicariously baptizing non-Mormons who have already died to give them a place in heaven, and teaching an unorthodox account of ancient American history based on the *Book of Mormon*. Largely because its young adults are required to spend two years as missionaries, Mormonism is among the world's fastest-growing religions. Beginning in 1890 with a quarter of a million people living on land that Easterners considered no more desirable than an Indian reservation, Mormons ended the twentieth century with five million US members and an equally large number around the world, especially in Latin America. Mormons and Orthodox Churches each had a one per cent slice of the US demographic pie, rivaling groups like Presbyterians and Muslims.[25]

The final group, which we will call positive thinkers, is more diffuse. In some ways it fits best in a map of new religions. However, parts of this loose-knit family tap into metaphysical traditions with deep roots in the past, while others exist as a current within Christianity. Thus, it is better to think of positive thinking as a theme or movement that cuts across multiple traditions, rather than a demographic slice in its own right.[26]

We have noted that Mary Baker Eddy's mental healing system, Christian Science, was a key alternative religion of the nineteenth century. Christian Science continued in the twentieth century and several spin-offs with similar themes also developed. These became loosely associated under the banner of New Thought. If we treat New Thought as the center of gravity in our map of positive thinkers and imagine this movement heading down a path that led in later years toward New Age healing and humanistic psychology, we will see complementary paths branching off in two directions. On the more esoteric and mystical of these paths is the Theosophical Society founded by Helena Blavatsky in 1875. Given its interest in Hindu and Buddhist philosophy and European traditions of hidden (or 'occult') wisdom, Theosophy's path also led toward the New Age movement, but along a route more deeply engaged with Asian traditions.

Meanwhile, pursuing a more pragmatic and middlebrow path were Christian preachers such as Norman Vincent Peale, author of the best-selling book, *The Power of Positive Thinking*. Peale touched lightly on compassion for the poor or conversion from sin; he concentrated on how faith could increase self-confidence, self-actualization, and wealth through cultivating the right mental attitude. Peale did not fit comfortably on either side of conflicts between Christian fundamentalists and modernists. In some ways he was the ultimate folksy evangelical (without much fire and brimstone); in other ways he was the ultimate banal modernist (without much social ethics), but in the end he always returned to prosperity through positive thinking. His path led toward later 'health and wealth' televangelists such as Oral Roberts and Joel Osteen.[27]

It is not entirely clear whether people as diverse as Mary Baker Eddy, Helena Blavatsky, and Norman Vincent Peale really should be mapped together. Group rivalries and the tension between elitist and middle-brow sensibilities make this a murky question. Nevertheless, scholars do attempt to group them. At a minimum they share enough interest in cultivating spiritual dimensions of the self and tapping into hidden energies of the universe – as well as harnessing these energies toward healing, wisdom, and self-actualization – that it is interesting to bring them into dialogue. As a group they are a significant current within US religion even though most New Thought organizations are quite small.

How should we chart the relationships among our growing (although still over-simplified) list of key players? Categorizing them by denomination or ethnic group – the main way we have proceeded so far – is not the only useful approach. Although such maps are a good place to start, there are family resemblances among many groups – for example, different forms of evangelicals and immigrants – and not all of their conflicts developed along denominational or ethnic lines. Irish Catholics and Southern Baptists worked together in the Democratic Party against northern Protestants who formed the backbone of the Republican Party. Black and white Protestants struggled bitterly, as did diverse Catholic groups. Although divides between corporate elites and working-class people often did break down along lines that matched denominations – for example, Episcopalian owners versus Catholic laborers – employers could be Christian, Jewish, or agnostic, and workers were drawn from nearly every religious group.

If we search for the factors that structure the most helpful maps, a leading contender is racial and ethnic difference. This should already be clear, and we will have more to say about it below. Other top contenders are class and gender. As we will highlight in Chapter 3, lines of class and religion often coincided and there were important associations between religion and gender; often it was hard to disentangle the distinction between normative feminine behavior and conventional religious behavior. Not to be forgotten is North–South conflict. Wounds were still raw from the Civil War at the turn of century, and North–South schisms in denominations such as the Methodists and Presbyterians remained a basic structural divide in US religion. Some of the bitterness between whites from the North and South healed during the years around World War I, due both to wartime co-operation and a sense of white Protestant solidarity against a tide of immigrants. Nevertheless, the religious and racial dynamics of the regions remained distinct.

Thinking about regional patterns from a different angle, a rural–urban split was highly consequential for religion. Although cities were rapidly growing, in 1920 half of all citizens still lived in rural areas. Catholics and Lutherans in eastern cities lived in a different world from Lutheran farmers on the plains or Catholic miners in the West. The Populist movement – the mobilization of impoverished southern and Midwestern farmers against bankers, railroads, and other corporate interests that were bleeding them dry – blended its economic goals (co-operative ownership of grain-shipping businesses, tax reform, and fairer banking policy) with a movement culture that blended democratic and co-operative values, religious rhetoric, and grassroots organizing that drew on church networks. The Populist leader, William Jennings Bryan, later defended fundamentalism over evolutionary theory at the Scopes Monkey Trial. For Bryan, Christian values supported grassroots democracy, whereas the survival of the fittest justified the rule of monopolistic railroad barons and bankers who threw farmers out of their homes.[28]

Each of these divides had a major effect on what one heard in church, whom one embraced as a religious ally, and where one's charitable donations went – yet none of them matches up reliably with lines on a pie chart based on denominations. One pattern alongside these others (neither more nor less important) does represent a fault line that later widened into the culture war discussed in the Introduction. This was the fundamentalist–modernist conflict that peaked in the 1920s, when Protestant liberals from establishment denominations battled conservatives from these same denominations (joined by many Holiness and Pentecostal people) over stances toward emerging intellectual and social changes. We will return to this conflict. For now let us simply note that liberals won most of the battles for control of large denominations, but fundamentalists did not respond by folding up and dying. They built their own network of schools, radio stations, publishing houses, and independent denominations. By the end of century these grew into the most powerful sector in US religion.

But we are getting ahead of our story. Let us close this chapter by underlining the multiple ways that our key players interacted – through co-operation, peaceful co-existence, or conflict – and looking ahead to upcoming chapters. These will select a few cultural–political issues of the early twentieth century and explore more concretely how religious people interacted with them.

Notes

1   Entry points to the literature on US Judaism include Hasia Diner, *Jews in America* (New York: Oxford University Press, 1999), Joseph Blau, *Judaism in America* (Chicago: University of Chicago Press, 1976), and articles by Jacob Neusner and Jonathan Sarna in *Religion and Immigration: Christian, Jewish, and Muslim Experiences in the United States*, Yvonne Haddad, Jane Smith, and John Esposito, eds, (Lanham: Rowman and Littlefield, 2003).

2   Irving Howe, *The World of Our Fathers* (New York: Galahad Books, 1994), Barbara Myerhoff, *Number Our Days* (New York: Simon and Schuster, 1978).

3   Solomon Schecter cited in Gaustad and Schmidt, *Religious History of America*, 215.

4   Declaration of the Union of American Hebrew Congregations, from 1898, cited in Egal Feldman, *Catholics and Jews in Twentieth Century America* (Urbana: University of Illinois Press, 2001), 40.

5   On Catholic history see James Fisher, *Catholics in America* (New York: Oxford University Press, 2000), Chester Gillis, *Roman Catholicism in America* (New York:

Columbia University Press, 2000), and Jay Dolan, *The American Catholic Experience: A History from Colonial Times to the Present* (Garden City: Image Books, 1985).

6 Hutchison, *Religious Pluralism in America*; Jenny Franchot, *Roads to Rome: the Antebellum Protestant Encounter with Catholicism* (Berkeley: University of California Press, 1994).

7 Laurie Maffly-Kipp, *Religion and Society in Frontier California* (New Haven: Yale University Press, 1994).

8 Dolan, *American Catholic Experience*, paints a vivid picture of immigrant Catholics; see also works of Colleen McDannell and Robert Orsi cited in Chapter 4.

9 Unlike Catholics, Jews had no central authority to enforce policy; each synagogue was autonomous. Unlike bishops who entered modernity with a centuries-old assumption that the Church should be an arm of the state ministering to a Catholic populace, Jews had an even longer experience of minority status and persecution.

10 Leo XIII's encyclical, *Longinqua Oceani* (1895) quoted in *Religion in America* (7th edn), John Corrigan and Winthrop Hudson, eds, (Upper Saddle River: Prentice-Hall, 2004), 272. Other key documents are Leo XIII's 1899 *Testem Benevolentiae* and Pius X's 1907 *Pascendi Dominici Gregis*.

11 A classic study is Will Herberg, *Protestant Catholic Jew* (revised edn) (New York: Anchor, 1960).

12 William Hutchison, ed., *Between the Times: the Travail of the Protestant Establishment in America, 1900–1960* (New York: Cambridge University Press, 1989); Robert Handy, *A Christian America: Protestant Hopes and Historical Realities* (2nd edn) (New York: Oxford University Press, 1984).

13 Sydney Ahlstrom, 'Annuit Coeptis: America as the Elect Nation,' in *Continuity and Discontinuity in Church History*, F. Forrester Church and Timothy George, eds, (Leiden: Brill, 1979), 315–37. Conrad Cherry, ed., *God's New Israel: Religious Interpretations of American Destiny* (revised edn) (Chapel Hill: University of North Carolina Press, 1998).

14 In addition to books cited above see Bill Leonard, *Baptists in America* (New York: Columbia University Press, 2005) and John Wigger, *Taking Heaven By Storm: Methodism and the Rise of Popular Christianity in America* (New York: Oxford University Press, 1998).

15 Surveys in US religion often slight Lutherans; an exception is Ahlstrom, *Religious History*. See also DeAne Lagerquist, *The Lutherans* (Westport: Praeger, 1999).

16 George Marsden, *Religion and American Culture* (New York: Harcourt Brace Jovanovich, 1990), 153.

17 This terminology follows Sam Hill, *One Name But Several Faces: Variety in Popular Christian Denominations in Southern History* (Athens: University of Georgia Press, 1996).

18 See Grant Wacker, *Heaven Below: Early Pentecostals and American Culture* (Cambridge: Harvard University Press, 2001); for further exploration see Edith Blumhofer, *Aimee Semple McPherson: Everybody's Sister* (Grand Rapids: Eerdmans, 1993) and Diane Winston, *Red-Hot and Righteous: the Urban Religion of the Salvation Army* (Cambridge: Harvard University Press, 1999).

19 Dennis Covington, *Salvation on Sand Mountain: Snake Handling and Redemption in Southern Appalachia* (New York: Penguin, 1995).

20 Wacker, *Heaven Below*.

21   In addition to general texts on the black church, see also Iain MacRobert, *The Black Roots and White Racism of Early Pentecostalism* (New York: St. Martin's Press, 1988) and Cheryl Sanders, *Saints in Exile: The Holiness-Pentecostal Experience in African American Religion and Culture* (New York: Oxford University Press, 1996).

22   John Erickson, *Orthodox Christians in America* (New York: Oxford University Press, 1999).

23   Laurie Maffly-Kipp places Russian Orthodox priests in Alaska within a rich mix of groups from Hawaii and the Pacific Rim in 'East-ward ho! American Religion from the perspective of the Pacific Rim,' in Tweed, *Retelling U.S. Religious History*, 127–48.

24   Quoted by Winnifred Fallers Sullivan, 'The State,' in Goff and Harvey, *Themes in Religion and American Culture*, 249.

25   Klaus Hansen, *Mormonism and the American Experience* (Chicago: University of Chicago Press, 1981), Philip Barlow, 'Shifting ground and the third transformation of Mormonism,' in Williams, *Perspectives on American Religion and Culture*, 140–53; Richard Ostling and Joan Ostling, *Mormon America: the Power and the Promise* (San Francisco: HarperSanFrancisco, 1999).

26   Donald Meyer, *The Positive Thinkers: Religion as Pop Psychology from Mary Baker Eddy to Oral Roberts* (2nd edn) (New York: Pantheon, 1980); Beryl Satter, *Each Mind a Kingdom: American Women, Sexual Purity, and the New Thought Movement* (Berkeley: University of California Press, 2000); Mary Farrell Bednarowski, *New Religions and the Theological Imagination in America* (Bloomington: Indiana University Press, 1989).

27   Craig Prentiss, 'Power of positive thinking,' in McDannell, *Religion of the United States in Practice*, 316–27; Carol George, *God's Salesman: Norman Vincent Peale and the Power of Positive Thinking* (New York: Oxford University Press, 1993); David Harrell, *Oral Roberts: An American Life* (Bloomington: Indiana University Press, 1985).

28   Lawrence Goodwyn, *The Populist Moment: a Short History of the Agrarian Revolt in America* (New York: Oxford, 1978); Michael Kazin, *The Populist Persuasion: an American History* (New York: Basic Books, 1995).

CHAPTER 3

Religion and Social Conflict in the Early Twentieth Century

In the Introduction we made plans to explore twentieth-century US religion at a pace analogous to a seven-day trip from New York to Seattle. We discussed how such a trip is inevitably selective. Rather than try to cover everything at a speed that would be like flying over cities and checking them off in a logbook, we planned a representative route through the landscape with a few stops along the way. Such stops cannot fully clarify the multi-leveled and dynamic nature of religion. They do, however, allow us to strike a balance between merely sketching the lay of the land, as we have done in the past two chapters, and treating a few issues in somewhat greater detail to give a feel for the concrete texture of religious life. In the second and third parts of each major section of this book – this chapter and the next one in the middle section, and Chapters 6 and 7 in the final section – we will make a few such stops.

A seven-day trip includes time for one mid-day break and one evening stopover every day. If we use our first day for orientation, the maximum number of cities, museums, natural landmarks, cultural events, and historic sites we can explore during such breaks – if we fill every time-slot – is only twelve, chosen from hundreds of possibilities. In New York alone it is hard to narrow a list of activities to twelve, much less explore the whole city in one night. Yet we are only projecting two or three choices from each of the above categories (cities, museums, landmarks, etc.) during our whole trip. Moreover, some of our choices – for example, attending a baseball game in Chicago, climbing a mountain in Colorado, or visiting the top museums of Washington, DC – deserve more time than we actually have.

In other words, by moving toward nuanced treatments of a few issues, the upcoming chapters intensify the problem of selectivity that we flagged from the outset. Each stop has its distinctive importance, but also represents many roads not taken – some of which readers might return to explore later. Also, even though we are slowing down slightly, we still cannot discuss issues in depth. We must move at a pace that is more like reading a guidebook than spending an extended period in any one place. Nevertheless, a cross-country trip can select a few cities, parks, and events to visit, in ways that serve as a model for later explorations. Likewise the upcoming chapters seek to dramatize the interplay of our key players in relation to a few major issues, giving our tour a blend of breadth and depth.

Religion, Wealth, and the Working Class

Between the mid-1700s and mid-1800s, the Industrial Revolution began to unfold in the coal and textile industries of England. Parts of the US shared in this trend, and some building blocks of an industrial economy fell into place, notably railroads. However, production was small-scale before the late 1800s. Horses, canals, and riverboats transported most goods, and the main labor force was composed of skilled artisans. After the Civil War the industrial machine took off, and the US recruited laborers from around the world for low-skilled jobs in large factories, mines, and other industries. This was a global phenomenon centered on cities in the US and Europe. Imagine a belt starting along a line in central Europe between northern Germany and Milan, Italy, then extending westward through northern Europe and the northern US to another line in the Midwest between Minneapolis and St. Louis. Rising cities within this belt acted like magnets, drawing workers from nearby rural areas and migrants from other countries. (A related process continues in today's post-industrial economy, with new cities like Atlanta, Tokyo, Mumbai, and Mexico City joining the 'belt' – now a global network – and more Asians and Africans among the workers.) Often cities specialized in particular industries; thus, Pittsburgh was a center for steelmaking, Chicago for agribusiness, and Detroit for cars. During the half-century centered on 1900, the main influx of US workers came from the rural South and places in southern and eastern Europe like Poland, Italy, and Russia; later the greatest influxes were from Mexico and Central America. As we have already discussed, many of these workers were Catholic, although most migrants from the US South were Protestant and many eastern Europeans were Jews or Orthodox Christians.[1]

Although elites became fabulously rich from their employees' hard work, wages were near the subsistence level; it was difficult for workers even to save money for emergencies, much less start independent businesses or send their children to universities. Hours were long and workplaces were often dangerous. Much work was mind-numbingly monotonous, especially after the turn of the century as managers broke the production process into small components and gave each worker a single task on an assembly line like an interchangeable cog in a machine. Children often worked to keep family economies afloat. People lived in crowded neighborhoods that sometimes lacked such basic resources as running water, or in company towns where they had to shop at company stores and could be evicted from their homes if they complained. In a divide and conquer strategy, employers hired workers who spoke a range of languages and fomented divisions between them.

Labor conflicts were intense and sometimes bloody. Strikes often escalated into gun battles between unions and hired police forces paid by employers. For example, such police might shoot unionists who were attempting to stop owners from bringing in strikebreakers; often blacks, prisoners, and vulnerable recent immigrants were used for this purpose. Unionists might respond by shooting back, sabotaging equipment, or calling on other unions to strike related industries or block trains carrying strikebreakers (in the 1930s general strikes closed down both San Francisco and Minneapolis-St. Paul). If such struggles escalated, troops from the National Guard or the federal army were sent in to 'maintain order' – almost always an order congenial to the owners. Thus, labor leaders did not perceive the government as a fair broker between themselves and corporate elites, much less as an ally in their efforts for better working conditions. Rather they saw politicians and judges as partners with management. This perception was especially strong at the high tide of US socialism, during World War I and the early 1920s. At this time, sweeping laws were passed to imprison or deport working-class leaders, suppress their newspapers, and crush their organizations.

In this context, no issue faced by our key players was more important than class. How should wealth be produced and who should control it? Who owned an unjust share of the goods produced by the society, and who lacked access to basic housing and medicine? Should children have to work? Were their workplaces safe? Who worked eighty-hour weeks, who had free weekends, and who lived a life of leisure? On what basis was this decided? We can adapt such questions to ask about religion and economics. Which business practices are moral and which are sinful? Which religions attract the rich and which attract the poor? What difference does this make to their weekly activities, understandings of sin, or behaviors during strikes? Do Biblical interpretations reinforce corporate hegemony? If the members of a parish and union overlap, do church and union activities compete for resources, work together, or exist in separate compartments? If a denomination votes Republican (the typical choice of business leaders and Midwestern farmers) do its religious ideas affect Republican policies or vice versa?

The answers to some of these questions are straightforward. Control of wealth is highly skewed toward the owners of corporations, and their decisions about how to use this wealth – and thus by extension what will be produced, under what conditions – are based on maximizing profits and reinvesting them to make their wealth grow further. Since businesses that grow tend to swallow up those that do not, the system has a ruthless structural logic. Suppose a Christian businesswoman wants to build affordable housing for homeless people and can do so for a profit. Even so, if she can make higher profits building luxury housing, she will face strong pressure to do so, since competitors who do this will thrive and threaten her business with extinction. This would hold true even if luxury housing damaged the environment and increased homelessness, because US law allows investors to 'externalize' most social consequences – that is, owners can pocket the difference between their product's market value and their short-term production costs, while disregarding the social and environmental costs as 'externalities' that the government and/or ecosystem are expected to absorb. According to free market theory, the benefits of this system outweigh the costs of absorbing externalities because markets efficiently allocate resources where they are needed most – with the proviso that this system can measure 'need' only in terms of market demand, which may imply, for example, that the homeless do not 'need' housing. In theory, everyone benefits as the economic pie grows and wealth trickles down to the poorest people. True believers in this theory would literally tell our Christian developer that she has a moral duty to build luxury housing.

In reality a pure free market does not exist. Workers can influence corporate policies directly through strikes and workplace negotiations or indirectly through community institutions and elected representatives. A city can recover costs that a luxury developer wants it to absorb – or prevent the costs in the first place – through zoning, luxury taxes, or environmental lawsuits. It can devise tax breaks that make affordable homes profitable, although by the same token, developers can bribe politicians to kill such tax breaks. Community groups can honor civic-minded builders in ways that override their economic losses or pressure builders not to pollute the environment. Importantly, governments provide benefits that businesses presuppose such as roads, police, and sewers; everyday politics is largely a negotiation about who should pay for such things. Government spending affects the market demand for everything from pencils to bombs, and politicians routinely allocate funds or create incentives to enable the projects they consider priorities. A classic example is the massive amount of land, stolen from Native Americans by the US Army, which was given to railroad companies in the 1800s. Railroad fortunes are the antithesis of self-made success through individual virtue in a free market; we could easily trace similar corporate welfare schemes down to the present.

Negotiations of this kind, in which the government and community set ground rules within which property owners make investment decisions, were near the heart of politics during the years that the US built its industrial economy. Elites worked to shape public opinion and buy political influence, with considerable success. As the century opened they presided over a system in which the state did little to direct the economy other than to promote corporate interests. Religion was part of this equation because elites interpreted their economic success as evidence of moral virtue; they pushed this idea as much through churches as through newspapers, radio stations, and advertisements. At the same time, working people had also had organized unions, political parties, and other organizations since the beginning of industrialization. They also had cards to play, including the vote, the strike, and religious traditions that called free-market hegemony into question. Let us consider some religious arguments about these matters, beginning with elite ideas and working our way down the class hierarchy.

The 'gospel of wealth' is a shorthand term for the idea that capitalism is inevitable and/or divinely ordained, that anyone who works hard can become rich on a 'level playing field' of the market, and that massive wealth is justifiable if used for community needs. Steel magnate Andrew Carnegie, who rose from poverty to become one of the world's richest people, made a classic argument for this gospel. He assumed that all social classes should celebrate the market as an engine of progress, and that in any case the system reflected impartial economic laws. Starting from these premises, Carnegie made a distinctive argument for philanthropy. He maintained that the rich should not pass their fortunes to their children, since doing so would corrupt them and prevent the ablest managers from rising in an economic struggle akin to Darwinian evolution. Rather elites should donate their money and business skills to build schools, libraries, hospitals, and parks. Carnegie believed that his plan to give back fortunes to the communities that helped produce them plus his support for inheritance taxes could 'solve the problem of rich and poor' and create Christian harmony (in theory he also supported the right to unionize, although in practice he was a union-buster.) However, he presupposed not only the beneficence of capitalism, but two further ideas: that entrepreneurs (not workers) played the key role in creating wealth and thus had the right to manage it, and that the poor deserved their poverty. According to Carnegie, 'those worthy of assistance ... seldom require assistance' and using philanthropy to 'encourage the slothful, the drunken, the unworthy' was anathema.[2]

Many elite voices echoed Carnegie. Horatio Alger wrote best-selling fiction about youth who rose from rags to riches through hard work. Sermons by elite clergy agreed. One minister toured the nation giving a speech called 'Acres of Diamonds' that spoke of the abounding opportunities for success that not only made it easy to become rich, but even made it one's *duty* to become rich. Such writings encouraged people to believe – although this was an outrageous distortion of real life – that being poor was evidence of laziness and immorality. In short, whether you were rich or poor, you probably deserved it.

The gospel of wealth was attacked from inside Protestantism by the social gospel movement and from outside Protestantism by Catholic social thought and the labor movement. The social gospel was an activist version of liberal Protestantism – the religious wing of a wider movement for Progressive reform and the politicized wing of Protestants whose theology was moving in similar modernist directions as the Reform Jews and Unitarians discussed above. Because most liberal Protestant clergy used some rhetoric of progress and social uplift, we must distinguish social gospelers from clergy like the author of 'Acres of Diamonds' – those who were complacent about business and quick to offer Biblical apologies for social Darwinism. Even within the moderate social gospel camp, one of the leading ministers led a congregation so dependent on John D. Rockefeller, Jr. that one critic suggested taking the cross off its building and replacing it with a sign reading 'SOCONY': Standard Oil Church of New York.[3]

A good example of a social gospel minister was Walter Rauschenbusch, a Baptist who worked first in an impoverished New York neighborhood and later as a seminary professor. He saw the economy betraying the promise of democracy, allowing aristocratic robber barons to treat workers little better than industrial peasants. Thus, he advocated broadly socialist reforms that would make the economy, as well as politics, more democratic. For Rauschenbusch, sin was not solely a matter of individual morality; it included the social sin of economic oppression. Progress toward greater justice was, in theological terms, associated with overcoming sin and moving closer to the kingdom of God. In later years, it became fashionable for scholars to ridicule Rauschenbusch for his supposed blindness to evil and the ambiguities of power. However, it is more accurate simply to see him as hopeful about making a positive impact.

Like other Progressives, social gospelers sought to impose order on the marketplace. Returning to our example of housing developers, we might imagine Progressives strengthening zoning laws, creating ground-rules to stop unscrupulous builders from gaining monopolies, and outlawing the use of child labor and unsafe building materials. Some Progressives even began to co-operate with labor unions – the least radical ones available – in the American Federation of Labor (AFL). Such unions focused on 'pure and simple' negotiation over wages. They organized by craft – one union for cigar-makers, another for pipe-fitters, and so on – such that corporations could use divide and conquer tactics to defeat several craft unions and a mass of unskilled laborers. Some managers felt that dealing with the AFL was more prudent than rejecting all unions and risking the growth of radicalism. Labor radicals included anarchists who advocated autonomous control of workplace decisions by laborers rather than managers. They included socialists who sought to use the vote to enact tax reform and public ownership of wealth – not only of a few small enterprises like libraries and municipal waterworks, but major industries like railroads and oil companies. Above all they included activists who organized workers across many jobs and industries rather than by craft. Early in the century their top organization was the Industrial Workers of the World (IWW); later they worked in the more radical sectors of the Congress of Industrial Organizations (CIO).

Most social gospel preachers had lives far removed from industrial workers. True, such preachers were often moderate socialists; although few supported the IWW, many fell somewhere on a continuum between participating in the Socialist Party and advocating cerebral socialist principles. However, these clergy preached to churches full of prosperous Republicans. They shied away from supporting strikes, preferring to call for compromise and co-operation in labor conflicts. We might consider them as expressing the guilty conscience of the middle class and trying their best to use their churches to atone for their guilt. At times their voice was important in calling for fair play and Progressive reform. For example, an ecumenical group called the Interchurch World Movement issued a report on the steel strike of 1919, bringing workers' grievances to a wider audience than they would have reached through the mainstream press or labor publications. As politicians hammered out decisions about how much to compromise with unions and support reforms that benefited working people, religious advocacy was a significant part of the public discourse.

Nevertheless, social gospelers had limited power because they had few troops to command. In the heat of battle in the Gastonia, North Carolina, textile strike of 1929, workers went to Baptist and Holiness churches and the union organizers were Communists. Managers belonged to the Episcopalian, Presbyterian, and Methodist churches that were home to most social gospelers – but if clergy from these denominations in Gastonia had supported the strike they would have lost their jobs. Such considerations were also relevant for northern church bureaucrats. The Interchurch World Movement, which was funded by Rockefeller money, ended in a highly publicized collapse shortly after its report on the steel strike. Although multiple factors were involved, observers felt that the timing was not coincidental.[4]

Turning to Catholic leaders, we find a different dynamic: many troops ready to mobilize (parishes were full of actual and potential union members), sympathy for their cause, but indecisiveness about whether to mobilize them. On the one hand, Catholic social teaching was clear, from Rome to the parish level: Catholic opposition to modernity included opposition to free-market economies, because these increased poverty and injustice, fomented the sins of individualism and greed by encouraging people to maximize personal profits, and pressured women and children to work when they should be at home. Pope Leo XIII made these points forcefully in his 1891 encyclical *Rerum Novarum*, 'On the Conditions of the Working Classes.' During World War I Catholics organized the National Catholic Welfare Conference, which was roughly similar to the Federal Council of Churches except that it coordinated dioceses rather than denominations (later it evolved into the US Conference of Catholic Bishops). Father John Ryan, the head of its Social Action Department, popularized Catholic social teaching through many books and the 1919 'Bishops Program for Social Reconstruction.' Ryan was the Catholic most analogous to Protestant social gospelers – an intellectual who largely lobbied clergy and policy-makers to be more concerned about economic justice.[5]

At the same time, Catholics were emphatic that their teaching was an alternative to (not an endorsement of) any labor movement that smacked of atheistic socialism. They also disapproved of unions that were structured as secret societies (many early unions were secret for self-defense reasons, and clerics compared them with the anti-Catholic Masons), supported women's independence (Catholics advocated a 'living wage' sufficient for a male breadwinner to support a wife at home, and unions that organized women were out of sync with this vision), or blended Protestants and Catholics in the same organizations. Rome's preferred strategy was to create all-Catholic unions guided by the church. US labor leaders considered such dual unionism utterly wrongheaded, and most US Catholics who cared about labor issues agreed with them. A key task of Americanist bishops was to persuade their colleagues that it was a bad idea to promote dual unions along with a dual education system, and a better idea to steer Catholics toward acceptable unions and away from unacceptable ones. Although the Americanists lost most of their battles, they did win this one.

Thus, the question shifted – case by case – to which bishops and priests actually made it a priority to support local labor struggles, and if so what unions they found acceptable. The Knights of Labor, a worker's organization drawn from many industries and led by an Irish Catholic, gained some support; Cardinal Gibbons convinced Rome not to condemn the Knights despite their secret status and religiously mixed membership. In 1910 Catholics organized a trade union group called the Militia of Christ for Social Service. However, any union seen as socialist was deemed unacceptable – which is not to say that all pious Catholics avoided such unions, but only that they had to join over their clergy's objection. Many labor leaders were radical enough to rouse bishops' suspicions. In 1886 they excommunicated a popular New York priest named Edward McGlynn for supporting Henry George, a politician who sought to increase property taxes and distribute the wealth more equally.

In the long run, the bulk of Catholic support came in behind the AFL, especially insofar as it forged alliances with Democratic politicians from the Catholic-dominated political machines that controlled cities such as Boston and Chicago. In 1928 such a politician, Al Smith of New York, won the Democratic nomination for President. Smith lost the election partly because Protestant clergy made a campaign issue out of the papal encyclicals that had earlier been used to silence Americanist bishops. Asked if he supported the papal condemnation of US religious pluralism, Smith reportedly responded 'Will somebody please tell me what in hell an encyclical is?'[6] He claimed that he had been a devout Catholic all his life but had never even heard of such teachings, much less used them to guide his policy decisions. Nevertheless, Protestants claimed that Smith would put his loyalty to the Pope ahead of the US Constitution.

Despite Smith's defeat, his nomination signaled how central Catholics had become to the Democrats. When the party's next candidate, Franklin Delano Roosevelt, came to power during the depths of the Great Depression, the stage was set for a major shift. At this time, capitalism was widely seen as a discredited failure. Up to a third of all workers were unemployed without a significant social safety net, people were literally starving, and radical movements were gaining strength. These included grass-roots self-help, left-wing parties such as the Communists, and a labor tactic called the sit-down strike in which unions took over factories from the inside rather than picketing outside them while owners ran strikebreakers through their lines. Socialist critique gained hegemony in many intellectual circles.

In this context, Roosevelt's New Deal committed the state to intervene more actively to guide the economy, for example, by stabilizing banks and expanding industrial planning. Such intervention in market decisions intensified during World War II; it remains a major feature of today's economy, especially in the overlapping territory between government and business known as the military–industrial complex. More controversially from a business perspective, the New Deal used taxes to create programs that addressed working-class problems, such as Social Security and a program that put unemployed people to work on projects such as building national parks. Importantly, the state stopped routinely intervening in strikes by sending police to side with owners; it guaranteed a right to collective bargaining and established ground-rules to facilitate this.

The New Deal represented a new social contract in which moderate unions and Democratic politicians – both with strong Catholic constituencies – won a place at tables of power, joined by Jews and to a limited degree by blacks. (Blacks, who had traditionally supported the Republicans since the Civil War, increasingly joined the Democratic voting bloc in the North but remained disenfranchised in the South.) We should not exaggerate the Catholic and Jewish breakthrough. Working-class ethnics were only one part of the Democratic coalition, alongside conservative southern Protestants who opposed Republicans because of their role in the Civil War. Unions were the weakest partner in negotiations between management, government, and labor. Conservatives despised Roosevelt and waited for a chance to roll back the New Deal, despite the fact that the New Deal largely represented an effort to co-opt radical dissent and channel it within the capitalist system. After the crisis of the 1930s passed, radicals were demonized and driven from power, and courts interpreted labor law in ways that curtailed the power of unions. Nevertheless, the new social contract was highly significant for the descendants of Catholic and Jewish immigrants. They were joining mainstream society, with relatively secure and well-paid jobs and a social safety net to reply upon in old age and times of economic difficulty.[7]

Catholics had a wide spectrum of economic views, both to the right and left of the main trend we have traced. We can gain a better sense of this spectrum's complexity by comparing three Catholic voices. We have already introduced one of these – the centrist John Ryan, who was nicknamed 'the Right Reverend New Dealer.' Secondly, and far better known, was the radio preacher, Father Charles Coughlin. Early in his career he advocated harmonizing the New Deal with Catholic social teaching, but at the height of his fame in the mid-1930s (when he was among the most popular radio personalities in the country) he spent more time attacking Roosevelt and the organized left than attacking conservative elites. By the late 1930s he was a notorious anti-Semite, as we will discuss further in Chapter 4. Most scholars map Coughlin as a right-wing populist with fascist sympathies, at least in the later stages of his career.[8]

A third voice, Dorothy Day, reminds us that not all Catholics opposed the radical left. Insofar as we consider bishops and immigrant enclaves as the heart of Catholicism, Day was about as unrepresentative a Catholic as one could imagine. Nevertheless, she became one of the nation's most famous Catholics. Day was raised as a middle-class Protestant and attended the University of Illinois. She became active in New York intellectual circles, where she had an affair with playwright Eugene O'Neill and studied left-wing anarchist thought. She converted to Catholicism because she felt a need for the community, spirituality, and grounded social critique that it provided, and she blended her anarchist and pacifist sensibilities with Catholic teachings against war and economic injustice. Out of this mix, Day co-founded a newspaper, *The Catholic Worker*, and an associated movement that ministered to poor and unemployed people throughout the country. The movement grew rapidly in the 1930s, branching out from a base in New York; after World War II it continued on a smaller scale.

By the standards of unions and political parties, the Catholic Worker Movement was decentralized and apolitical. It focused on the communal lives of its local groups and on directly feeding and housing needy people using donated goods and labor. Participants in the movement lived simple lives of voluntary poverty. In some ways their houses of hospitality were like communities of monks or nuns even though they did not ordain people; volunteers passed through their doors for whatever time period they wished. Although Day's vision was small-scale and in some senses apolitical, in other ways it was radically politicized. She was scathingly hostile to capitalism, which she saw as utterly incompatible with Christianity, and she was a strict pacifist even during World War II. After 1945 the Catholic Worker Movement engaged in protests against nuclear weapons. Alongside Quakers, Day and her colleagues helped keep a religious peace movement alive from the 1930s until it revived in the 1960s.[9]

Religion and the Politics of Gender

By now it should be clear that we must be careful before lumping together all members of large religious groups. For example, black and white Baptists disagree on major issues, and Catholic Worker activists are very different from conservative Catholics. When describing a given group it is sometimes safe to assume that one's descriptions apply equally to men and women. But often this is not a safe assumption, because gender conflicts are near the heart of US religion. This section discusses the difference it made to be a religious woman rather than a man during the late nineteenth and early twentieth century, as well as the role of religion in movements for women's rights.[10]

At the turn of the century, opportunities for women were far more limited than they are today. Women lacked the right to vote. They were excluded from industrial jobs, professions, and many service jobs that are considered pink-collar today. In financial and legal contexts, they were treated more like dependent children than the equals of men. For example, husbands controlled their wives' property, and laws against marital rape and abuse were weak to non-existent since marriage gave a husband rights over his wife's body. Business, politics, and war were male domains; women were supposed to exist in the private world of home and family. According to the ideal of domesticity, a girl should be brought up in a loving home, learn the womanly roles of humility and religious sentiment, and find a husband to take over her father's role as caretaker. She should devote herself to being a mother and maintaining her home, while her husband spoke for her in public contexts like voting and the courts.

This ideal was most attainable for white urban women in affluent families. However, many women's lives were far removed from this model: rural wives who worked on farms alongside their husbands; working-class mothers who took in boarders; black women who worked as caretakers for white people's children; unmarried daughters who worked in textile mills; and women of all ages who worked in jobs open to them such as teaching, nursing, sweatshops, clerking in department stores, and prostitution. Not all women had children, not all women with children had husbands, and not all women with husbands were sexually attracted to men. (The latter case was not necessarily seen as a problem, since the dominant ideology held that lust was a male trait and virtuous women were passionless.) Nevertheless, insofar as women's choices and circumstances diverged from the ideal, they were seen as falling short of a 'true womanhood' that was their natural vocation. Because they were dependent on fathers and husbands, women had limited options if they wanted to leave abusive fathers or unloving marriages, or if they felt a calling to pursue 'male' vocations such as law, preaching, or medicine. If they sought to expand their options through social reform, they had little leverage as long as they lacked the vote.

In a society that polarized most aspects of life into a public sphere for men and a private sphere for women and the family, religion had an ambiguous in-between status. On the one hand, Christianity maintained a strong public role, building on the ways it had long informed US law and policy. Preaching was a man's job with a prestige comparable to the highest professions. Clergy spoke of a God who was the Father of humanity and creator of the universe, and they did not hesitate to address 'masculine' policy issues (for instance, when pro- and anti-slavery factions battled in Kansas during the 1850s, a famous minister named Henry Ward Beecher sent rifles – nicknamed 'Beecher's Bibles' – to the anti-slavery forces). Nevertheless, by the 1800s religion was associated with the private sphere. The Constitution defined religion as a matter of individual conscience – but more importantly, it became associated with teaching morality in the home and glorifying motherhood. Evangelicals stressed sentimental themes like following one's heart, letting God lead one like a mother leads a child, and resting in the bosom of a gentle Jesus – a way of imagining Jesus which portrayed him as rather androgynous if not feminine.

Women, religion, and the private sphere became linked largely because most US religions have had strong majorities of female participants – with only a few exceptions, usually religions which made no distinction between being born into a culture and being part of its religion. This is a striking pattern given that men have monopolized most leadership roles (especially before the 1970s) and taught that God commands female submission.[11] The pattern of female majorities among the laity was already strong in the colonial era. When Puritan clergy lamented declines in their group's piety, they were largely worrying that fewer men than women were joining their churches. The pattern intensified after 1800 due to disestablishment. As churches came to depend on people voluntarily investing their time, women volunteered more than men – no doubt partly because they lacked other social outlets. By the late 1800s, more than seventy per cent of participants in many churches were women.

Scholars treat nineteenth-century Protestantism as a classic example of this trend. Some argue that women strengthened churches; others speak about a 'feminization of religion' and lament that this trend watered down the Protestant heritage. In any case, the trend of laywomen outnumbering laymen cut across many groups and time periods. Much of Jewish religion centered on home Sabbath observances led by women. Catholics had a full-blown version of religion that glorified mothers and the home, as discussed below. African-American churches and their associated network of women's clubs shared in the trend.

Female majorities could create a spiraling dynamic in which religion became identified as feminine, which in turn made men less comfortable in churches, which led to even larger gender imbalances and less male interest. In this context, we should add a set of all-male organizations called lodges – the Masons, the Odd Fellows, and many more – to the list of alternative religions that we earlier identified as a collective key player. The years when lodges grew the most in comparison with churches – as well as when lodges most emphasized elaborate initiation rites – were years when churches seemed most feminized and when boys were expected to make the sharpest transition from a mother-dominated world of childhood to a man's world of adult success. If churches were too female-oriented to help young men negotiate this break, perhaps fraternal initiation rituals could do better. Men joined lodges in huge numbers, and if we were traveling at a more leisurely pace, exploring their rituals would reward a longer stop.[12] However, rather than pursuing male responses to the emerging gender system, let us stay with the female majority in the churches. Why did they participate so enthusiastically? What did they do with the religious groups they created? How did this affect the gender system over time?

According to the dominant ideology, women were not oppressed by being confined to the home. Rather they were being placed on a pedestal and encouraged to thrive in a sphere that matched their nature – which was increasingly understood as pure and virtuous (with the Virgin Mary as a role model) rather than weak and prone to temptation (as one might expect from a daughter of Eve). The world of business and politics was brutish and amoral; it lowered men's quality of life and reflected badly on men's nature. Women should welcome their vocation of providing a shelter from this world. After all, males could only enjoy this refuge during their hours away from work, politics, and war, but women could enjoy it all the time (once again, note how the ideal fitted the experience of middle-class whites better than others). Moreover, if women did not provide a refuge from the dog-eat-dog world of the market, what would become of morality and virtue in the modern world? Thus, defenders of the domestic ideology hotly denied that the women's sphere was any less important than the public sphere.

Clergy added that this division of roles was part of the order of nature ordained by God. The emerging modern family – a nuclear rather than extended family, based on a public–private distinction that reflected an urban market society but made limited sense for other times and places – came to be seen as 'the Biblical model.' Although groups like the Mormons and Shakers noted that Biblical patriarchs practiced polygamy and St. Paul counseled celibacy, most Christians assumed that the Bible supported the hegemonic system. God was male, the first human (Adam) was male, and the first woman (Eve) was created from Adam's rib. Sin entered the world through Eve's disobedience, with the result that God had cursed women to be ruled by men. The chain of authority passed from God, through (male) political leaders, to (male) heads of families, and then to wives, children, and animals.

Granted, there was debate about interpreting the Bible. Genesis can be read as teaching that Adam and Eve were created at the same time in God's image, with Eve created out of Adam's side to symbolize equality and companionship. The text that curses women to ruled by men can be read not as a command to emulate forever, but as an unfortunate result of sin, somewhat like the mark placed on Cain after he murdered Abel. If so, just as churches can work to prevent murders instead of taking them for granted, so also churches can treat women's oppression as a problem to overcome. Some fundamentalists do not allow women to take drugs to ease the pain during childbirth because Genesis 3:16 curses Eve with the words 'in pain you shall bring forth children.' Most Christians consider this absurd – yet this is exactly the same verse that includes the words 'your husband ... shall rule over you.' Feminists became expert at finding texts that supported gender equality, presenting them as the Bible's core teaching, and using them to trump texts that teach women's subordination. They stressed Galatians 3:29 ('There is no longer Jew or Greek, there is no longer slave or free, there is no longer male and female; for all of you are one in Christ Jesus') and explained away Ephesians 5:22 ('Wives, be subject to your husbands, as to the Lord').

Pro-equality readings of the Bible were a distinct minority until the 1970s (after which they became common in liberal churches) and have been controversial in every decade.[13] Many scholars argue that the continuum of debate about women's roles will remain tilted toward conservatism as long as the debate is primarily grounded in the Bible; it will range from strong misogyny at one pole to weaker claims of gender-blind neutrality at the other. Although arguments from the gender-blind pole do challenge male hegemony in some ways, in other contexts they can discount the importance of gender. Consider that many people have used the Bible to deny that God is literally a male and that the Bible necessarily supports the supremacy of human fathers when it speaks of God as Father; perhaps 'he' transcends gender, parents are equal in 'his' eyes, and divine parenthood allows one to appeal to a higher authority if one's human father is oppressive. However, hardly anyone uses the Bible to contend that God the Mother transcends 'her' gender and that this supports female supremacy. What they more commonly debate is whether feminism is un-Biblical when it presupposes gender conflict, given the spiritual equality of the sexes. In other words, even though feminists can advance powerful Biblical arguments, when they do so they build on a text with many anti-feminist dimensions.

Thus, the nexus between Christian teaching, women's participation in churches, and domestic ideology was largely an example of male-dominated religion gaining hegemony and limiting the life prospects of women. Even scholars who grant that women could use religion as a base to struggle for equality tend to stress the limits that churches placed on such struggles; they judge that arguments based on secular law and advocating equal rights, rather than arguments based on the Bible and promoting the welfare of families, provided the best route toward women's power. From this perspective, early feminists who urged women to reject Christianity – for example, Elizabeth Cady Stanton, the author of a critique called *The Woman's Bible* – were the pioneers of twentieth-century feminism; their central task was to throw off the shackles of domestic ideology.

However, this is only half the story. Although Christians were not the most radical part of the first wave of US feminism, they were the largest part, and their work laid a foundation for later progress. Recall how religion occupied a space midway between private and public and how women were considered guardians of morality. This allowed women to expand on their (semi-private and thus culturally accepted) religious roles and make them an avenue for self-assertion and empowerment. Working from (semi-public but still respected) spaces in religious organizations, women boldly addressed public issues – notably slavery, temperance, and mission. On the first two fronts their efforts led to Constitutional Amendments abolishing slavery and instituting Prohibition; on the third they formed a key part of the cultural fabric of US global expansion and established precedents that led toward women's ordination.

By the early twentieth century, female reformers focused on winning the right to vote (finally accomplished in 1920) and working on social gospel causes such as ending child labor, aiding immigrants through settlement houses like Chicago's Hull House, regulating industries like meat packing, and marching for peace (some also pushed to make birth control legal and accessible, scandalizing more moderate social gospelers). Parts of the New Deal social safety net, especially its programs for women and children, grew from this activism. Although male social gospelers also championed such causes, women supplied many of the movement's foot soldiers and leaders.

Foremost among these leaders was Frances Willard, who headed the Women's Christian Temperance Union (WCTU), in the latter part of the nineteenth century. Working from a base in Protestant churches,

Willard built the WCTU into a mass movement, complete with an elaborate structure of national, state, and local organizations, twenty international affiliates, and a state-of-the-art Chicago skyscraper called the Woman's Temple. Temperance activists addressed the problem of alcoholic men who abused or neglected their families; we might compare it with recent campaigns against domestic violence and fathers who do not pay child support. The WCTU also addressed underlying issues that compounded the problems of women with abusive husbands, especially economic dependency and lack of legal rights. Its 'do-everything policy' approached temperance as just one plank in a comprehensive platform of reform. The WCTU fought for the vote, built orphanages and kindergartens, promoted women's health, attacked sexual double standards, sought prison reform, and promoted causes like animal rights, vegetarianism, and educating Native Americans. Willard was a socialist who strongly supported labor and tried to build bridges between the WCTU, the Knights of Labor, and the Populist movement.[14]

Not all WCTU activists were as progressive as Willard. Few were as committed to socialism, and despite the roots of women's reform in abolitionism and its continued activism against lynching, parts of the suffrage campaign took a racist turn. Suffragists complained that upstanding matrons like Willard were denied the right to vote while purportedly less civilized males from black and immigrant communities abused their voting rights. Although the core motives of temperance were feminist, and although many Catholic priests promoted temperance, Prohibition also represented a crusade in which middle-class Protestants looked down upon, and attempted to police, the behavior of immigrants. In this regard, the battle lines in the war for Prohibition were as much between the Protestant middle class and Catholic working class as between women and men. Largely for this reason, Prohibitionists lost their war against alcohol in the long run, despite their temporary victory when the Eighteenth Amendment passed in 1919. Prohibition proved to be unenforceable and was repealed in 1933. Since then the popular image of temperance has centered (rather misleadingly) on blue-haired, backward-looking church ladies who refused to let modern urban dwellers have any fun.

Far more than Protestants, Catholics had an established role for women who opted not to become wives and mothers. This was taking the vows of poverty, chastity, and obedience to become nuns. Before the mid-1800s, most US nuns lived cloistered lives as contemplatives.

However, nuns soon organized themselves to work as teachers, nurses, heads of orphanages, and related roles in orders such as the Sisters of Loretto, Sisters of St. Joseph, and many others – eventually 200 in all. The women who led large orders, such as Elizabeth Ann Seton of the Sisters of Charity, became some of nation's most powerful women, even though they served under the formal authority of priests. As noted above, nuns were the backbone of Catholic institutions; at the turn of the century 40,000 of them – four times the number of priests – ran 265 hospitals and 4,000 schools. Although Dorothy Day was not a nun, it is hard to imagine her Catholic Worker Movement succeeding outside the context of earlier work by nuns and Protestant women's reform. In later years many nuns saw Day as a role model.[15]

Protestants had closed convents and forced nuns to marry during the Reformation; for them the closest approximation to becoming a nun was becoming a missionary. Of all the causes promoted by Protestant reformers in the nineteenth and early twentieth centuries, this was the most popular. (Judaism had a related dynamic; the women's group called Hadassah, first formed to aid Jews in Palestine, became the largest and most vibrant of all Zionist groups.) After the mid-1800s many women volunteered as missionaries, either in foreign countries or in home missions to the frontier or inner city. At first they went as wives of clergy or as 'female assistant missionaries' under male authority, but they soon became leaders in their own right. Their adventures captured the imaginations of Protestant women. Most denominations had women's mission societies, and these often rivaled the power of official denominational structures. In 1920 the leader of the northern Baptists' missionary society was elected head of her denomination. Three million women belonged to missionary societies, and they supported 5,000 unmarried female missionaries – double the number of male missionaries. These societies became so wealthy that the leaders of several denominations merged them into their bureaucracies in the twentieth century. In effect these were hostile male takeovers of autonomous women's organizations, done in the name of efficiency.[16]

Mission work was a step toward women's ordination, which has tended to proceed in stages: from the right to speak in worship and vote on congregational policies; through roles like Sunday School teacher and missionary; and eventually to full status as clergy. (Of course, many groups still resist some of these steps.) During the revivals of the 1700s and 1800s, many women found callings to speak in public, which was considered scandalous at the time. In settings where openness to the Holy Spirit took precedence over education and a call from God took precedence over the authority of husbands, women began to give testimony in worship, speak as exhorters at revivals, and become lay preachers. Holiness and Pentecostal churches moved rapidly in this direction, and in the early twentieth century most of the women who led churches – around three per cent of all clergy – were in this movement. (Women commonly lost these roles as Holiness churches institutionalized and/or were influenced by fundamentalism; from the beginning to the end of the twentieth century, the percentage of women ministers in the Church of the Nazarene fell from twenty to one per cent.)[17]

Meanwhile, establishment churches had ordained only a handful of women by the late nineteenth century, mainly in liberal denominations such as Congregationalism which gave individual congregations autonomous power. However, pressure for ordination was building. The option of mission work siphoned off some pressure in the short run, but it ratcheted up the pressure in the long run. After World War II the process bore fruit.

The decline of female Holiness ministers was just one manifestation of the gender politics of fundamentalists. Scholars often explain the rise of fundamentalism as resulting from two factors: cultural discomfort with a pluralist urban society and theological resistance to modern science and Biblical study. No doubt these factors were important, but a third and equally important factor also accounts for fundamentalism – its opposition to emerging changes in gender roles. Fundamentalists presupposed the nineteenth-century gender system, with its sharp public–private split and its glorification of women as mothers. In large part, fundamentalism was an effort to maintain this system in the face of emerging challenges to it. These challenges included women's progress in entering the public sphere, especially their growing access to higher education and paid work. The challenges also included the sexual mores of so-called 'new women,' symbolized by flappers who shocked conservatives by smoking cigarettes, bobbing their hair, approaching men in nightclubs, and pushing to legalize contraceptives.

Both of these changes – women winning public roles and the emergence of new women – undermined the ideal of a separate women's sphere. Both changes also reflected a shift from an economy based on small-scale production on farms and in small towns – with their associated emphasis on thrift and hard work – toward an urban consumer economy that emphasized spending and leisure entertainment. Sparkling personalities and consumer style began to eclipse the value of traditional moral character. Since fundamentalists saw women as the guardians of morality, they were especially worried when women moved in these new directions. At the peak of fundamentalist mobilization in the 1920s, they often symbolized these challenges through the image of the faithful Christian wife versus the ungodly flapper.[18]

Fundamentalist concerns about gender were not a mere afterthought. In sermons and journalistic writings, concerns about the family were deeply integrated into fundamentalist arguments, often to the point of shaping them. When believers searched their Bibles and newspapers for signs of the end-times, they stressed the breakdown of the family. Preachers railed against evolutionism partly because they saw it as undermining sexual morality. When they spoke about the central institutions of faith, they often ranked the Christian home as equally important as the church. As we will see, fundamentalist alarm about women's equality remained important throughout the century. Many of the arguments that conservatives currently use to condemn abortion rights and the civil rights of gays and lesbians are quite similar to arguments they used earlier against legalizing contraceptives and allowing women to attend universities.

If we interpret fundamentalism as a form of resistance to women's empowerment, this complicates maps of US religion that draw their main boundary lines between Catholics, fundamentalists, and Protestant liberals. All of these groups were dominated by men who responded defensively to changes in the gender system. From this perspective we need another map that charts how clergy as a group (whether Catholic or Protestant, liberal or fundamentalist) responded to women. True, liberals were more open to certain changes and women's reform had a larger place among liberals than fundamentalists. Our new map must continue to acknowledge these points. Nevertheless, gender created surprising convergences. Fundamentalists spoke warmly about Catholic teachings on the family despite their overall hostility to Catholicism (at this time they routinely identified the Pope as the anti-Christ). Also, despite pitched battles between fundamentalist and modernist clergy in other arenas, both agreed on the need to defend the Christian home. Leaders on all sides promoted a 'muscular Christianity' and felt that overly feminized churches should be 'reclaimed for men.'[19]

An interesting question arises if we interpret fundamentalism largely as a male reaction to the success of feminism. There were at least as many fundamentalist women as Christian feminists like Willard, and many of them embraced the most conservative domestic ideologies. How did such women perceive these issues? There is no easy answer to this question. Some women believed that the Bible demanded their submission and saw this as more important than seeking equality. Others felt that the family was under such stress that defending it should be their top priority. However, there were also subtle negotiations about gender inside conservative sub-cultures. Women's committees and informal social networks created semi-autonomous spaces in which women could support each other and address their concerns. We must not underestimate how much of the day-to-day energy in congregations flows through such channels, as opposed to the pronouncements of clergy. Conservative clergy, like their liberal counterparts, learned that many of the constituents they most needed to please were women: the church secretary; the head of religious education; the president of the mission board; the women who controlled the church kitchen, and so on. As we will see, behind a solid front of anti-feminist language, there were significant changes in evangelical gender practices as the century unfolded.

Debates about War, Peace, and Foreign Relations

US Christians have largely supported the war efforts of their government. We have noted religious support for conquest in the colonial era, civil millennialism during the Revolutionary era, and claims by both North and South that God was on their side in the Civil War. Manifest Destiny justified wars of conquest during the 1800s, and similar justifications continued as US expansion moved from a national to an international stage after 1890.

Not surprisingly given the ugliness of war and the Bible's many teachings about peacemaking, support for US war efforts has not been unanimous.[20] Even people who generally supported specific wars – not to speak of those who questioned them – were capable of feeling uneasy about the bloodshed that accompanied battle, regretting the corruption that accompanied conquest, and/or debating whether expansion risked weakening the nation's unity and virtue. Significant minorities opposed the Mexican War. Missionaries often sided with Native Americans against settlers and traders. When US elites began to debate after 1890 whether they should build a navy and continue their expansion southward to Cuba and westward to China, it became difficult to sustain the hegemonic idea that US behavior was a righteous (democratic, God-ordained) alterna-tive to the naked imperialism of Europeans. A sizeable anti-imperialist movement developed, often mobilizing religious sentiments to oppose rather than promote US empire. During the bitter struggle to subdue resistance to the US takeover of the Philippines, Mark Twain imagined a stranger entering a church and praying as follows: 'O Lord God, help us to tear their soldiers to bloody shreds with our shells; help us to cover their smiling fields with the pale forms of their patriot dead ... help us to lay waste their humble homes with a hurricane of fire ... We ask it in a spirit of love.'[21]

Despite such reservations about Manifest Destiny, the momentum of expansion and its associated religious justifications won the day. Presi-dent McKinley told a group of clergy that he did not want to colonize the Philippines 'when they came to us a gift from the gods.' In an effort to discern what to do, McKinley 'went down on [his] knees and prayed Almighty God for light.' In this way he perceived that he could not give the Philippines independence since 'they were unfit for self-govern-ment.' Nor could he allow Spain, France, or Germany to control them. 'There was nothing left for us to do but to take them all and to educate [them], and uplift and civilize and Christianize them, and by God's grace do the very best we could by them, as our fellow men for whom Christ also died.'[22]

The tendency to conflate God's will, US political goals, and religious virtue continued during World War I and II and the Cold War. After initial hesitancy (and despite a few hold-outs like the Jehovah's Witnesses) most denominations supported World War I in the name of spreading democracy around the world. The tradition of fusing US global goals with a sense of Christian mission flowered into one of its classic expres-sions in the 1940s and 1950s, when the US fought first Germany and Japan in World War II and later the Soviet Union and China in the Cold War. During these years, issues as diverse as capitalism, democracy, religious freedom, US military objectives, and Christian values were seen by many people as tightly connected – although it is obvious in retrospect that these are independent variables that were often mutually contradictory. In 1954 the words 'under God' were added to the Pledge of Allegiance, largely to underline a contrast with 'godless' Communism. Although much of the world perceived the US building a neo-colonial empire, most people at home saw the issue as military defense against totalitarians – whether Hitler on the right or Stalin on the left.

Religious leaders linked God and country with varying degrees of subtlety. Well-heeled establishment clergy took pains to deny that they were baptizing a crusade or a greedy power grab that they associated with European colonialism. They saw themselves as responsible world leaders – supporting global co-operation through trade and the United Nations while restraining totalitarianism. Conservative religious leaders were less nuanced. The leading evangelical preacher of the twentieth century, Billy Graham, launched his career largely through a revival that began three days after the 'Godless' Soviets exploded their first atomic bomb. Graham's sermons (heavily promoted by the Hearst newspaper chain) built on fears that this escalation of the Cold War was part of prophetic scenarios about the end of history. Around this time, Graham's father-in-law joined a group of leading conservative Protestants in calling for a nuclear attack on Russia. Meanwhile, Catholic groups such as the Militia of the Immaculata publicized lurid apocalyptic visions of the Virgin Mary in which she exhorted her children to battle Communism. Such Catholics stressed themes like praying the rosary and using the eucharist as weapons in spiritual warfare. Senator Joseph McCarthy, who led the effort to purge leftist influence from US national life in the 1950s, saw himself as a pious Catholic. Francis Spellman, who was both the Cardinal of New York and vicar of the US military, was a vocal supporter of US efforts in the Cold War and Vietnam. Fulton Sheen, a popular priest with a prime-time television show, called Communism 'the Mystical body of Satan.'[23]

In light of this longstanding tradition of Christian support for the US military that reached a crescendo around 1950, it may seem surprising that mainline Protestant social thinkers – not just a few Quaker activists and Jehovah's Witnesses but a wide spectrum of social gospel leaders – were deeply committed to peacemaking and anti-imperialism during the 1920s and 1930s. Many of these leaders opposed the US entry into World War II even after Hitler invaded Poland in 1939, right up to Japan's attack on Pearl Harbor in 1941. Reinhold Niebuhr, the best-known Protestant social thinker in the middle years of the century, became famous by arguing against pacifist forms of the social gospel and moving Protestants toward his so-called Christian realist support for US military policy. Let us retell his story, both as a case study of intra-religious struggles for hegemony, and because the common sense that emerged from this struggle eclipsed the social gospel as the dominant stance of establishment Protestants until the 1970s.[24]

Niebuhr and his antagonists debated their response to Hitler near the end of a long-running dispute about whether changes were needed in the social gospel. As we have seen, the social gospel was the activist wing of liberal Protestantism; it advocated various reforms and stressed God's immanent presence in history. Social gospelers saw themselves making progress toward fulfilling God's will on earth – a vision they described as building the kingdom of God. As we will discuss in Chapter 4, fundamentalists vilified this theology from the outside. However, criticisms also emerged from within the social gospel world. Questions about World War II arose in the wake of three earlier events that called social gospel idealism into question: the debacle of World War I, failures of Prohibition that symbolized a loss of Protestant hegemony, and the collapse of the economy during the Great Depression. Debates about World War II gained resonance because they built on these earlier challenges.

Social gospelers invested much energy in supporting World War I and Prohibition, and this led to disillusionment when it became obvious that there was a huge gap between the results they hoped for and the actual experience on the ground. Prohibition symbolized Protestant efforts to maintain hegemony in a new urban context; thus, the widespread flaunting and ultimate collapse of Prohibition – which reflected the power of immigrants, popular entertainment, and new women – has led scholars to speak about a second Protestant disestablishment.[25] This was a cultural disestablishment, as opposed to the earlier constitutional one that left an informal establishment intact. However, many clergy refused to accept this second disestablishment as a settled issue, and they redoubled their efforts to maintain their influence. They responded similarly to the carnage and corruption of World War I, which led many US intellectuals to repudiate the whole idea of US-led wars for democratic progress. Social gospelers responded less by repudiating the idea of progress, and more by conceiving war as a form of backsliding on the road to progress. Rather than abandoning hope for a democratic world, they recast this hope by making pacifism and international co-operation central to their vision of the kingdom of God. It is hard to overstate the centrality of anti-war themes for social gospelers of the inter-war years.

Thus, although social gospelers emerged scarred and battered from the challenges of the early century, they felt they had made the proper adjustments to keep moving forward. Early in his career Niebuhr presupposed this background. Like many of his colleagues, he had become a pacifist after World War I. He became a parish pastor in Detroit, a popular lecturer on college campuses, and an activist involved with many groups including the pacifist Fellowship of Reconciliation and the New Deal-oriented Americans for Democratic Action, in which he became friends with many people who later rose to high positions in the Democratic Party. After 1928, he taught at the flagship school of liberal Protestantism, Union Theological Seminary in New York.

In the 1930s Niebuhr turned his attention toward a third challenge to Progressive optimism that proved harder to assimilate than World War I or the collapse of Prohibition. This was the frustration of hopes for democratic socialism – both because of the general power of US capitalism and the shock of the Great Depression. In the face of bitter labor conflicts in the 1920s and 1930s, social gospel appeals to labor–management co-operation and progress toward socialism appeared increasingly illusory. Niebuhr became famous for attacking the New Deal from the left. In the mid-1930s some of his students flew the flag of the Soviet Union from the Union Seminary flagpole, largely but not entirely as a joke. Niebuhr was not distinctive because he called for economic justice – other religious activists were also active on this front – but because he attacked social gospel ideas about peaceful progress toward justice. In a book called *Moral Man and Immoral Society* he dropped a bombshell on his social gospel comrades by proposing a model of class conflict and inevitable group self-interest. He stressed that moral idealism could not solve problems of class oppression, which were rooted in deep-seated human sinfulness. A realist, as opposed to a sentimental utopian, had to admit that political coercion – possibly including violence – would be needed to create change.[26]

Could this suggestion – that progress toward a just society was only possible through class struggle – really be the route to the kingdom of God? For old-school social gospelers this was no better than cutting out the heart of Christianity. One reviewer wrote that 'Jesus's serene trust in human nature ... his sunny optimism, his radiant passion would all have seemed a little ridiculous to Niebuhr ... and with what relief he would have turned to the "cynical and realistic" Pilate as the man of the hour!'[27] Although Niebuhr was outraged by this review, he granted that he had drastically lowered his expectations for progress. The upshot was complex: Christians should participate in political struggle, but only as the pursuit of lesser evils in a fallen world.

In the wake of such controversies, Nazism posed a decisive challenge to the social gospel. If we compare shifts in worldviews to earthquakes, we might say that the debacle of World War I created a fault line. Cultural disestablishment and frustrated hopes for economic justice were ongoing sources of pressure. However, it was the rise of Hitler that shook the foundations and rearranged the landscape. As the power of fascism grew, it seemed absurd to argue that God was working through immanent processes of history. Could Nazi conquests represent progress toward the kingdom of God? Appeals to a 'serene trust in human nature' seemed out of touch; didn't it make more sense to stress human capacities for evil? Peacemaking appeared as an irresponsible utopianism that – however well intentioned – caused more harm than good. Wasn't fascism a greater evil? Wasn't a less-than-peaceful defense of a less-than-perfect society needed to combat it? Through such arguments, Niebuhr shifted the form of sinful pride that was the focus of his critique. Earlier he had mainly worried about economic injustice; he had insisted that class struggle was a fact of life and that joining this struggle was a lesser evil. Now he focused on sin expressed in fascist tyranny. Just as he had accused his colleagues of naiveté about class struggle, he now insisted that their hopes for peace blinded them to Hitler's threat.

A leading religious magazine called the *Christian Century* refused to abandon the anti-militarist plank of its social gospel platform. In terms of our earthquake analogy, the *Century* was trying to hold on to its inherited landscape as the ground shifted. The *Century*'s opposition to World War II was not based on sympathy for Nazism or lack of interest in global issues. Rather it reflected their judgment that the most fundamental conflicts were internal to the US. On one side the *Century* placed democratic socialists and anti-imperialists; on the other side were military and industrial leaders who envisioned a post-war global order led by the US – a vision then being promoted in *Time* and *Life* magazines as the 'American Century.'[28] Thus, the *Century*'s battle lines pitted Christianity, democracy, and peacemaking against capitalism, imperialism, and militarism. Although the *Century* worried about Hitler, it worried even more that US imperialism would lead to a long series of wars that would destroy US democracy.

Niebuhr perceived reshuffled battle lines: Christianity, democracy, capitalism, imperialism, and the US military ('the arsenal of democracy') *together* against totalitarians on a global stage and irresponsible peace activists at home. He said that the *Century*'s concerns were like redesigning one's garden while a tornado threatened to destroy one's house. To discredit the *Century* he started a competing magazine called

Christianity and Crisis, in which he wrote that 'the sin of imperialism ... may well be a less dangerous form of selfishness than an irresponsible attitude toward the task of organizing the human community.' All nations needed to keep their sinful pride in check, but fortunately the US had checks and balances that accomplished this goal better than other countries. Moreover, 'only those who have no sense of the profundities of history would deny that various nations and classes, various social groups and races, are at various times placed in such a position that a special measure of the divine mission in history falls upon them. In that sense God has chosen us in this fateful period.'[29]

For Niebuhr the principle of choosing lesser evils justified the use of force – including nuclear weapons – to uphold democracy and US postwar economic plans against totalitarians. If people who claimed Jesus as a role model felt uneasy about such compromises, they should review the Bible's teachings about the fallen human condition. They should trust God to clean their dirty hands rather than try to save the world. Although critics called this stance an apology for US global empire, Niebuhr called it international responsibility.

As the top sin targeted for prophetic critique changed from domestic inequality to foreign tyranny, the Protestant mindset became more defensive. Whereas the social gospel had stressed progress toward a more just society, realists stressed defending the US status quo against an external evil. Less and less they rallied democratic socialists to win greater economic justice; more and more they called all citizens to unite behind the New Deal and defeat foreign enemies and the naive idealists who closed their eyes to their threat. Niebuhrians drew two morals from the 1938 Munich Agreement that appeased Hitler. Politically, they concluded that tyrants cannot be stopped by idealistic pronouncements; they must be stopped by force, and better sooner than later. Theologically, they interpreted the Bible's prophetic tradition less as a vision that called people toward a better society, and more as a weapon that unmasked the abuse of power.

Four aspects of the Niebuhrian mindset came to dominate mainline Protestant social thought for decades to come. First, his way of framing questions stressed God's transcendence, especially as a judgment on human pride, rather than God's immanent presence. Secondly, he highlighted the inevitability of sin, conceptualized as self-centered pride. Sin implied that all political movements abused power, so that left-leaning activists should not get carried away with optimism. Thirdly, as already noted, his mindset encouraged a defensive posture, always on the lookout for Munich analogies and quick to use countervailing power against leaders whose sin led them to abuse power. Fourthly, at the same time, Niebuhrians continued to promote social action for goals that they deemed realistic. These actions simply needed to be self-critical and realistic. Thus, the questions arose: what options were realistic, and who decided?

With only two additional changes the classic Christian realist world-view fell into place. Niebuhrians extended their arguments against Hitler's fascism into arguments against all forms of totalitarianism; soon they advanced such arguments mainly to support resistance to Communism through US military and economic power. Meanwhile, they qualified their earlier socialist commitments so heavily as to largely abandon them – or, more precisely, to transmute them into advocacy for the New Deal. After the 1940s they portrayed unrepentant socialists – both at home and abroad – as naive and unrealistic. They used their arguments for Christian social action to support Cold War liberalism – the blend of New Deal economics, anti-Communism, and bullish visions of international development associated with presidents like Harry Truman and John Kennedy. Despite the overtly defensive way that Niebuhrians framed their arguments, in practice this carried forward the tradition of religious support for US foreign policy, as well as optimism about the US as the standard-bearer for progress in the world.

Notes

1 A short overview of US cultural and social history is Peter Carroll and David W. Noble, *The Free and the Unfree: A New History of the United States* (2nd edn) (New York: Penguin, 1992). See also Howard Zinn, *A People's History of the United States* (revised edn) (New York: Harper Perennial, 2003).

2 Carnegie, *The Gospel of Wealth and Other Timely Essays*, Edward Kirkland, ed. (Cambridge, MA: Harvard University Press, 1962), 26–7, 29.

3 John Roach Stratton cited in Albert Schenkel, *The Rich Man and the Kingdom: John D. Rockefeller, Jr. and the Protestant Establishment* (Minneapolis: Fortress Press, 1995), 176. For more on the social gospel see Gary Dorrien, *Soul in Society: the Making and Remaking of Social Christianity* (Minneapolis: Fortress Press, 1995).

4 On relations among clergy, workers, and business leaders see Henry May, *Protestant Churches and Industrial America* (New York, Harper and Bros: 1949); Liston Pope, *Millhands and Preachers: a Study of Gastonia* (2nd edn) (New Haven: Yale University Press, 1965), and Robert Craig, *Religion and Radical Politics: an Alternative Christian Tradition in the United States* (Philadelphia: Temple University Press, 1992).

5 Mary Hobgood, *Catholic Social Teaching and Economic Theory* (Philadelphia: Temple University Press, 1991); Edward DeBerri et al., eds, *Catholic Social Teaching: Our Best Kept Secret* (Maryknoll: Orbis, 1988).

6   Smith cited in James Hennesey, 'Roman Catholics and American politics,' in *Religion and American Politics*, Mark Noll, ed. (New York: Oxford University Press, 1990), 311.

7   Steve Fraser and Gary Gerstle, eds, *The Rise and Fall of the New Deal Order, 1930–1980* (Princeton: Princeton University Press, 1989).

8   Alan Brinkley, *Voices of Protest: Huey Long, Father Coughlin, and the Great Depression* (New York: Vintage, 1983).

9   Nancy Roberts, *Dorothy Day and the Catholic Worker* (Albany: SUNY Press, 1984); Patricia McNeal, *Harder Than War: Catholic Peacemaking in Twentieth Century America* (New Brunswick: Rutgers University Press, 1992).

10 See also Rosemary Ruether and Rosemary Shinner Keller, eds, *In Our Own Voices: Four Centuries of American Women's Religious Writing* (San Francisco: HarperCollins, 1995); Susan Lindley, *You Have Stept Out of Your Place: a History of Women and Religion in America* (Louisville: Westminster, 1996); Margaret Bendroth and Virginia Brereton, eds, *Women and Twentieth-Century Protestantism* (Urbana: University of Illinois Press, 2002).

11 Braude, 'Women's history IS American religious history,' in Tweed, *Re-Telling American Religious History*, 87–107.

12 See Mark Carnes, 'Victorian fraternal rituals,' in Hackett, *Religion and American Culture*, 317–26.

13 Entry points to these complex debates include Virginia Ramey Mollenkott, *Women, Men, and the Bible* (2nd edn) (New York: Crossroad, 1988) and Cullen Murphy, *The World According to Eve* (New York: Houghton Mifflin, 1999).

14 Carolyn DeSwarte Gifford, ed., *Writing My Heart Out: Selections from the Journal of Frances Willard* (Urbana: University of Illinois Press, 1995); Barbara Leslie Epstein, *The Politics of Domesticity: Women, Evangelism, and Temperance in Nineteenth Century America* (Middleton: Wesleyan University Press, 1981).

15 Numerical estimates in this section from Braude, *Women and American Religion*, 86, 96, and 116, and Braude, 'Women's history IS American religious history,' 106.

16 On Baptist resistance to such a takeover see Paul Harvey, 'Saints but not subordinates: the Women's Missionary Union of the Southern Baptist Convention,' in Bendroth and Brereton, *Women and Twentieth-Century Protestantism*, 4–24.

17 Nancy Hardesty, *Women Called to Witness: Evangelical Feminism in the Nineteenth Century* (2nd edn) (Knoxville: University of Tennessee Press, 1999).

18 Betty DeBerg, *Ungodly Women: Gender and the First Wave of American Fundamentalism* (Minneapolis: Fortress Press, 1990); Margaret Lamberts Bendroth, *Fundamentalism and Gender, 1875 to the Present* (New Haven: Yale University Press, 1993).

19 Gail Bederman, '"The women have had charge of the church long enough": the Men and Religion Forward Movement of 1911–1912 and the masculinization of middle-class Protestantism,' *American Quarterly* vol. 41, no. 3 (1989), 432–65.

20 Ira Chernus, *American Nonviolence: the History of an Idea* (Maryknoll: Orbis, 2004), Lawrence Wittner, *Rebels Against War: the American Peace Movement* (New York: Columbia University Press, 1969).

21 'The War Prayer,' cited in *Mark Twain's Weapons of Satire: Anti-imperialist Writings on the Philippine–American War*, Jim Zwick, ed. (Syracuse: Syracuse University Press, 1992), 159–60.

22 Cited in Zinn, *People's History of the United States*, 312–13.

23 Cited in Fisher, *Catholics in America*, 325. Entry points to this subject include Mark Silk, *Spiritual Politics: Religion and America Since Word War II* (New York: Simon and Schuster, 1987) and Sara Diamond, *Roads to Dominion: Right-wing Movements and Political Power in the United States* (New York: Guilford Press, 1995).

24 On Niebuhr see Dorrein, *Soul in Society*, Richard Fox, *Reinhold Niebuhr: A Biography* (New York: Pantheon, 1985), and Mark Hulsether, *Building a Protestant Left:* Christianity and Crisis *Magazine, 1941–1993* (Knoxville: University of Tennessee Press, 1999). The following section is adapted from pp. 12–22 of this book.

25 Handy, *Christian America*, 159–84. Hutchison, *Between the Times*, explores relationships between the Protestant establishment and key 'outsiders.'

26 Reinhold Niebuhr, *Moral Man and Immoral Society* (New York: Scribners, 1933). See also David Nelson Duke, *In the Trenches with Jesus and Marx: Harry F. Ward and the Struggle for Social Justice* (Tuscaloosa: University of Alabama Press, 2003).

27 John Haynes Holmes review cited in Fox, *Reinhold Niebuhr*, 152–3.

28 Henry Luce's 'American Century' essay first appeared in *Life* in 1941 and is widely reprinted, including in William Appleman Williams et al., *America in Vietnam: a Documentary History* (New York: Anchor, 1985), 22–8. On foreign policy see Thomas McCormick, *America's Half-Century: United States Foreign Policy in the Cold War* (Baltimore: Johns Hopkins, 1989). On ideas of secular intellectuals that paralleled the Niebuhrians, see Richard Pells, *The Liberal Mind in a Conservative Age* (New York: Harper and Row, 1985)

29 Niebuhr, 'Imperialism and irresponsibility,' *Christianity and Crisis*, 2/24/41, 6. Niebuhr, 'Anglo-American destiny and responsibility,' in Cherry, *God's New Israel*, 303, 304 (subsequent citations from *Christianity and Crisis* are abbreviated *C&C*).

CHAPTER 4

Cultural Aspects of Religion
in the Early Twentieth Century

As we explored cases of religion intersecting with political issues of the early twentieth century – wealth and poverty, women's rights, and foreign policy – our goal in Chapter 3 was not to be comprehensive, but rather concrete and evocative. Nor were we trying to distinguish sharply between politics and the cultural issues that we will highlight in this chapter. Religious politics has a cultural dimension, religious culture has a political dimension, and our plan is to circle through related issues more than once to gain a multifaceted understanding. Nevertheless, the cases we will explore in the 'mid-day breaks' and 'evening stopovers' of the current chapter – immigrant traditions and devotions, commercial popular culture, and the fundamentalist-modernist controversy – tilt the balance toward culture.

Cultural Dimensions of Immigrant Religious Enclaves

In Chapter 2 we flagged the importance of ethnic traditions for Jewish and Catholic immigrants. In Chapter 3 we discussed the struggles of immigrants to move from poverty to a relatively comfortable life in the middle class. Still deserving more attention, however, is how religious culture shaped distinctive ways of life in ethnic communities and how this related to the process of entering the mainstream. This is a tangled problem that we cannot map in detail, since there are so many ethnic groups and each one is internally divided. Complicating the picture is a push–pull dynamic created by the dual fact that immigrants wanted to be accepted by the mainstream and overcome biases that were used as weapons against them, yet at the same time wanted to maintain distinctive aspects of their heritage that set them apart. This section explores the richness of immigrant religion and the textures of this push–pull dynamic, using examples from the Jewish and Italian Catholic experience.

Recall the pattern in which the first immigrant generation tries to maintain Old World traditions, the second generation runs away from these traditions, and the third generation seeks to recover what the second generation rejected – but recover it selectively from a base closer to the mainstream, rather than adopting it as a total way of life. In the long run, the third generation experience – as extended by later generations – is what we most need to understand. However, we must not underestimate the difficulty of arriving at a 'third generation' perspective in the first place. Hostility and misunderstanding from hegemonic groups could tempt immigrants to remain in a 'first generation' posture of resistance or continue a 'second generation' strategy of rejecting tradition to fit in.

The breakthrough of immigrants to the middle class is hard to disentangle from their cultural acceptance by hegemonic groups. Sometimes economic tensions were expressed in religious terms; sometimes religious attitudes helped create economic differences. Either way, immigrants faced resistance in which economic and cultural factors reinforced each other. Ever since the influx of Irish in the 1840s, nativism had been a strong force in US culture. Protestants had hated and feared Catholics since the earliest years of the Reformation; one school primer in the colonial era instructed students to 'abhor that arrant Whore of Rome and all her blasphemies.'[1] After 1840 this hostility spilled over into riots in which Catholic buildings (most famously a Boston convent) were burned and many people died. Nativism fueled political movements such as the Know-Nothing Party and the American Protective Association. The 1884 Republican presidential candidate attacked Democrats as the party of 'rum, Romanism, and rebellion.' Popular novels portrayed Irish as drunkards and convents as brothels for priests. Anti-Catholic themes informed discourses about political corruption and the unworthy poor.

Anti-Semitism often took a back seat to anti-Catholicism among nativists because Catholics posed a greater threat to Protestant hegemony. Nevertheless, anti-Semitism was also widespread, and it has deeper roots reaching back to the founding of Christianity. Since we focused on Catholics when discussing the economic struggles of immigrants – although we could tell a broadly similar story about Jews, with a larger role for socialist politics and a smaller role for formal social teachings – let us focus on Jews in our discussion of nativism, although we could tell a similar story about Catholics.[2]

Although Jews prospered in the US and entered the mainstream, this did not happen without resistance. In the 1920s universities such as Harvard feared that too many Jews were applying and limited Jewish enrollment to 10 per cent; such quotas did not end until after mid-century. Jews often faced social and professional barriers; for example, they had difficulty getting jobs as university professors before mid-century, and many elite neighborhoods signed covenants against selling homes to Jews (by 1970 such covenants were outlawed or seen as embarrassing, and ten per cent of all professors were Jewish). More alarming was the revival of the Ku Klux Klan (KKK) as a nationwide group that gave equal time to demonizing blacks, Catholics, and Jews. The original Klan had atrophied after the North stopped pressing the South for reconstruction, but in the 1920s a new set of leaders reinvented it. They recruited 2.5 million members from throughout the country, including middle-class professionals along with farmers and blue-collar workers. The KKK's new emphasis was defending '100 per cent Americanism' against immigrants who were seen as 'mongrelizing' US society. Other groups chimed in with related ideas and open sympathy for European fascism. Conspiracy theories popular among such groups held that Jews controlled both the global banking system and world communism; a document called *The Protocols of the Elders of Zion* – highly implausible at best and soon shown to be a fake – purported to prove this conspiracy. In 1915 a group from this network lynched a Jewish businessman from Atlanta named Leo Frank. As in the case of many lynched blacks, there was a flimsy charge that he had sexually abused an Anglo-Protestant woman.

We could easily misperceive what the KKK and kindred groups were like during the 1920s, because after the 1940s they were perceived as far-right extremists – that is, as fairly marginal even though they retained some influence that occasionally bubbled into the mainstream, for example, when televangelist Pat Robertson published a book that echoed the *Protocols of the Elders of Zion*.[3] This perception of marginality reflects a change in the character of these groups after World War II. Mass followings melted away from groups seen as sympathetic to fascism, leaving only the most rigid and strident members. The KKK had this fringe reputation when it revived in yet another form to fight the civil rights movement of the 1950s. During the 1920s the most disturbing thing about the KKK from a Jewish perspective was less its extremism (as one might suspect from its later reputation) than how it tapped into a nativism that was widely shared in the mainstream. '100 per cent Americanism' was popular with leading politicians. Some Populists focused a disproportionate amount of their hostility on Jews when attacking bankers and other corporate elites, which could create a sense of scapegoating and demonizing Jews as a group – although we should not overstress this point, given that the core conflict for Populists was rich versus poor rather than Protestant versus Jewish. The Populists' upper-class enemies were equally guilty of anti-Semitism; for example, Henry Ford, the founder of Ford Motor Company, promoted the *Protocols of the Elders of Zion.*

Father Coughlin, the radio preacher introduced above, became a prominent anti-Semite in the 1930s. Coughlin had begun to broadcast in response to the KKK burning a cross at his Detroit church, and early in the decade he defended the New Deal against its conservative enemies using Catholic teachings on social justice. However, he became obsessed with Roosevelt's perceived betrayal of principle – which Coughlin called the 'Jew Deal' – and sympathetic to Hitler. This became increasingly disturbing as his sermons became more strident and his popularity grew. Before the 1936 election, many people saw an alliance between Coughlin and Louisiana Senator Huey Long as the strongest threat to Roosevelt's re-election. (Roosevelt adopted many of the New Deal policies that most helped working people during the years that Long and Coughlin were cutting into his working-class support.) For his part, Long controlled Louisiana through ruthless suppression of his enemies and a Biblically infused rhetoric calling for heavy taxation of the rich to 'Share Our Wealth.' Although his enemies denounced him as a mere demagogue, his policies really did shift significant resources toward working people. Some people worried that Long was anti-Semitic and that a Long–Coughlin alliance could develop into an American version of Hitler's right-wing populism. Probably these fears were overstated, but one of Long's top associates, a demagogic preacher named G. L. K. Smith, did turn to the extreme right in the 1940s. We will never know what Long would have done if he had gained more power because he was assassinated in 1935; efforts to continue the incipient coalition without him self-destructed.[4]

The combined weight of the KKK, Ford, Coughlin, Long, and fascist extremists like Smith was more than enough to make Jews fear that quotas and social exclusion were only the tip of an iceberg of anti-Semitism. In the face of such pressure, it is easy to understand why Jews – and by extension other immigrants – were attracted to approaches such as Reform Judaism and the Americanist tendency in Catholicism. They often went to great lengths to express their patriotism. In the years around 1920, communities that had not yet switched from Old World vernacular languages to English did so on a large scale. They changed for many reasons: the desires of second and third generation children; the impact of public schools; a climate of repression during World War I; and the emergence of a shared multi-ethnic popular culture. When religious groups switched to English, older generations often felt this as a wrenching break with tradition. Catholics were partly insulated from this shock at worship because all Catholics used the same Latin Mass, but questions still remained about what language to use in other contexts. Most Reform Jews had already made the linguistic switch, but more recent Jewish immigrants moving from Yiddish-speaking neighborhoods to suburban synagogues felt the impact keenly – as did families from every immigrant group making the switch at home.

It is also understandable that hostility from the dominant culture could lead immigrants – especially communities like Jews and Irish with long histories of being persecuted – to circle their wagons and hold tightly to their culture. A classic example is the rise of Zionism, as discussed above. In light of patriotic US rhetoric celebrating religious freedom, it was common for outsider groups to combine an insistence on freely practicing their religion with staking a claim to be true Americans. Scholars argue that US religions have often thrived not so much by blending into the mainstream as by defining themselves in tension with the mainstream and insisting that this choice was part of their birthright as Americans.[5] This dynamic helps explain why Conservative Judaism grew faster than Reform Judaism among third generation immigrants. It also helps account for the importance of the Yiddish press and community arts movement in Jewish neighborhoods. Immigrants did not have to depend for information solely on English language newspapers and Horatio Alger books checked out of Carnegie-endowed libraries. They could read their own newspapers such as the *Jewish Daily Forward* and attend local theater productions in which they dramatized issues of their own choice in their own words.

By no means were Jews the only immigrants who faced such issues. For example, after the propaganda machine for World War I took hold, any German-American who publicly identified with German culture had heavy costs to pay. Only a small fraction of the community identified with nationalist political movements in Germany – a path that led toward far-right extremism by the 1940s. However, there were strong anti-war sentiments in German-American communities (especially those with a strong socialist presence) during the run-up to World War I. As an example of the push–pull dynamic in immigrant communities – the simultaneous motivation to remain distinct from mainstream culture and to merge with it – there are few cases more dramatic than the pressures faced by German-Americans between 1910 and 1920. They had a natural desire to maintain their language and customs, worry about relatives in Germany, and critically examine a case for war that seemed unpersuasive to people ranging from the Socialist Party to Secretary of State William Jennings Bryan. Yet they also felt intense pressure to prove their patriotism by joining the army, speaking English, possibly changing their names, and generally conforming to 100 per cent Americanism.

Nor were Zionists the only immigrants who identified with ethnic-religious compatriots in other parts of the world. Irish tensions with Anglo-Protestants resonated with memories of Irish oppression by the English. Catholic clergy sympathized with Francisco Franco in the Spanish Civil War and conservative factions in the Mexican revolution of 1910–20; these alliances inflamed tensions between Catholics and the US left. Although Italian-Americans felt limited loyalty to elites in Italy – they came from the southern part of Italy which was historically exploited by the industrialized north – they followed the news from the old country, sympathized with Italy's fascist leader Benito Mussolini, and celebrated Columbus Day with markedly more gusto than other groups (Columbus was from Italy even though he sailed for Spain).

Importantly, many Italians and Mexicans came to the US as temporary migrants rather than permanent settlers. More than half of all Italians who arrived after 1900 returned home. Mexicans have a long history of two-way border crossings, based partly on choice and partly on US government policy. Many Mexicans were deported in the 1930s; later the Bracero Program created a legal structure for annual migrations from Mexico to the US and back.

Devotional Catholicism is the cultural expression of immigrant religious life that we most need to explore. The term refers to a nexus of prayers, rituals, and pious practices: lighting votive candles; wearing crosses; praying the rosary using special beads; fasting; meditating in front of (often bloody) pictures of saints; building shrines; joining processions during holidays like Easter; and many others. When we spoke in Chapter 2 about the sacramental sensibility of Catholics, we were not referring solely to worship in Catholic churches, but also to a wider texture of life in homes and neighborhoods. Likewise, when we spoke in Chapter 3 about Catholic women's experience, we were not referring solely to nuns; devotional Catholicism is strongly informed by a version of domestic ideology.[6]

Compared with Catholics, Protestants favor more conceptual forms of spirituality, although they did develop their own paler forms of devotion, such as sentimental songs, daily prayers, semi-iconic paintings of Jesus, societies to decorate churches with flowers, and holiday traditions. There was no ambiguity about the embodied quality of Catholic devotions: putting plaster-cast statues of saints in gardens; burning incense; using holy water from places where the Blessed Virgin appeared; wearing scapulars (special pieces of cloth that fit around one's neck); not eating meat on Fridays; and so on. A standard theme of Protestant preaching was to attack such practices as abnormal and foreign. Evangelicals perceived devotional Catholicism as a distraction from true Christianity and an example of trust in external works instead of Christ's saving grace. Liberal Protestants added that it was irrational and superstitious. Complicating the situation, some Catholics (such as Americanist priests) agreed with aspects of the Protestant critique, creating intra-Catholic tensions somewhat comparable to debates between Reform and Orthodox Jews.

This set the stage for many levels of experience – communal, personal, and generational – to come together in particular devotions. At a communal level, patron saints (such as the Virgin of Guadalupe for Mexicans) or rituals of respect for community symbols (such as the US flag for 100 per cent Americans) can resonate deeply as symbols of an ethnic or national group. If outsiders attack such practices, community members rally behind them. Such was the response, for example, when Protestants insulted Irish culture or when Irish bishops were disrespectful to Polish culture. Yet devotional practice did not solely express collective pride. It was also near the heart of immigrant life because of its personal dimensions: the ways it structured people's attitudes, coping strategies, and spiritual imaginations. Moreover, since individuals have varying needs – for example, they reflect different generations and genders – internal tensions arose within the multiple levels of devotional practice.

One example of this complexity is the *festa*, or community festival, dedicated to the Madonna del Carmine, the patron saint of Italian-Americans from East Harlem, New York.[7] To understand this festival we must bear four factors in mind. First is the economic struggle of the community. (We could easily pursue the story of how its support for the radical politician, Fiorello La Guardia, relates to our discussion of economics in Chapter 3.) Second is the tendency of Italian immigrants to mistrust priests. Unlike in Ireland and Poland where people rallied behind their bishops against foreign oppressors, in Italy the bishops were more likely to *be* the oppressors. A third factor is how Italians centered their religion on the home. Not only did they stress devotions that were practiced at home, they saw loyalty to the family as the heart of being a religious person, whether or not one attended mass regularly. Devotions focused on the relation between Mary and Jesus, which mirrored the centrality of the mother and her eldest son within the Italian family. Although the culture excluded women from many public roles, its domestic ideology made mothers the dominant power in the religious realm.

A final factor was the tendency of Irish priests and Anglo-Protestants to look down on Italian religion. One reason was the Italian reputation for anti-clericalism. Another was the Italians' ambiguous place within the US racial system, midway between black and white and sharing the same skin tone with Puerto Ricans who increasingly moved into their neighborhood. Just as other ethnic groups changed over time from being considered semi-American to 100 per cent American, the reputation of Italians changed from racially ambiguous to just another white ethnic group. However, early in the century this outcome was not yet clear.[8]

Italian behavior at the *festa* threatened to reinforce an outside perception that they were racially exotic at best and perhaps just backward and superstitious. The ritual center of the festival – which also involved a week-long party in which families reunited, ate traditional foods, and generally had a good time – occurred when a statue of the Madonna was taken from the church and paraded through the neighborhood. Although other ethnic groups organized similar processions, some of the Italian practices were dramatic by Catholic standards. Devotees made extravagant sacrifices as part of their prayers for blessings. They walked the hot streets barefoot, carrying candles weighing up to 200 pounds on their heads. They made candles in the same size and shape of body parts that needed healing and offered them to the Madonna. At an extreme, women asked family members to carry them up the aisle of the church to the Madonna's altar as they dragged their tongues along the floor.

Such behavior did not match the image of decorum and progress that many priests sought to cultivate. Priests tried to bring the *festa*, which was organized by a church-related committee, under their control. For years they made the Italians keep their statue of the Madonna in the church basement rather than its sanctuary. (This tactic backfired when the Italians appealed to higher-ups in Rome, who overturned the policy and recognized the church as a special shrine.) Predictably, such resistance increased the Italians' expression of pride through the *festa*.

In addition to the straightforward ways that the *festa* expressed Italian pride, there were conflicts internal to the festival over women's roles and generational behavior. The most dramatic sacrifices like dragging one's tongue along the floor were made by mothers. As we have noted, mothers exercised more power in Italian religion than any other group including priests. Thus, it made sense for mothers to be the leaders in a ritual focusing on a divine mother – the Madonna – whose importance rivaled that of Jesus or God the Father. However, we must not forget that mothers wielded this power within a society that confined them to the home, and that a key way that they exercised power in the home was through sacrificing for their families. Since the *festa* was one of the few times during the year when women played a public role, it makes sense that the ritual dramatized both sacrifice and power.

Scholars speculate that the *festa* expressed two more things. One is a venting of pent-up frustration at being confined at home through taking to the streets in the parade. Another is the way that sacrifice functioned in a battle of generations. By no means did all Italian daughters want to grow up just like their mothers in a culture that taught, for example, that respect for the family included marrying the first person one dated. (We need only consider that Madonna, the pop star, grew up in a such an Italian family, before spending much of her career rebelling against it.) When mothers at the *festa* modeled for their daughters how to give proper respect to the Madonna – and more pointedly when they undertook extreme sacrifices for the sake of their daughters – their sacrifices were potent ways to pressure upcoming generations to stay loyal. One scholar asks whether this form of power through sacrifice, into which mothers sought to initiate daughters, may be somewhat masochistic.[9] However we answer this question, it is clear that if we approach Italian gender roles as a hegemonic system, the *festa* tends to support the system, albeit in complex and conflicted ways. At the some time, the response of women like Madonna (the pop star) makes it clear that gender roles are not always stable over time.

This *festa* is only one example of immigrant devotion. It has similarities and differences with the festivals of other groups such as Polish-Americans and Mexican-Americans. The Italian form of domestic ideology is not the same as the Irish form, and the *festa* early in the twentieth century was not the same as the *festa* practiced today. However, by exploring this celebration's levels of meaning we can begin to see the hidden complexities and cultural depth of immigrant religion. Given that the total amount of time that immigrants spent studying theology was only a fraction of the time they spent on devotional practices, it is crucial to have maps that can focus on such practices and analyze them in depth.

Religion and Popular Culture

Some of the most important cultural changes of the twentieth century happened in the field of popular culture and mass-mediated entertainment. Although little was entirely new in this field – entertainments including saloons, dime novels, theater, minstrel shows, baseball, and boxing had long been important – commercial culture grew rapidly in importance. New technologies like radio and film transformed it. New musical forms such as blues and jazz gave it great vitality. The diversity of a multi-ethnic working class and the energy of urban life enriched it. It was near the heart of changes associated with the shift from an economy based on production and its associated virtues of hard work, thrift, and moral character – the classic building blocks of the Protestant work ethic – toward an economy based on consumer spending and its virtues of leisure, pleasure-seeking, and cultivating an attractive appearance and sparkling personality. The latter were building blocks of what came to be called consumerism and materialism – and sometimes also individualism, although it is not clear whether individualism actually increased in a consumer society or simply took a distinctive form. Popular culture benefited from all these changes and intensified them.[10]

In contrast to the contemporary situation in which overtly religious forms of popular culture are often derivative versions of more respected forms – for example, much Christian contemporary music is a pale imitation of the best popular music and most overtly Christian films are notably inferior to Hollywood films – evangelical themes were near the center of popular culture during the nineteenth century. Best-selling works such as *Uncle Tom's Cabin* taught hegemonic religious values, and clergy were cutting-edge innovators. Protestant leaders had perceived a challenge from innovations such as cheap popular literature, and had opted to 'fight fire with fire' by producing their own market offerings. They wrote tracts and 'true tales' that were equally lurid as their secular competitors but with edifying morals, organized educational programs called Chautauquas, and so on. Although critics feared that they were watering down and sensationalizing religion by entering this market, their success was part and parcel of their status as a cultural establishment.[11]

We have seen that cultural change early in the century dovetailed with demographic trends to produce a second disestablishment of Protestantism – a cultural disestablishment that forced Protestant elites to share influence with immigrants and secular mass culture. To be sure, religious leaders did not give up without a fight, nor did they lose all their fights. They policed popular culture and continued to create influential religious market offerings, for example, Coughlin's radio sermons and a widely-read novel called *In His Steps* that imagined the wonderful results from a group of Kansas Protestants vowing not to do anything for a year without asking 'What Would Jesus Do?' Nevertheless, the clergy's power to set the standards for cultural taste was slipping, along with their ability to hold their market share of people who chose their books and weekend activities over secular alternatives.

Before turning to a case study of such change, let us step back and reflect on how to approach the phenomenon of popular religion. Recall how we asked in the Introduction whether activities like following baseball or playing jazz could be considered religious if they became central enough to a person's identity. We have been assuming that religion is about the everyday life of ordinary people as well as the teachings of clergy – so that, for example, the *festa* and the home are near the heart of Italian Catholicism. It is only a small additional step to ask whether spending every weekend going to a nightclub, ballpark, theater, or department store – and, more pointedly, gaining one's sense of meaning and experience of community through such activities – should be considered 'consumer religion.'[12]

We decided not to adopt a definition of religion so broad that our selective tour of religion ballooned into a survey of everything considered important by anyone in the country. Nevertheless, we must pay attention when inherited religious practices – for example, setting aside one day each week for community rituals, teaching values to children, and seeking aesthetic experiences that cultivate spiritual depth – either overlap with commercial culture or are forced into a zero-sum competition with it. What difference does it make if people spend Sabbaths at amusement parks instead of churches and synagogues? What if children identify with rock musicians more than the heroes of Horatio Alger books and learn Bible stories at the movies? If worship is no longer the main place that people hear music, does this diminish the importance of worship? If radio becomes the main place people hear religious music, does this change this music's meaning? Nineteenth-century clergy opted to enter the entertainment market – to fight fire with fire – because they felt that they could not pass their values to upcoming generations without a strong presence in this realm. When many twentieth-century clergy came to feel that they lacked the firepower (or the stomach for crass commercialization) to compete with secular popular culture – so that at best they could try to guide it, consume it selectively, and create enclaves of partial shelter from it – this was a significant change.

Nevertheless, we could overestimate how thoroughly secular culture displaced popular religion and underestimate how much the two overlapped and converged. If we use a broad definition of religion, we can see that religion changed in form and interpenetrated with commercial culture more than it lost importance. American Studies scholars often assume that by the twentieth century, religion had become culturally marginal and less interesting than higher priority subjects. In effect they assume that exploring religious aspects of popular culture is like listening to mediocre Christian rock when they could be listening to cutting-edge musicians. However, consider how many of the best US musicians – Bob Dylan, John Coltrane, Madonna, Johnny Cash, and Ruben Blades among others – weave religious themes deeply into their music. There is barely even a market niche for 'Contemporary Christian *Country* Music' because mainstream country is already so Christian. Rhythm and blues – and by extension rock and hip-hop – are built on a foundation of black gospel. Whatever one thinks about evangelical record labels – which, to be fair, have become quite diverse and of higher quality compared with the years when they earned their reputation for mediocrity – dismissing religious forms of popular music is not a promising foundation for an argument against exploring popular religion.[13] This analogy holds for other parts of popular culture.

Somewhat surprisingly, scholars in Religious Studies are almost as likely as American Studies scholars to underestimate the complexity of US popular religion. They limit themselves through an approach that overstresses commodification and secularization. Consider that there are at least four meanings of the term 'popular religion.' First, it can mean *prevalent* or pervasive practices, such as attending church or reading the Bible. Secondly, it can mean *authentic traditions* of the folk (as opposed to elites) such as Italian *festas*, old-time Appalachian hymns, or Native American ceremonies. Note how this second meaning can be nearly the opposite of the first, and how it is often defined in opposition to the third: religion in the form of *mass-mediated entertainment*, such as sermons by Father Coughlin or Hollywood films about Jesus. Fourthly, popular religion can mean *counter-hegemonic expressions* of 'the people' versus hegemonic elites. This fourth sense – the favorite one for cultural studies – means various things in practice depending on what kinds of hegemony are in focus, but examples include the *festa* as an expression of Italian pride versus Protestant hegemony, Dorothy Day's religion as a challenge to the hegemony of capitalism, and the role of progressive black churches in the civil rights era.

These four senses overlap. The *festa* is both a counter-hegemonic expression of ethnic pride (sense four) and an authentic tradition (sense two). Politicians who say 'God Bless America' are both prevalent (sense one) and mass-mediated (sense three). Some anti-war music of the late 1960s was prevalent, mass-mediated, and counter-hegemonic at the same time. However, it is hard to imagine practices that are popular in all four senses at the same time.

Scholars who approach popular religion through a commodification paradigm focus on change – usually seen as decline – from the second of these senses (the authentic) to the third (the mass-mediated). They stress how such change trivializes religion by smoothing off its rough edges, reducing it to tiny sound bites, and forcing it to compete with soap advertisements and amusement park rides as a commodity for sale. Moreover, if religion becomes a consumer choice, it may also become an example of secularization. Secularization theorists do not necessarily try to argue that religion is disappearing or belabor the point that religion and the state have largely separated in many countries. They may simply claim that religion is weakening because it is becoming a matter of private individual choice. Pursuing this line of thought, one might conclude that US religion is between a rock and hard place: if it fails to engage with popular culture it becomes culturally marginal, but if it enters the cultural market, the price of admission is privatization. Either way, secularization wins.

Analyses based on this approach are undoubtedly valuable – but also overstressed by scholars in US religion. We can point to many examples that fit the approach, such as certain activities of New Agers or a 1925 book called *The Man Nobody Knows* that presented Jesus as the world's greatest advertising executive.[14] Nevertheless, this is not the only useful approach, and at times it distracts from two important questions: what forms of religion are most prevalent; and what forms are most counter-hegemonic. Consider how many additional examples come into view if we draw on all four senses of popular religion rather than narrowing our attention to decline from sense two to three. Consider, also, that expressing religion in popular forms – fighting fire with fire – does not always represent decline. In many cases we are better off taking for granted that religion inevitably has commercial dimensions – so that the commodification of tradition is unsurprising or even uninteresting – and exploring why certain forms of popular religion are more prevalent than others, or are counter-hegemonic alternatives to others, in a context where none of them escapes the logic of the market. This is a promising approach for building bridges between religious studies and cultural studies.

If we approach US culture within this framework, we are quickly forced to abandon any lingering impression that religion and popular culture are divergent fields with limited overlap. Instead, what is striking is how deeply they interpenetrate. In both the nineteenth and twentieth centuries, major building blocks of popular culture have been part and parcel of popular religion. For example, consider the rise of radio. From the beginning, religious broadcasters accounted for a healthy share of radio stations. Religiously-inflected content – music, sermons, dramas with religious characters, and diverse moralistic discourses – helped fill the airtime of secular stations, and clergy had a significant voice in discussions about regulating the airwaves. Or consider the rise of jazz and blues. True, this music made its home in nightclubs and juke joints that some people considered the antithesis of religion. True, respectable white Protestants (as well as many black ministers) were scandalized by the music. However, this music also made its home in churches in the form of gospel music, which became part of the foundation for later styles. It is much better to understand jazz and blues simply as a new style of music – one attuned to African-American sensibilities, with religious and non-religious dimensions tightly interwoven – than as a displacement of religious music by secular music.

In light of the inter-racial quality of early Pentecostalism that we discussed above, it is fascinating to compare two related dynamics in US race relations: on the one hand, the blend of white establishment disdain for Pentecostalism and white grassroots fascination with it, and on the other hand, the blend of white establishment disdain for jazz and blues (a music largely created by blacks) and white grassroots fascination with it. Of course, neither Pentecostalism nor the jazz subculture was an anti-racist utopia. Nevertheless, each was an important site for black innovation and inter-racial contact and communication, and in both cases there was eventually a rich blend of contributions from both sides of the racial divide. The mutual influence of religion and popular music suggested by this comparison goes beyond mere speculation in at least one sense: many singers at the heart of black popular music – as well as Elvis Presley, the music's most famous white popularizer – learned to sing in Pentecostal churches.

We lack the space to address every important form of popular religion – or, for that matter, even *one* form if we work in depth, giving attention to new technologies, major artistic texts, the interplay between artists and audiences, and the relationships between art and historical trends such as transformations in the work ethic or gender system. We must narrow our attention to cases. The rise and fall of the Hollywood Production Code and the censorship apparatus that enforced this code (best known as the Hays Office) is a fascinating case study for exploring the relations among religious reformers, media corporations, and consumers of popular culture. It is also a significant case study since the Code helped to establish the ground rules for the content of popular film during an era when film and radio were the nation's leading media.[15]

Before mid-century, movies had an impact comparable to television in later years; in 1930 the weekly attendance at films was 90 million out of a population of 120 million. Moreover, Hollywood's power was centralized in a handful of studios that monopolized the production and distribution of films, so that Will Hays, the head of the studios' unified bureaucracy, could enforce standards for films. Regulation by the Hays Office evolved through various stages, but the underlying issue was that film-makers did not want to fight a patchwork of local censorship boards that emerged as movies became the leading form of entertainment. Hollywood either wanted no censorship at all – which was not in the cards – or a centralized form of censorship that matched its business needs. These desires forced it into negotiation with religious reformers.

Censorship boards built on a long tradition in which clergy and associated moral watchdogs – groups that by the twentieth century were typically part of Progressive reform networks – sought to safeguard public morals from corruption by undesirable forms of art and entertainment. Reformers worked both through shaping public opinion and imposing laws. Their classic cause was Prohibition but there were many more. Sunday closing laws outlawed many forms of weekend recreation, and even in places without such laws churches often policed their members' behavior. There were conflicts over the use of parks and other public spaces. The 1873 Comstock Act criminalized the circulation of any 'obscene' writing, including information about birth control. The New England Watch and Ward Society used similar laws to prevent the sale of books it judged immoral; these laws were not overturned until 1930, after the society suppressed an article about prostitution in H. L. Mencken's *American Mercury* and acclaimed novels by D. H. Lawrence and Theodore Dreiser.[16]

Such watchdogs became especially worried about film because early movie houses, called nickelodeons, built upon the so-called 'low' entertainment of vaudeville and were typically in working-class neighborhoods. By the 1920s film-makers were upgrading their image by building opulent theaters and pressuring audiences to behave on a model of decorum more like attending church or the opera, as compared with the casual behavior in nickelodeons and saloons. However, watchdogs became even more worried about the corrupting effects of films on youth as audiences grew. Reformers worried about what young lovers did in dark theaters and how immigrants who built the film industry – who were largely Jewish – were using films to address issues such as labor struggles and changing gender roles. Initially, some people thought that films could develop on a model similar to journalism, as opposed to 'mere entertainment' – thus, suggesting a need for free speech guarantees and encouragement to address controversial issues. In practice, however, film came to be defined as a commercial product that could be regulated for the public good and subjected to stronger censorship than journalism or the theater. A key case that established this precedent concerned a black prizefighter, Jack Johnson, who scandalized whites by knocking out white challengers and sleeping with white women. His fights were deemed too controversial for screening.[17]

Since regulation was inevitable, Hollywood wanted a single standard for the whole country; dealing with a separate censorship board in each city was a nightmare. Moreover, producers did not want a rating system that would restrict their audience. They wanted the power to regulate their own films, either in-house or working with a weak censorship board of their choice. Thus they developed internal guidelines and co-operated first with a board of reviewers drawn from a Protestant social gospel network and later with a similar Catholic group. Hays paid people involved with these boards, including leaders of the Federal Council of Churches. Although this raised questions about the reviewers' independence, it reveals the stature of Christian elites who assumed, as a matter of course, that they deserved input into Hollywood policies.

During the 1930s Hollywood experimented with more controversial themes and bolder social criticism, notably in gangster films, and more risqué sexual plots featuring independent women such as Mae West. Such trends led a group of Catholic reformers – including clerics, the publishers of two Catholic journals and one film industry journal, and a journalist named Joseph Breen – to press for tougher censorship. Their efforts led in 1933 to the Legion of Decency, which operated under the umbrella of the National Catholic Welfare Conference. The Legion's influence reached into parishes throughout the country. Priests publicized its lists of approved (A) and condemned (C) films, plus a B category that later evolved into the PG and R ratings. Laypeople took solemn oaths not to watch condemned films. Local applications of this model varied – few bishops matched the zeal of the Cardinal of Philadelphia who ordered all Catholics in his city to stop attending theaters entirely – but the point to accent is that Hollywood faced a credible threat of large-scale boycotts.

In response, Hays agreed to put teeth into industry guidelines, which film-makers had earlier found fairly easy to evade. In 1934, the classic version of the Production Code emerged and the Hays Office began to enforce it aggressively. It forbade all negative portrayals of religion, law, and US public authorities – as well as birth control, miscegenation, homosexuality, divorce, revenge, sex outside marriage, and lustful kissing. It also proclaimed Hollywood's responsibility to promote public morality. Every film was required both to portray unambiguous lines between good and evil, and to ensure that good was rewarded and evil punished. Breen was hired to enforce the Code, and nothing could be produced without his approval. Thus, a dual apparatus emerged – the Hays Office as the internal police for the industry, and the Legion of Decency monitoring the Hays Office for any sign of weakening resolve. Together they mediated between those who desired less censorship (notably producers) and conservative church people. Thickening the plot was the fact that many film-makers were Jewish but several of the moral watchdogs were anti-Semitic – including Breen, who called Hollywood

Jews 'the scum of the earth' and 'a rotten bunch of vile people with no respect for anything beyond the making of money.'[18] This was not a case of seamless and harmonious co-operation between religious reformers and film producers! Nevertheless, they forged a compromise that put conservative Catholic values at the heart of popular entertainment – not solely in the role of punishing films that transgressed religious sensibilities, but near the center of decision-making and at the roots of Hollywood's stated mission.

During the production process, scripts ping-ponged between Breen and the producers. If the producers accepted Breen's demands, the Legion of Decency usually followed with an A or B rating. However, sometimes the Legion still condemned the film and there were more rounds of negotiation. The case of *The Outlaw* (1943) dragged on for six years as the producer flaunted censorship, released the film outside industry channels – a difficult move at the time – and focused his advertising campaign on his star's breasts. Eventually, after censors had viewed the film twenty times, the producers cut enough from the film's rape scenes and sexual dialogue for the Legion to lift its condemnation.

Films could be altered in striking ways. By the time censors finished with *Black Fury* (1935) it no longer portrayed coal miners striking against greedy owners and their hired thugs. Instead a well-treated miner who resented his corrupt labor bosses foiled the plans of outside thugs whose violence was contrary to the wishes of the mine-owners. Censors would not permit a Catholic missionary in *Keys to the Kingdom* (1944) to say 'there are many gates to heaven; we enter by one, these new preachers by another.'[19] He was only allowed to show Christ-like tolerance for people of other religions (in this case Methodists) even though he knew they were wrong. These were films that made it to a stage of negotiation; many projects were ruled out from the start.

Of course, films managed to glamorize sex and question authority despite censorship. One scriptwriter, after learning about the behavior required of heroes, simply produced plots that exclusively featured villains. Often Breen could only ensure that charismatic gangsters and renegades received pro forma punishments in the final reel, or that plots based on glamorizing sexual transgression ended in marriage or death. In Biblical epics, earnest Christian heroes appeared against a background of Roman debauchery that seemed more fun; for example, *Sign of the Cross* (1932) featured such lurid temptations for its pious heroes as a dance with lesbian overtones and a sensuous milk bath. Censors struggled with producers over the ending of a Western called *Duel in the Sun* (1946), which earned the nickname *Lust in the Dust*. Everyone agreed that its lovers must die in the final reel, but would their sins be adequately punished if they died in each other's arms, or must the plot kill them before they reached each other's arms? Although the film's steamiest parts were cut and its opening credits coached viewers to watch for the supposed moral – that a 'grim fate lay waiting for the transgressor of the laws of God and man' – critics felt that such editing merely papered over deeper problems.

Despite efforts by producers to stretch the boundaries of what could be screened, we should not exaggerate how much of Hollywood's creative effort pushed against the Code's constraints, as opposed to flowing comfortably within the channels created by its ground rules and philosophy. Hollywood would have produced many films with strong religious themes even without the Code, given the interests of its audience and many of its producers, and the Code reinforced this tendency. Dozens of films portrayed Biblical characters, model priests and nuns, and heroes of faith like Joan of Arc. The list expands dramatically if we add films with overtly Christian heroes – several versions of *Uncle Tom's Cabin*, hundreds of films about soldiers with God on their side, and so on. If we identify values that are central to religion – sacrifice, faith, courage, mother's love, and so on – and include films that champion such values, the list can expand indefinitely. The Code's overt goal was to make *every* film religious in this latter sense.

We cannot understand the blend of interests in this story about religion in Hollywood – especially if we bring the story down to cases of specific audiences responding to particular films – if we approach with the simple idea that religion is marginal to popular culture or that popular religion declined due to commodification. Rather, we need to explore the diverse ways in which films – and by extension other forms of popular culture – interact with religious actors and how decisions about producing popular culture relate to struggles for hegemony.

Battles for the Soul of Protestantism

We have discussed how Catholic and Jewish immigrants debated how to adapt to the dominant culture. Sometimes they resisted assimilation, sometimes they grudgingly accepted it, and sometimes they created new religious forms. In a curious way, Protestants who were by no means outside the cultural mainstream – who, indeed, *constituted* the mainstream – faced analogous choices as the century opened. Without moving to a foreign country, they perceived a cultural context that felt foreign moving toward them. When they traveled to the city from close-knit rural communities, they might experience a culture shock as strong as an immigrant's. Many Protestants feared for the future of cities full of labor conflict and cultural diversity; they worried about prostitution, political corruption, and immoral entertainment as well as challenges to their hegemony. Some saw the emerging society as a modern-day Babylon and tried to remain aloof from it; others embraced emerging trends and tried to Christianize them.

In addition to the changing sociopolitical landscape, Protestants entered a new conceptual landscape – one increasingly shaped by science, Enlightenment values, and historical thinking. Although we have already touched on their responses to such challenges – for example, as background assumptions of social gospelers and evangelical anti-feminists – it will be useful to unpack these positions more fully. In general, liberal Protestants judged that trends such as science and historical criticism were intellectual advances, or at least changes that they could not ignore; they developed a way of thinking about religion that made peace with these trends. This provoked bitter opposition from conservatives who were coming to call themselves fundamentalists.

Who spoke for Christianity? What sources could Christians use for authority, whether their goal was explaining a Biblical approach to women's rights or the truth status of Trinitarian doctrine in an age of science? Broadly speaking, liberals approached such issues much like the Deists, Unitarians, and Reform Jews that we have already discussed. They tested inherited teachings against Enlightenment reason and historical scholarship, and they focused their religious energies on ideas that were supported by, or at least consistent with, the best modern intellectual work. Before the late 1800s, relatively few Protestants had been deeply concerned about harmonizing Enlightenment themes with orthodox traditions. True, there were exceptions to this rule. One was a tendency to correlate mission with the progress of reason and democracy. Another was the way that polemics unfolded between abolitionists and people who quoted the Bible to support slavery. Abolitionists moved some distance toward liberal theology when they pointed to core Biblical themes such as equality before God and used these overarching themes to trump individual texts such as 'Slaves, obey your masters.' Nevertheless, compared with later years there was limited stress on such reasoning. By late in the century this was changing; liberal theological trends reached deep into mainstream seminary training, popular Protestant magazines, and worship in downtown churches.

The challenge to inherited teaching was formidable. Earlier Protestants had accepted orthodox doctrines and assumed that they could defend them through direct appeals to the Bible. Although they had not always claimed that every Biblical passage was literally true, they did assume that readers could discover the Bible's common-sense meanings and use them as building blocks for a true understanding of the world, in harmony with truths discovered by scientific observation. Now science seemed to contradict orthodox teachings – most famously in the clash between Darwinian theory and traditional readings of Genesis. Moreover, a method called higher criticism analyzed the Bible as a set of historical and literary texts; this made direct appeals to the Bible difficult by presenting it as a book written by humans – one that had changed over time and was self-contradictory even in its canonical version, to say nothing of its many textual variations. Intellectuals increasingly believed that scientific reason made 'dogmatic' and 'magical' ideas inappropriate for a modern age.

In response to such challenges, liberal Protestants steered a middle course between fundamentalists who refused to accept modern arguments, on the one hand, and secularists who abandoned religious belief on the other hand. Making their home within modernity, liberals rethought theology within its horizon. They presupposed historical methods and scientific assumptions, and they recast theological themes like sin and salvation in terms consistent with them. For example, rather than questioning discoveries of historians on Biblical grounds, they used historical methods to learn as much as they could about the Bible. They looked for the deep truths of faith, as distinguished from the changing forms that people had used to express such truths over the years. In the process of such sifting, they often rejected orthodox dogmas as outmoded at best, if not distortions of deeper truths. Liberals felt that some pre-scientific language, such as stories of miracles, expressed truth in ways useful to pre-modern people – but that modern people must express their faith in modern ways, somewhat like world travelers might translate the same story into different languages from place to place.[20]

Modernists used such reasoning to defend several characteristic themes. Like Deists they based their claims on rational thought about human experience, as opposed to leaps of faith and special revelations.

More than Deists, they stressed God's immanent presence in nature and history, as opposed to God's transcendence. They stressed Jesus' life as role model and teacher more than his status as God and savior. They focused their spirituality on living a moral life; thus they continued to move (like both Deists and revivalists before them) away from Calvinist teachings about human depravity. One of their trademarks was to link these themes to the idea of progress: God was immanent in the progress of history, Jesus taught a moral life of progress toward the kingdom of God, and so on.

Shailer Matthews, a professor at the University of Chicago Divinity School, wrote a set of 'affirmations' – not creeds (which he rejected) but model claims for modernists. They began, 'I believe in God, immanent in the forces and processes of nature.' Others included 'I believe in the Bible, when interpreted historically, as the product and trustworthy record of the progressive revelation of God' and 'I believe in the practicability of the teaching of Jesus in social life.' Matthews charged fundamentalists with 'giv[ing] up intelligence … and forc[ing] men to choose between the universally accepted results of modern culture and diagrams from the book of Daniel.' If every Biblical text that recorded any belief of early Christians were taken as 'the teaching of the Bible' – and by extension as timeless truth – then moderns would be forced to believe 'in a flat earth, the perpetuation of slavery, [and] submission to rulers like Nero.' Another liberal scholar added that 'We shall not come nearer to the truth about God if we cut loose our idea of God from the highest human moral standards.' Defending his focus on Jesus as a human role model, he attacked scholars who 'exalt the absolute supremacy of Jesus Christ and at the same time suggest that his teachings are relatively unimportant.'[21]

Traditionalists were appalled by such innovations. J. Gresham Machen, a professor at the Presbyterians' flagship seminary, argued in his book, *Christianity and Liberalism*, that modernists taught a new and different religion, not a form of Christianity at all. Fundamentalism became the name for people who, starting from such perceptions, engaged in militant struggles against modernism. They included many Pentecostals and Holiness believers, but centered on the conservative wings of mainstream denominations like Presbyterians and Baptists. Not all evangelicals became fundamentalist militants, but enough did so to define the movement's dominant character early in the century. Fundamentalists rallied behind doctrines that they refused to compromise, notably beliefs about Jesus' virgin birth, literal resurrection, and ability to perform miracles. They insisted on an interpretation of salvation called substitutionary atonement, which held that a human debt of sin was paid through a blood sacrifice by Christ, and that no one could be saved without a personal relationship with Christ based on this sacrifice. Most fundamentalists felt that the Bible foretold a decline of history before Christ's return, including an apostasy of liberal church leaders that they were currently witnessing.[22]

Above all, fundamentalists stressed Biblical inerrancy. Given Protestantism's stress on Biblical authority, historical criticism raised a specter of relativism. Fundamentalists refused to consider even the most basic methods of higher criticism, such as comparing different versions of a text or studying how passages written later revise earlier ones. They felt that such methods would start them down a slippery slope that ended in destroying the Bible's authority; people could simply pick and choose which parts to believe. To avoid this slide, fundamentalists read the Bible literally and claimed that it contained no errors. True, they made *de facto* concessions that qualified their commitment to inerrancy. Confronted with undeniable evidence that the Bible has variant versions, they retreated to a claim that its 'original autographs' (before translation mistakes) had no errors. Forced to grant that some passages are absurd unless taken as metaphors (as when Jesus told his disciples, 'you are salt for the earth') they maintained that readers could discover the plain meaning of texts and take those meanings as literally true. However, fundamentalists tried to dwell on such subtleties as little as possible. Often they took as settled truth the King James Version of the Bible (an English translation from the 1600s) as interpreted through their impression of its plain meaning. Their best defense was a good offense – confronting liberals with favorite texts, asking them to affirm the literal truth of these texts, and complaining about answers they found evasive. A top revivalist of the early twentieth century, Billy Sunday, ridiculed 'deodorized and disinfected sermons' of preachers who tried 'to make religion out of social service with Jesus Christ left out.'[23]

Fundamentalists smoothed out some of the Bible's internal tensions through a theory called dispensationalism. Whereas modernists were not troubled by the Bible's running disagreements about issues such as slavery or Jewish–Gentile relations – they saw these debates enriching the Bible's meaning – such disagreements appeared as outright contradictions if one approached the Bible as a set of timeless propositions that must all be literally true. Dispensationalists evaded this problem by teaching that history from the Garden of Eden to the Battle of Armageddon was divided into stages (dispensations) in which different rules applied. For example, there are Bible passages that both require and forbid temple sacrifice; one can hold that they all apply literally, but some apply before Jesus' lifetime and others afterward. Treading on thinner ice, one might teach that at some stage of history, owning slaves changed from a divine blessing to a sin. Since pro- and anti-slavery texts both appear throughout the Bible (and since US Christians were willing to go to war over slavery) this second example suggests why dispensationalists did not fully succeed in ironing out conflicts among Biblical texts. They mainly moved interpretive conflicts to new places – to overt disagreements about which dispensational systems were correct, and (more commonly) to a habit of quoting favorite verses while ignoring verses inconsistent with them. Thus, for example, Pentecostals and Baptists debated whether speaking in tongues was solely for the dispensation of the early Church or for all true believers. Christians debated how to reconcile passages like 'Blessed are the peacemakers' with endorsements of holy war and speculated ceaselessly about signs of the end-times. Each fundamentalist group presented its dispensational theory as the timeless truth of an inerrant Bible.

In a campaign that peaked in the 1920s, fundamentalists tried to purge modernist leaders from top denominations – for example, Shailer Matthews was president of both the Federal Council of Churches and the northern Baptists in the 1910s. By the late 1920s fundamentalists had lost this fight, written off their former comrades as apostates, and retreated to their own institutions. Although they had many sympathizers in mainline denominations, the leading fundamentalists formed breakaway denominations. They called themselves 'come-outers' – an allusion to Revelation 18: 2–4, which details the lurid sins of Babylon which have marked it for destruction and concludes 'Come out of her, my people, that ye be not partakers in her sins and receive not of her plagues.'

Although liberals largely ignored fundamentalism from this point until the 1970s – they expected it to die with its older generation – in fact, fundamentalists thrived in local and regional institutions. One example is William Bell Riley, leader of fundamentalism's top national organization of the 1920s. Riley began as the head of a Minneapolis church that sponsored ministries associated with the social gospel, although he stressed its more conservative manifestations like Prohibition and charity as opposed to labor activism (by the 1930s Riley was a vocal anti-Semite who supported extreme right-wing politics). Beginning from a Bible study program in his church, Riley built a Bible school – later a liberal arts college – which anchored a regional network of congregations. He provided church members (and anyone else who would tune in) with radio stations that broadcast throughout the upper Midwest. Riley ruled his network like an empire through his charisma, ability to make or break the careers of seminary students, and control of the resources his school provided. Churches in his empire depended on educational curricula produced at his school and labor provided by his students. By 1936 Riley controlled the Minnesota Baptist Convention. In a typical Baptist pattern, this led to conflict with the national denomination and multiple schisms – but his college, his radio network, and most of the churches associated with them remained standing in the end. Riley's story is not unique. Dozens of Bible colleges sprang up around the country – Moody Bible Institute in Chicago and Bob Jones University in South Carolina are the best known – along with publishing houses, mission societies, touring faith healers, radio ministries, and many more. They became a seedbed for the return of fundamentalists to the public eye after the 1960s.[24]

We will dangerously oversimplify our maps if we lump all Protestants into two clusters on a single continuum from modernism to fundamentalism. Consider some of the differences among people who co-existed near the liberal end of this scale. Modernists who were Lutheran, Baptist, and Presbyterian had major liturgical and doctrinal differences. John D. Rockefeller, Jr. and Reinhold Niebuhr moved in some of the same ecumenical circles. Men and women, blacks and whites, pacifists and soldiers, Northerners and Southerners all joined mainstream churches and heard sermons informed by liberal premises.

People near the conservative end of the continuum were equally diverse. Liturgies ranged from formal and solemn among Presbyterians and Missouri Synod Lutherans, to improvisational and nearly cacophonous among Pentecostals. Machen was an erudite scholar, whereas some Holiness preachers quoted the Bible from memory because they were illiterate. Holiness churches were in the vanguard of ordaining women, yet fundamentalism as a whole was anti-feminist. Some fundamentalists voted and some boycotted elections – and if they did vote they were more likely than establishment Protestants to support Democrats. Billy Sunday had few rivals in drumming up support for World War I – 'If you turn hell upside down,' he stated, 'you will find "Made in Germany" stamped on the bottom.'[25] Yet other conservatives – including Jehovah's Witnesses, Adventists, and many Pentecostals – took Biblical injunctions to separate from the world seriously enough to be pacifists. In a landmark case in 1943 on freedom of religious dissent, the Supreme Court ruled in favor of Jehovah's Witnesses who refused to pledge allegiance to the flag. If we are charting stances toward war, we need a map that can place Billy Sunday near his liberal nemesis Reinhold Niebuhr, while placing Adventists (usually mapped as conservatives) near both Quakers (usually considered liberals) and Mennonites (who fit uneasily on either side of a liberal-conservative spectrum).

One of the deepest divides within the conservative sub-culture fell between Pentecostals on one side, and more doctrinally-oriented Calvinist fundamentalists, including conservative Presbyterians and most Baptists, on the other. Pentecostals enraged the latter group (let's call them Baptist-types for short) by suggesting that only tongue-speakers were true Christians; they also embarrassed respectable Baptist-types with their emotional style, impoverished constituents, and inter-racial character. One leading fundamentalist denounced Pentecostals as 'the last vomit of Satan.'[26] Skeptics felt that tongue-speaking was a shallow and self-deluded emotional technique unanchored by sound doctrine, rather than a genuine experience of being filled by God's spirit. Whereas Pentecostals saw themselves following the Holy Spirit wherever it led, skeptics simply saw them as undisciplined and unprincipled.

The most famous battle in the fundamentalist–modernist war, the Scopes Monkey Trial, dramatizes the internal complexity of Protestant religious conflict.[27] This 1925 trial took place in a small Tennessee town, but it became a national media event – complete with trained monkeys, songs with monkey themes, editorial cartoons about monkeys who did not want to evolve into humans, and related diversions – when it was broadcast live on national radio and hyped by elite intellectuals such as H. L. Mencken. The trial concerned a teacher named John Scopes who broke Tennessee law by teaching Darwinian theory to a high school biology class. That is, he argued that different species did not come into existence through creation by God six thousand years ago (as Biblical literalists held), nor through God guiding an evolutionary process over millions of years (as some evangelicals held). Rather life developed through natural selection; species that successfully adapted to challenges passed their genes to upcoming generations, and this could explain how they had filled every ecological niche without any appeal to God. In sharp contrast to Bible stories about God creating humans in God's image, Scopes used a textbook with a diagram of evolution that did not even have a separate category for humans. They were simply lumped in a tiny circle labeled 'mammals,' amid larger circles for such groups as mollusks and insects.

Although Christians had been disturbed by Darwin's theory since he published *Origin of Species* in 1859, this became a hot button issue only after 1900, as liberal theologians stressed evolutionary themes and scientists stressed atheistic interpretations of evolution. Tennessee outlawed the teaching of evolution, and Scopes broke this law as part of a strategy to overturn it in the courts. When the renowned liberal lawyer Clarence Darrow agreed to argue the pro-evolution side, William Jennings Bryan signed up to defend the fundamentalists. Bryan had been a three-time Democratic presidential candidate and a major Populist leader; he had also been Secretary of State from 1913 to 1915, until he resigned in opposition to World War I. Given such star power, Scopes' fate became a side issue (he was convicted and fined a few dollars, preparing the way for a legal appeal) compared with the radio debate between Darrow and Bryan. It seemed at first that their epic battle would be a bust because the judge did not allow pro-evolution witnesses to testify. However, Bryan allowed Darrow to cross-examine him as an expert witness on the Bible, and Darrow made him look foolish by exposing far-fetched ideas and contradictions in his position. Bryan expected to have the last word in his closing arguments, but a legal maneuver by Darrow denied him this chance, and then Bryan died five days later. This seemed to give evolutionists the last word; in popular mythology the Scopes Trial came to symbolize the last gasp of a sub-culture that irrationally resists modernity.

In fact, this mythology masks several complexities. First, as already noted, fundamentalists thrived instead of dying. Secondly, although the trial was a public relations disaster for fundamentalists, they largely won their war to keep evolution out of schools until the early 1960s. They did so by pressuring textbook publishers not to include much about it. As we will see, they also won a long-term war for public opinion. Thirdly, the battle line pitting the Bible against science was only one among several conflicts in play at the trial. Fundamentalism was not solely about intellectual issues; it was also about upholding traditional gender roles and defending Protestant hegemony in the face of pluralism. Evolution was a hot button issue for fundamentalists because it symbolized the amorality of modern cities and breakdown of the family. The Scopes Trial was also about urban–rural conflict and the legacy of the Civil War. Legal wrangling at the trial often returned to the charge that pro-evolution lawyers were northern liberal interlopers in Tennessee. How would Darrow feel, one of the anti-evolution lawyers asked, if Tennesseans came north and tried to overturn the laws of New York?

Importantly, Social Darwinists like Andrew Carnegie and Theodore Roosevelt – supported by intellectuals like Mencken – used the idea of the survival of the fittest to argue that capitalism and imperialism were inevitable. If southern farmers and old-time Populists had been asked to rank their concerns about social Darwinism, Biblical authority, and scientific theory, their anxiety about science would have been well back in third place. The crucial point, however, is that for Bryan all three issues formed one fabric. Evolutionary theory eroded democracy; it strengthened militarism and Social Darwinism. Bryan worried as much about this as about the Bible – or, more precisely, when he worried about Biblical authority he was largely worrying about maintaining a foundation from which to fight Social Darwinism. He also saw himself upholding the rights of local communities to set their own educational goals and defending the dignity of rural folk against elites who called them 'hicks' and 'hillbillies' – or, as Mencken did on the occasion of Bryan's death, compared them with 'gaping primates from the upland valleys of the Cumberland' and 'cocks crowing on a dunghill.'[28] For Bryan such considerations overshadowed debates about scientific explanation. In this sense the Scopes Trial was not primarily about science at all, and the trial's popular image that has come down through the years is a fascinating example of how history is written by the victors.

Notes

1 Cited in David Bennett, 'Nativist movement,' in *Oxford Companion to United States History*, Paul Boyer, ed. (New York: Oxford University Press, 2001), 543.

2 General works on issues of this section (supplementing books already cited on labor and immigration) include David Bennett, *The Party of Fear: from Nativist Movements to the New Religious Right* (Chapel Hill: University of North Carolina Press, 1988); Robert Bellah and Frederick Greenspahn, eds, *Uncivil Religion: Interreligious Hostility in America* (New York: Crossroad, 1987); John Higham, *Send These to Me: Immigrants in Urban America* (revised edn) (Baltimore: Johns Hopkins University Press, 1984).

3 This book is discussed in Chapter 6.

4 Brinkley, *Voices of Protest*; Leo Ribuffo, *The Old Christian Right: the Protestant Far*

Right from the Great Depression to the Cold War (Philadelphia: Temple University Press, 1983).

5 A key statement is Moore, *Religious Outsiders and the Making of Americans*.

6 Colleen McDannell, *Material Christianity: Religion and Popular Culture in America* (New Haven: Yale University Press, 1996), Robert Orsi, *Between Heaven and Earth: the Religious Worlds People Make and the Scholars Who Study Them* (Princeton: Princeton University Press, 2004).

7 Robert Orsi, *The Madonna of 115th Street: Faith and Commitment in Italian Harlem, 1880–1950* (2nd edn) (New Haven: Yale University Press, 2002).

8 Entry points to this literature include Noel Ignatiev, *How the Irish Became White* (New York: Routledge, 1995); Mike Hill, ed., *Whiteness: A Critical Reader* (New York: New York University Press, 1997); Peter Kolchin, 'Whiteness studies: the new history of race in America,' *Journal of American History* vol. 89, no. 1 (2002), 154–73.

9 Orsi, *Madonna of 115th Street*, 203.

10 For an orientation see Jim Cullen, *The Art of Democracy: a Concise History of Popular Culture in the United States* (New York: Monthly Review Press, 1996). On how religion relates to this history see Bruce Forbes and Jeffrey Mahan, eds, *Religion and Popular Culture in America* (2nd edn) (Berkeley: University of California Press, 2005), Diane Winston and John Giggie, eds, *Faith in the Market: Religion and the Rise of Urban Commercial Culture* (New Brunswick: Rutgers University Press, 2002); Stewart Hoover and Knut Lundby, eds, *Rethinking Media, Religion, and Culture* (Thousand Oaks: Sage, 1997).

11 A classic analysis is R. Laurence Moore, *Selling God: American Religion in the Marketplace of Culture* (New York: Oxford University Press, 1994); see also Jane Tompkins, *Sensational Designs: the Cultural Work of American Fiction, 1790–1860* (New York: Oxford University Press, 1985).

12 See David Chidester, 'The church of baseball, the fetish of Coca-Cola, and the potlatch of rock and roll,' in Forbes and Mahan, *Religion and Popular Culture in America*, 219–37.

13 Studies taking up aspects of this phenomenon include Michael Harris, *The Rise of Gospel Blues: the Music of Thomas Andrew Dorsey in the Urban Church* (New York: Oxford University Press, 1994), Anthony Pinn, ed., *Noise and Spirit: the Religious and Spiritual Sensibilities of Rap Music* (New York: New York University Press, 2003), and Cecelia Tichi, ed., *Readin' Country Music: Steel Guitars, Opry Stars, and Honky Tonk Bars* (Durham: Duke University Press, 1995). On contemporary Christian music see Jay Howard and John Streck, *Apostles of Rock: the Splintered World of Contemporary Christian Music* (Lexington: University Press of Kentucky, 1999).

14 Bruce Barton, *The Man Nobody Knows* (New York: Charter Books, 1962). Widely cited books that reflect the approach I have in mind include Moore, *Selling God* and Neil Postman *Amusing Ourselves to Death: Public Discourse in the Age of Show Business* (New York, Penguin, 1985).

15 On the Code see Gregory Black, *Hollywood Censored: Morality Codes, Catholics, and the Movies* (New York: Cambridge University Press, 1994) and Frank Walsh, *Sin and Censorship: The Catholic Church and the Motion Picture Industry* (New Haven: Yale University Press, 1996). To place it in context see Steven Ross, ed., *Movies and American Society* (Oxford: Blackwell, 2002), Lary May, *The Big Tomorrow: Hollywood and the Politics of the American Way* (Chicago: University of Chicago Press,

2000), and Mark Hulsether, 'Sorting out the relationships among Christian values, U.S. popular religion, and Hollywood films,' *Religious Studies Review* vol. 25, no. 1 (January 1999), 3–11. Some of the following paragraphs are adapted from this article.

16 P.C. Kemeny, 'Banned in Boston: commercial culture and the politics of moral reform in Boston during the 1920s,' in Winston and Giggie, *Faith in the Market*, 133–52. To relate censorship to the everyday lives of working people, see Roy Rosenzweig, *Eight Hours for What We Will: Workers and Leisure in an Industrial City, 1870–1920* (New York: Cambridge University Press, 1983).

17 Lee Grieveson, *Policing Cinema: Movies and Censorship in Early-Twentieth-Century America* (Berkeley: University of California Press, 2004).

18 Stephen Vaughn, 'Morality and entertainment: the origins of the Motion Picture Production Code,' *Journal of American History* no. 77 (1990), 62–3.

19 Walsh, *Sin and Censorship*, 232–6.

20 William Hutchison, *The Modernist Impulse in American Protestantism* (Cambridge, MA: Harvard University Press, 1976).

21 Shailer Matthews, 'The Faith of Modernism,' in *Documentary History of the Religion in America*, Edwin Gaustad, ed. (Grand Rapdis: Eerdmans, 1983), 398; Matthews cited in Gaustad and Schmidt, *Religious History of America*, 308–9. John Bennett, 'A changed liberal – but still a liberal,' *Christian Century*, 2/8/39, 179.

22 Nancy Ammerman, 'North American Protestant fundamentalism,' in *Fundamentalisms Observed*, Martin Marty and R. Scott Appleby, eds, (Chicago: University of Chicago Press, 1991), 1–66; George Marsden, *Fundamentalism and American Culture* (New York: Oxford University Press, 1980), and Marsden, *Understanding Fundamentalism and Evangelicalism* (Grand Rapids: Eerdmans, 1991).

23 Cited in Marsdsen, *Understanding Fundamentalism and Evangelicalism*, 31.

24 William Vance Trollinger, *God's Empire: William Bell Riley and Midwestern Fundamentalism* (Madison: University of Wisconsin Press, 1991); C. Allyn Russell, *Voices of American Fundamentalism* (Philadelphia: Westminster Press, 1976).

25 Cited in Marsden, *Religion and American Culture*, 179.

26 Ruben Archer Torrey, President of Moody Bible Institute (later dean of the Bible Institute of Los Angeles) quoted in Clyde Wilcox, *Onward Christian Soldiers? The Religious Right in American Politics* (2nd edn) (Boulder: Westview Press, 2000), 29.

27 Jeffrey Moran, ed., *The Scopes Trial: a Brief History with Documents* (New York: Palgrave Macmillan, 2002); Edward Larson, *Summer for the Gods: the Scopes Trial and America's Continuing Debate Over Science and Religion* (New York: Basic Books, 1997).

28 H. L. Mencken, 'In Memoriam: W.J.B.' in Laderman and León, *Religion and American Cultures*, 816; see also Michael Kazin, *William Jennings Bryan: a Godly Hero* (New York: Knopf, 2006).

CHAPTER 5

Shifts in the Religious Landscape from World War II to the Present

It should be clear that American religion has never lacked diversity. From the beginning Native Americans practiced hundreds of religions. In the colonial era African-Americans practiced Islam, Christianity, and traditional African religion. Colonies like Pennsylvania and New York welcomed British Quakers, Swedish Lutherans, Dutch Reformed, Sephardic Jews, Scottish Presbyterians, and German Amish. Alternative religions (Mormons, Spiritualists, Shakers, and dozens of others) flourished. Workers from throughout the world (Ireland, Italy, Russia, Greece, Syria, Chile, Japan, China) brought their faiths (Christianity, Judaism, Islam, Rastafarianism, Buddhism, Taoism) to the Americas.

In some ways this diversity narrowed by the mid-twentieth century. More people spoke English, interacted with shared aspects of US culture, and embraced the hegemonic pattern in which religions 'normally' had to persuade people to join them on a voluntary and privatized basis. (This is not to say that all healthy communities dissolved or that political aspects of religion disappeared, but only that the state – and by extension other public actors such as the media – aspired to be neutral with respect to religious difference, and that this implied some pressure to redefine religion as individualized and disengaged from the public sphere.) Catholics and Jews moved to the suburbs and organized their congregations in ways that looked less like their grandparents' parishes and synagogues and more like Protestant churches. Native Americans – even those who accented resurgent cultural pride – increasingly became urban and pan-tribal, often using English as a *lingua franca*. The fastest-growing branches of religion bought heavily into the logic of consumerism, which led to a huge supply of religious brands to choose from, but also to some homogenization of differences among them. In short, religious difference carried decreasing weight within the fabric of everyday life compared with practices shared by many citizens such as watching television, eating at chain restaurants, following professional sports, or surfing the internet. Deeper forms of religious difference – distinctive rituals, ethnic enclaves with sharp group boundaries, and strong oppositional identities – lost momentum compared with religions that found a comfortable niche in the dominant culture.

Despite such trends, the point to accent is a continuing – and in important ways increasing – diversity of religious life, especially after the 1960s. New players emerged to counterbalance processes of homogenization; the growth of Asian and Latino/a religions was especially notable. Even more important was the increasing recognition of diversity that had long been important – especially differences based on race, ethnicity, and gender. There was also growing conflict within mainstream Christianity that eroded its hegemony. The mere existence of such conflict was not new – earlier divisions such as Protestant–Catholic strife, schisms over slavery, and the fundamentalist–modernist conflict were at least as deep – but emergent conflict polarized local communities internally along lines of gender, race, and a liberal–conservative culture war. At mid-century Christians could still think of themselves as a united front capable of teaching common moral-religious values to the society – however much this exaggerated their influence and discounted minorities. By the century's end they were more likely to take sides in a culture war. Those who nursed hopes for a society based on common Christian values assumed that they were fighting an uphill battle against secularism and moral anarchy; those who embraced pluralism assumed that the best-known Christian leaders opposed them.

A Changing Map of Dazzling Religious Diversity

The most important force driving the increased visibility and acceptance of pluralism after World War II was the mobilization of African-Americans – as well as other racial minorities with similar struggles – for civil rights and an equal share of power. Starting in the 1940s and peaking in the 1960s, blacks mobilized for equal rights both in the South, where a largely rural population had suffered disenfranchisement and petty apartheid since the end of Reconstruction, and in northern cities where blacks increasingly migrated during the first part of the century. The civil rights movement brought politicized preachers such as Martin Luther King, Jr. and Jesse Jackson into the national limelight. In addition, more radical black religious leaders were active during the civil rights era, building on the separatist and culturally nationalist legacy of Marcus Garvey, who during the 1910s and 1920s had built the largest mass movement in African-American history. As the freedom movement radicalized, especially in northern cities after the early 1960s, such voices become well known and sometimes dominant in the movement. Malcolm X, the slain leader of the Nation of Islam (NOI) became an icon of black resistance. Among the many accomplishments of black activism was a growing visibility and respect for a range of African-American religious movements. Despite backlash in some quarters, a broad spectrum of citizens came to appreciate distinctive aspects of black religion such as gospel music and the chanted sermon, which in earlier years had often been ignored or considered exotic and backward. Black Christians gained the most from this change, but Muslims and Afro-Caribbean religions also benefited.[1]

Native Americans and Latino/as who had long been oppressed along racial lines mobilized at the same time, partly following the model of the black freedom movement and partly forging their own paths. There was a resurgence of Native American culture from a low point around 1900. By the 1930s, with the arrival of a so-called Indian New Deal that laid the foundations for tribal governments as they exist today, some of the overt legal suppression of native religion began to lift, although mission schools continued their efforts at assimilation. By the 1970s the American Indian Movement (AIM), put treaty rights and the police harassment of native people in the headlines through flamboyant actions like a protracted gun battle with the FBI at the site of the Wounded Knee massacre. Practices such as sweat lodge ceremonies, Sun Dances, and prayer meetings of the Native American Church (in which devotees use a hallucinogenic cactus called peyote to seek visions) – all of which had existed throughout the century in semi-underground forms – came to be practiced more openly on a larger scale. It became popular for white seekers to try, with varying degrees of sensitivity, to tap into the benefits of such spiritual practices. Indian and pseudo-Indian artists, healers, and writers made money responding to this demand, sparking debate within native communities about whether their activities were defensible.[2]

In 1978 Congress passed the American Indian Religious Freedom Act (AIRFA), in a belated effort to extend First Amendment rights to Native Americans. This law lacked teeth to protect religious practices in cases where native priorities conflicted with those of the mainstream; for example, in the 1990 *Employment Division* v. *Smith* case, the Supreme Court ruled that members of the Native American Church could be fired for failing a drug test that had nothing to do with working under the influence of drugs; they simply had ingested peyote at prayer meetings on their own time. Critics compared this with firing Catholics for using communion wine during the years when Prohibition was in effect. Nevertheless, AIRFA did reflect a growing sense that traditional native practices were a respected form of religion. Through AIRFA and related initiatives, Indians won significant battles for control of sacred sites and forced the repatriation of many skeletons and artifacts that anthropologists and art collectors had stolen from native cemeteries. By 2004 there was a National Museum of the American Indian in Washington, DC – with a profile comparable with that of the Holocaust Museum and major war memorials – under native control. Most importantly, many native communities were rebounding. Despite ongoing problems of unemployment, alcoholism, and loss of traditional languages, nevertheless a range of communal religious practices (both traditional and Christian) thrived and a new generation of artists and activists made important contributions to the larger US culture.

Mexican-American civil rights organizations and a Chicano Power movement organized in ways roughly parallel to movements for black civil rights and black power. As in the African-American case, politicized religious leaders played significant roles. Cesar Chavez, the head of the United Farm Workers, stressed the religious dimensions of his movement and worked closely with sectors of the Catholic Church. The Virgin of Guadalupe, the most revered saint in Mexican popular Catholicism largely because of her associations with pre-Christian tradition, became a symbolic focus of Mexican-American identity. Within US Catholicism, Latino/a parishes and clergy pushed for greater power and recognition, with considerable success.[3]

Deep differences existed beneath the umbrella of Latino/a identity. Latino/as were divided by national origin and lived in many parts of the country; Puerto Ricans in the Northeast, Cubans in Florida, and Mexicans and Central Americans in the Southwest were especially important. Latino/as varied in their degree of blending with African-American and Native American culture, as well as their level of assimilation and appetite for oppositional politics. Due to large-scale immigration, both legal and illegal, their population increased rapidly. Early in the twenty-first century they account for nearly fifteen per cent of the population, and scholars expect this percentage to rise well over twenty per cent by 2050.[4] In light of their rising influence, it has become impossible to relegate Latino/a religion – for example, Cuban Catholic parishes, a rapidly growing Latino/a Pentecostal community, or the popularity of Mexican cultural practices such as honoring ancestors on *el Día de los Muertos* (the Day of the Dead) – to the margins of US religion.[5]

In addition to the rising power and recognition of such groups that had long been key players on the landscape (however underappreciated), new players also emerged in the second half of the century. The most visible were immigrant practitioners of Islam, Buddhism, Hinduism, and Afro-Caribbean religion who came to the US from places like India, Pakistan, Vietnam, China, Kenya, and Haiti after US immigration law was liberalized in 1965. Fully ten per cent of the population was foreign born by the year 2000; if we count their native-born children the number rises higher. Unlike earlier waves of immigrants who were overwhelmingly European, now Asians outnumbered Europeans two to one and the majority of newcomers were from Latin America. In many cases sizeable communities grew from almost nothing in one generation. For example, before 1965 only 15,000 people from South Asia (mainly Sikhs) had entered the US, but by the year 2000 the community grew to 1.7 million.[6]

Because we have no standard way of counting adherents to US religions, it is hard to assess the numerical trends caused by this immigration. For example, we might be tempted to count most of the 1.7 million South Asians as Hindu, since eighty per cent of Indians are Hindu at least in a broad cultural sense. However, some of these immigrants are Muslim, Christian, or Sikh. Many are highly secularized, and it is not clear how – if at all – we should distinguish between religious and cultural Hindus, given that Hindus traditionally are not members of temples in ways comparable to Christian church membership, and given the overlap between Hindu ideas and Western psychologies associated with the New Age. Approaching the same problem from another direction, at what point – if at all – should we count a suburban Jew who attends yoga classes as part of Hinduism? Even to frame a question this way – as a problem to quantify in order to place such a person in the proper slice of demographic pie – seems to miss the point, distracting from the cultural blending that makes the case interesting. Turning to another example, we could spin the data to suggest that there are twice as many US Muslims as Presbyterians if we compare the official membership rolls of Presbyterian churches to the highest published estimates by Muslim spokespeople – estimates that might, for example, count most Iranian immigrants as Muslim. However, if we compare the larger group of people who tell pollsters they consider themselves Presbyterian to the lower estimates of Muslims discovered by scholars who count people connected with mosques, we could claim more than three times more Presbyterians than Muslims.[7]

By drawing selectively on such flexible numbers, many commentators – some of whom celebrate diversity and others who are alarmed by it – overestimate the impact of non-Christian immigration. It is clear that immigration does not yet account for a slice of demographic pie large enough to make a significant dent in Christian numerical dominance, even if we lump all non-Christians into one group. According to one estimate, the total number of Jews, Muslims, Hindus, Buddhists, and Sikhs accounts for less than five per cent of the population – not much higher than the percentage of Jews alone a century ago.[8] This low estimate makes sense despite massive immigration because two-thirds of new immigrants are Christian – including majorities of Latin Americans and Koreans, sizeable minorities of Chinese and Vietnamese, and significant numbers even from places like the Middle East. The key religious trend related to recent immigration is 'not the de-Christianization of American society but the de-Europeanization of American Christianity' – above all, through the impact of Latino/as on Catholicism and Pentecostalism.[9]

Nevertheless, both the surging raw numbers and the rapid percentage growth of non-Christians are highly significant. For example, the numbers of Muslims and Jews are now about the same and the numbers of Buddhists are comparable with Presbyterians. Moreover, many immigrants are prosperous professionals who are easily visible to the general public, and some immigrant religions are strikingly different from Christianity. Consider how the rise of heterodox Mormons and non-English-speaking Catholics was a greater shock to nineteenth century society than the mere creation of another Protestant denomination; similarly the growth of Asian religion attracts much attention today.

One development which we will discuss more fully below, but which deserves mention in this inventory of key trends, is the growth of African-Caribbean religions like Santería and Vodou. We could equally well treat them under the rubric of new immigration or as a revival of tradition among some of our longest-established key players. Moreover, these religions blend with Catholicism and involve both African-Americans and Latino/as; we must remember them when treating all of these groups. However we map the trend, it represents traditional

African practices – suppressed under US slavery, or at least circum-scribed and forced underground – returning to the US from places where these traditions were better able to survive.

Islam has been the most successful of the new immigrant groups as measured by numbers, ability to gain converts, and overall cultural weight. Fully a third of US Muslims are converts, drawn largely from among African-Americans. A small number are descendants of immigrants who arrived between 1880 and 1920 from places like Syria and Lebanon; such a community in Iowa built the oldest US mosque in 1934. Another sizeable group includes people who live in the US on temporary work visas or as students; US universities are centers for inter-national dialogue about the future of Islam because they attract Muslims from around the world. The largest group consists of people who have arrived since 1965 and their children and grandchildren. This latter bloc is diverse since US Islam is in many ways a microcosm of world Islam. Immigrants came not only from the historical cradle of Islam in the Arab world, but also from Iran, Pakistan, India, Indonesia (the world's most populous Muslim country), Africa, and the Philippines – with the largest contingents from the Middle East and especially South Asia. We must not underestimate the differences among these cultures, which run as deep as the differences among Christians from England, Korea, Mexico, Egypt, Russia, and Nigeria. Yet in some US cities all of these groups coexist in the same mosques.[10]

Beyond its geographical differences, Islam has longstanding insti-tutional and doctrinal divides somewhat comparable to those among Protestant, Catholic, and Orthodox Christians. One is between the Sunni majority and the Shi'a tradition centered on present-day Iran. Another is a tension between the elite, male-dominated, and relatively centralized traditions of Islamic scholars, on one side, versus local practices that have developed in various places, perhaps in dialogue with Hindu influences in Pakistan or African traditions in Nigeria, but in any case with more scope for the innovations of ordinary people, including women. A tendency in many places is Sufism, the tradition within Islam that stresses mysticism, contemplation, and direct experience of the divine. In many parts of the world, Muslims stress learning from Sufi teachers and worshipping at shrines of local saints. Other places (importantly including Saudi Arabia) stress purifying perceived abuses introduced by such practices.

As a universal faith stressing the equality of all people before an all-powerful and compassionate God – a religion founded by the Prophet

Muhammad in the seventh century and built on a base shared with Judaism and Christianity – Islam is in a good position to unite such a diverse group in a community called the *ummah*. All Muslims accept the authority of a book of revelations to Muhammad called the Qur'an; since they teach that the Qur'an cannot be fully translated from its original Arabic, this language is used in worship and is a *lingua franca* for educated Muslims, who often devote much effort to studying Arabic and reciting Qur'anic texts. All Muslims agree on practicing five pillars of their faith: (1) professing that there is only one God (known in Arabic as Allah) and that Muhammad is his prophet; (2) praying five times daily; (3) fasting as a spiritual discipline during the month of Ramadan; (4) contributing generously to support the needs of the community, especially needy people within it, and (5) making a pilgrimage to the center of world Islam in Mecca at least once in their lifetime. Muslims are proud of their history and tradition; during much of the time between the founding of Islam and the modern era, the Islamic empire (not Christendom) was the center of Western civilization. There are complex traditions of interpreting Islamic law, or Shariah, that developed out of the Qur'an and later traditions.

Within this common ground, there are significant tensions in US Islam. One divide is between immigrants with long traditions of Islamic practice, and converts who have a shorter history practicing Islam but a longer history in the Americas. Even when immigrants and converts enter the same mosques as believers in the same doctrines, they bring diverse cultural baggage (food, music, family structure, knowledge of US history) and ideas about adapting Islam to US society. Who is the expert on adapting Islam to the US – someone whose ancestors have a millennium of experience practicing Islam or three centuries of experience dealing with white Protestants? Compounding such tensions is the fact that some converts earlier belonged to groups considered heretical by orthodox Muslims, including the Moorish Science Temple founded by Noble Drew Ali and the Nation of Islam (NOI) long led by the Honorable Elijah Muhammad and made famous by Malcolm X before he converted to orthodox Islam.[11]

At least as important as immigrant–convert tensions are generational differences. These constitute something like an Islamic version of debates about liberalization and assimilation that earlier raged between Reform and Orthodox Jews or traditionalist and Americanist Catholics – but with a higher profile for issues of race, such that one can imagine

Muslims entering the US mainstream as smoothly as Reform Jews did in earlier years or on a rockier path suggested by resistance to the empowerment of blacks and Latino/as. Although new generational voices are emerging, it is hard to predict the pace and outcome of change. It is clear, however, that Islamic centers are growing throughout the country – one study found more than a thousand of them – that Muslim Student Associations are strong on many college campuses, and that many forms of Muslim thought and practice are thriving.[12] These range from a secularized 'cultural' Islam that we might compare with Reform Judaism, through a more conservative and pious practice that we might compare with Orthodox Judaism, through scattered sympathizers with radical Islamists (in some ways comparable with ultra-Orthodox Zionists), to white converts who focus on aspects of Sufism (comparable with New Age fascination with Jewish mysticism, or Kabbalah).

Buddhism and Hinduism have also become key players, largely due to post-1965 immigration, although both have longer histories in the US. Ideas from these traditions have sparked the interest of US intellectuals since the nineteenth century, dating back to the Theosophical Society and Transcendentalists like Ralph Waldo Emerson. Before 1965 there was sizeable Buddhist immigration from China and Japan as well as considerable mainstream interest in Zen Buddhism. However, both Hinduism and Buddhism grew rapidly after 1965 through immigration and conversion, and both traditions are now deeply divided between new immigrants and native-born converts.[13]

In contrast to Muslims, who share common roots and core sensibilities with Christians and Jews, Buddhists and Hindus have traditionally approached the basic categories and purposes of religion quite differently. Although we cannot do justice to this subject – embedding a micro-survey of world religion inside this book is out of the question – we should note that Buddhism and Hinduism both originated in India with a similar background assumption that the human condition was a series of births, deaths, and rebirths known as samsara.[14] One's station in any given lifetime was determined by karma, or the principle that one's actions have later consequences. Religion was partly about performing the duties and rituals appropriate to one's station in life – thus creating positive karma for the future – but ultimately it aimed toward release from the sufferings and disappointments caused by being bound to the wheel of samsara. Just as contemporary Christians and Jews debate how to interpret their traditional teachings in light of modern science, Hindus and Buddhists do the same with these ideas.

Neither Hindus nor Buddhists assume – as Jews, Christians, and Muslims do – the existence of a single personal God conceived as the creator and judge of the universe, on a different plane of existence from sinful mortals and communicating with them through prophets. Hindus are polytheistic; they teach that there are 330 million gods – or in other words that the universe has an infinite number of divine manifestations – and they practice devotion (*bhakti*) toward particular deities such as Shiva, Vishnu, and forms of the Goddess. For Hindus the distinction between gods and humans – especially between gods and human teachers known as gurus – is more a continuum than an unbridgeable gulf. Sometimes even this continuum dissolves. Hindu philosophers speak of a single impersonal Absolute (Brahman) encompassing all reality. They teach that with the proper insight and training, one can recognize that there is ultimately no difference between the Absolute and the depths of the individual human soul. In light of such teaching, it is equally possible to describe Hindus as monotheistic, monistic, or polytheistic.

Buddhism complicates this picture even further. Although this religion began as an offshoot of Hinduism, with similar understandings of karma and samsara, its classic forms deny the existence of God. Many Buddhist converts are strongly anti-supernaturalist; one of their leaders has called for a 'Buddhism without beliefs' that promotes an 'existential, therapeutic, and liberating agnosticism.'[15] Yet major parts of the Buddhist tradition focus on celestial Buddhas who are loosely comparable with Hindu gods. Buddhists also have subtle teachings somewhat akin to Hindu ideas about the divine being manifest in all existence; some branches stress that all beings share in a perfect Buddha-nature. Meditation and other rituals (whether these presuppose atheism or ask for help from celestial Buddhas) stress perceiving this underlying perfection and the connections among all beings. Many Buddhists feel they can harmonize such insights with Christian mysticism and postmodern science.

Even this oversimplified presentation hints at the great diversity represented by Asian religions, but we are still only scratching the surface. Let us consider Hindus further. It can be misleading even to speak of a unified entity called Hinduism, since this family of traditions has as much internal diversity as Judaism, Christianity, and Islam combined (imagine lumping all three together as 'Middle-Easternism'). Hindus recognize three paths to release from samsara – doing one's duty in the world, performing devotion to particular gods, and gaining wisdom through contemplative disciplines called yoga. Although popular images of Hinduism stress the path of yoga, most Hindus pay more attention to the other two paths. How should they adapt the duties and customs of Indian culture – its famed caste system that still informs much of Hindu culture despite changes due to urbanization and secular law – to conditions in the Americas, especially as their children enter the mainstream? How should they transplant their devotional practices? Challenges include building temples and home altars, recruiting priests (and deciding how much priests should adjust their roles to become like Christian ministers), celebrating holidays, and teaching children about gods like Krishna. Since many Hindus are affluent professionals, they have been able to build impressive temples throughout the US; sometimes these temples blend devotion to multiple gods in the same building, which would not happen in India. A key practice in Hindu temples is seeing and being seen by statues in which gods are understood to be embodied; Hindus undertake elaborate rituals to prepare such statues and the temples that house them. Sometimes they parade statues through the streets in festivals that are interesting to compare with the Italian-American celebrations discussed above.[16]

Devotional Hinduism has sparked the interest of a few white converts – notably members of the International Society for Krishna Consciousness, or Hare Krishnas, who became famous in the 1960s for chanting hymns to Krishna, soliciting donations in airports, and forming counter-cultural communes. Other small groups led by Indian gurus and populated by middle-class youth also gained attention. However, the main attractions of Hinduism for US whites have been the selective use of yoga in aerobics classes, watered-down versions of its meditation techniques, and its philosophical ideas. Influential authors from Emerson through novelist Aldous Huxley to New Age guru Deepak Chopra have popularized selected Hindu philosophies. For the small subset of their readers who have desired to explore Hindu ideas in a communal context, the leading organization has been the Vedanta Society, which centers on a network of meeting rooms for study and meditation.

The founder of the Vedanta Society, the missionary and reformer Swami Vivekananda, became famous largely through speeches at the World's Parliament of Religions. This 1893 gathering, part of a world's fair in Chicago, brought Asian religious leaders to the US for the first time. The Parliament had decisive limitations as a global dialogue. Most Muslims and many Christians boycotted the meeting, no one thought to invite Native Americans, African-Americans and women of all races were under-represented, and in general the participants represented the most educated and Westernized parts of their traditions. Many of the Parliament's organizers expected that liberal Christianity – something in the ballpark of Unitarianism – would emerge as a framework within which the deep truths of all the gathered traditions could be harmonized and purified. Despite these limitations the meeting became a landmark in the history of US pluralism because of the unprecedented range of voices that the organizers did invite.

Vivekananda shared the organizers' goal of harmonizing religions but added a twist. For him it was not that the wisdom of Asia should be purified and taken up into a higher truth framed by Unitarians. Rather all religions (including parts of Christianity that needed purification) should be taken up into the universal truths of the Hindu philosophy called Vedanta. This teaching assumed that the divine was manifest in millions of forms as discussed above, but stressed the existence of an impersonal monistic Absolute that encompassed all these forms. For Vivekananda, all religions are 'a coming up of different men and women ... to the same goal. Every religion is only evolving a God out of the material man ... In the heart of everything the same truth reigns ... the Lord has declared to the Hindu in his incarnation as Krishna, I am in every religion as the thread through a string of pearls.'[17]

To a large extent, the diverse manifestations of US Hinduism – Vivekananda's cerebral world of religious dialogue, yoga exercises at the gym, counter-cultural communes led by gurus, and devotions to specific gods and goddesses at temples and home altars – exist in separate worlds. However, the point to accent is that devotional practices at the center of South Asian Hinduism have grown rapidly through post-1965 immigration. So far there has been limited cross-pollination between convert and immigrant Hindus, although white converts sometimes visit temples and immigrants sometimes find their way to Hare Krishna meetings or Vedanta Centers. Such exchanges are likely to increase as the children of immigrants decide what forms their tradition will take in the US.

Buddhism entered the mainstream faster than either Islam or Hinduism, measured by its ability to gain sympathetic media coverage and attract famous converts such as novelist Jack Kerouac, basketball coach Phil Jackson, rock singer Tina Turner, and movie star Richard Gere. Zen Buddhism has sparked wide interest, and the leader of Tibetan Buddhism, the Dalai Lama, is a celebrity rivaling the Pope in the popular respect he commands. There is a long-established Japanese-American Buddhist community, and since 1965 immigration from China, Korea, and Southeast Asia has increased rapidly. Thus, on many levels US Buddhism is well rooted and growing. As in the case of Hinduism, there is a gap between immigrant Buddhists – based in ethnic communities, often concerned with venerating ancestors, standoffish toward women's rights, and relatively uninterested in meditation or the counterculture – and native-born converts who practice Zen meditation or Tibetan visualization during weekend retreats and approach religion with a counter-cultural sensibility, often insisting on equal participation by women at all levels of the community. In general, it is hard to generalize about US Buddhism because it mirrors and intensifies the decentered nature of Buddhism worldwide.[18]

We will return to the question of who speaks for Buddhism in Chapter 7. For now let us simply note that Buddhist converts have built a strong network of meditation centers, rural retreats, activist groups, publishing houses, and other institutions informed by many forms of world Buddhism. Meanwhile, immigrant Buddhists are establishing temples throughout the country, from the opulent Hsai Lai Temple built by Taiwanese in Los Angeles to small home-based centers built by refugees from Southeast Asia. By the 1990s Cambodian Buddhists alone had built forty-one temples; there were 300 Buddhist temples in Los Angeles and 1,500 nationwide.[19] Along with issues that face other immigrants – adapting customs, learning English, celebrating holidays that are out of sync with Christianity, and so on – a key question for Buddhists is how to adapt their traditional emphasis on male monasticism to a society that largely assumes women's equality and lacks the infrastructure that undergirds Asian monasticism – both historic endowed institutions and everyday customs through which monks and laity support each other.

Collapse and Restructuring in the Old Protestant Establishment

Amid the diversity of US religion, white Protestants remained by far the largest bloc. They accounted for half the population by themselves, and they helped to establish patterns that influenced other Christians: black and Latino/a Protestants, Catholics, Orthodox Christians, Asian immigrant churches, and so on. They also remained deeply divided. This section explores trends in the Protestant mainstream; later we will return to distinctive developments among Catholics and expand on the

Protestant story. Let us begin by considering how a liberal–conservative culture war emerged after the 1960s. Culture war analysis is not a one-size-fits-all map; it does not always fit the experience of non-whites and it can divert attention from class and gender since rich and poor people, as well as women and men, fall on both sides of its battle lines. Nevertheless, as a framework for exploring the white mainstream, it is a good place to start.

Culture war polarization took place against a dual baseline of suburbanization and a perception of post-war consensus. After 1945 Protestants joined the exodus of Jews and white Catholics from inner city neighborhoods – as well as from rural areas that dwindled as a percentage of the population – to the suburbs. These suburbs were created largely by tax breaks for homeowners and government decisions to subsidize expressways for automobile commuters. They were overwhelmingly white, fueled by a dynamic of white flight from inner cities that resulted in the US making virtually no progress in *de facto* residential integration between 1950 and the present.[20] In the 1950s there was a huge wave of spending on suburban churches. Not unlike in the Jewish case discussed above, building congregations became a key way that Christians organized their communities in new suburban neighborhoods. Religious membership surged to the highest levels in US history, in the fifty to sixty per cent range. Week-to-week socializing, volunteer work, and charitable giving were channeled through congregations. Although churches and synagogues competed for people's energies with schools, lodges, social service agencies, and other civic organizations, there was often co-operation among these groups and overlap in their leaders. The community functions of congregations were especially important for women, who often did not hold paying jobs during these years. Although the overall curve of women's paid labor was upward throughout the century, and although the industrial mobilization for World War II was a step forward in women's quest for equal access to good jobs, in the 1950s middle-class women were pressured to stay at home and locked out of most professions.

Intellectuals of the 1950s perceived the US entering an era of liberal consensus, as opposed to conflict between labor and capital or cultural strife between liberals and conservatives. Their idea was not that everyone had become liberal in the sense of supporting the New Deal or voting for Democrats, but rather that a social contract had been hammered out in the 1930s and 1940s – enforced by the purges and blacklists of the 1950s that set limits to dissent – such that there was little disagreement about the legitimacy of electoral democracy and a regulated capitalist economy.[21] Scholars who promoted this vision spoke about a moral responsibility to defend democracy through fighting the Cold War and promoting a US-led global market; they believed that socialism threatened greater evils because it was naively optimistic and did not provide checks against the abuse of power. On the home front, liberals upheld what they called a vital center against people to their left and right. They portrayed unrepentant social gospelers as dupes of left-wing extremists, labeled fundamentalists as backward-looking proto-fascists, and imagined both groups to have been neutralized and replaced by an emerging consensus. The commanding US position in the global economy offered unprecedented material prosperity, making it possible to buy off much dissent and imagine that an affluent middle-class society was the wave of the future. Some people even dared to hope that zero-sum conflicts over distributing wealth could be finessed indefinitely through technocratic management and endless economic growth.

Culture war analyses highlight two changes from this baseline; both unfolded amid a wider breakdown of consensus as the perception of stable centrism gave way to conflict over race, gender, the Vietnam War, and the future of the New Deal. First, in the suburbs differences among Protestants, Catholics, and Jews carried less weight for determining the make-up of workplaces and neighborhoods, patterns of friendship and marriage, and forms of identity. As inherited cultural distinctions weakened, tensions loomed larger between people from all three groups – Protestants, Catholics, and Jews – who responded to emerging social conflicts as conservatives versus liberals. Each denomination had its own distinctive character and center of gravity, but in general this polarization pitted liberal members of large denominations against conservatives from the same denominations. Thus, although we can still draw denominational pie charts with lines that represent important nuances of theology and ritual, increasingly the lines that mattered – especially for charting divides among white Christians – were between people who clustered at the poles of a spectrum that cut across denominations.[22] Conservatives (whether Baptist, Catholic, or Lutheran) taught what they called traditional family values and complained about vacuous liberals (also Baptist, Catholic, and Lutheran) whom they perceived as failing to preach the gospel and accommodating to secular relativism. Many conservatives enjoyed reading apocalyptic novels that imagined the gruesome deaths of such liberal church-going neighbors whom God punishes for their foolish choices. Meanwhile, secularists and liberal churchgoers embraced multiculturalism and sexual equality; they complained about conservative neighbors whom they saw as shockingly anti-intellectual, and marveled that such people could stand to be associated with televangelists and Republican politicians.

Secondly, this realignment occurred at the same time that centrist religious leaders – people who took their influence for granted at mid-century, such as Methodist bishops who oversaw suburban church-building campaigns and ecumenical activists who championed the New Deal – declined in power due to falling memberships and the loss of allies in elite circles. There was a drop-off in loyalty among the children and grandchildren of people who founded the mainline churches of the 1950s. Between 1965 and 1985, evangelicals continued to grow steadily – indeed spectacularly in the case of the fastest growing groups such as Pentecostals – while the mainline lost members at a striking rate: twenty-eight per cent for Presbyterians, seventeen per cent for Methodists, and so on. The ratio of liberal versus conservative congregations shifted between the early 1970s and late 1990s from fifty-seven per cent versus forty-three per cent in favor of liberals to forty-seven per cent versus fifty-three per cent in favor of evangelicals.[23]

The drop in liberal demographic strength is better understood as a long-term slide that reached a critical stage in the 1970s than as an overnight collapse. Mainline Protestants had long been a minority; their mid-century sense of being an establishment that could speak for the whole society was ripe for unmasking, since this discounted blacks, Catholics, and evangelicals among others. Moreover, their trend of losing market share to evangelicals and immigrants had been underway since 1800, with the 1950s church-building boom as a partial exception to this rule. The percentage difference between the growth rates of evangelicals and liberals was smaller in the 1970s, when journalists began to trumpet the gap, than it had been earlier in the century.[24] Nevertheless, the cumulative impact of long-term trends was important, and two associated changes made the trends stand out starkly during the 1970s. One was the vocal alienation of mainline youth, linked to interest in the counter-culture and a sense that churches were boring and complacent. The other was the contrast between the travails of liberals and the rising power of evangelicals. At mid-century, mainline clergy had dared to hope that they were rebounding from their cultural disestablishment of the 1920s and assuming a role as senior partners in an ecumenical establishment alongside liberal Catholics and Jews. By the 1980s this vision seemed out of touch with reality. Denominational budgets dwindled, liberal seminaries struggled to survive, and ecumenical bureaucracies were drastically downsized. Whereas earlier politicians had courted liberal Protestants, the newly ascendant Republicans discounted them as irrelevant while Democrats fretted about how to attract evangelicals.

In this context, mainline leaders who traditionally aspired to speak for a society-wide consensus saw movements to their left and right seize the initiative in the realm of public religion. On the left flank of Christianity an impulse akin to the social gospel revived in both Protestant and Catholic forms, starting in the 1950s with civil rights activism and continuing in the 1960s and 1970s with liberation theologies. This was spearheaded by leading clergy and often sparked conflict between centrists and radicals in church networks. Its momentum was part of a wider constellation of forces that challenged the 1950s status quo: the black freedom movement; the student left; feminism; green politics; and so on. We will return to this development in Chapter 6. It is important to underline the religious dimensions of left-liberal movements since mid-century, since scholars often stress these movements' secular aspects more than their religious ones. Some culture war maps leave an impression that a left-to-right spectrum is really, at root, a secular-to-religious spectrum. If we frame the issue this way, the term 'religion' is effectively captured by the right; its *de facto* understanding narrows to hegemonic conservative religion. Although this view gains plausibility if we interpret the demographic trends as showing liberal Christianity in a process of terminal decline – so that, in effect, it is a mere transitional stage on a slippery slope from authentic Christianity through religious privatization to institutional death – we will see that this is a dubious reading of liberal fortunes.

At the rightward end of a culture war spectrum, evangelicals – whom we last met building come-outer institutions such as William Bell Riley's network of churches and radio stations – re-emerged between the 1950s and 1970s from years of neglect by scholars and journalists. Old-time fundamentalists like Riley held fast to militant separatism and Biblical literalism. More influential was an emerging group known as neo-evangelicals led by Billy Graham, *Christianity Today* magazine, and schools like Wheaton College and Fuller Seminary. Neo-evangelicals continued to stress born-again conversion, but they embraced theories of

Biblical authority that did not insist on the literal truth of every word, and their stance toward the cultural mainstream was more open.[25] (Unfortunately there is no standard terminology for discussing these groups. We are using 'evangelical' as an umbrella term for born-again believers who are strict fundamentalists, neo-evangelicals, or Pentecostals. However, neo-evangelicals often claim the term 'evangelical' solely for themselves, and pundits often use 'fundamentalist' as their umbrella term.)

Although evangelicals played a significant cultural-political role throughout the century, after the 1960s their political mobilization became more self-conscious and emphatic. Leaders of the New Christian Right (NCR), such as Baptist minister Jerry Falwell and televangelist Pat Robertson came to stress redeeming this world alongside otherworldly and individual concerns; they built a powerful network of organizations focused on a wide range of issues, which we will explore in more detail below. The NCR played a major role in Ronald Reagan's election and by the turn of the new century it constituted the base of George W. Bush's electoral support. In light of evangelicals' growth and elite alliances, it became increasingly difficult for pundits to interpret them as marginal or apolitical.

Although culture war polarization is important both on its own terms and as an analytical framework that focuses attention on certain issues over others, we must not exaggerate its prevalence. Many people from outside white Christianity do not see this war's hot button issues as priorities compared with economic justice, racism, and various religious differences that are not easily reduced to a culture war calculus. Inside white Christianity, the middle range of the culture war continuum is not an empty space, vacant because everyone has moved to extreme positions; many people do not see themselves taking sides in a war. It is better to imagine the culture war spectrum as a bell curve with most people in the middle rather than as a battlefield where two armies shoot at each other across a free-fire zone.

Scholars are especially prone to underplay the power of moderate evangelicals and the ongoing strength of mainline Protestants. Many people underestimate how many evangelicals oppose the NCR. Although the evangelical center of gravity does tilt to the right, the sub-culture includes many political moderates and liberals. There is no clear-cut way to measure evangelicals. When pollsters simply ask people whether they consider themselves born-again, the numbers run as high as forty-seven per cent of the population, or three-quarters of all US Protestants.

However, if we count only members of conservative denominations like the Southern Baptists, we find numbers around twenty per cent, or a third of Protestants. A rough estimate of people who support a full range of NCR positions is also twenty per cent – enough to dominate the Republican Party, but a distinct minority of the overall population.[26] We could spin these numbers up or down by counting black and Latino/a evangelicals in a separate category, or not. In any case, a solid minority of evangelicals – perhaps a third or more depending on how we count – is liberal on most cultural-political issues. Many neo-evangelicals followed a trajectory of voting for Presidents Eisenhower, Nixon, Carter, and Clinton; they are quick to point out that both Carter and Clinton are evangelicals. Important evangelical leaders speak out about global warming and Third World poverty. After the 2004 election, in which the official popular vote was essentially a tie, culture war analysts stressed that the vote for George W. Bush was highly skewed toward evangelicals while the secular vote was skewed toward the Democrats. However, it is also true that the majority of Democratic voters were Christian and many of these were evangelicals. Although pundits stressed that abortion and gay marriage were concerns for 'values' voters, twice as many people considered war as their top moral concern compared with abortion and same-sex marriage combined. In the 2006 election, a third of white evangelicals voted Democratic.[27]

In other words, although few evangelicals are leftist by the standards of American Studies scholars, the alliance between Republicans and evangelicals is far from monolithic. In fact it is vulnerable on issues of the economy, the environment, and war. The political instincts of black evangelicals are largely liberal – with a partial exception for their stances toward sexuality and gender – and an influential minority of white evangelicals are strong critics of militarism and advocates of justice for working people. Their best-known leader, Jim Wallis of *Sojourners* magazine, likes to claim that he is neither liberal nor conservative – rather that he is equally opposed to secular liberals and religious conservatives – but on most issues his ideas dovetail with progressive Democrats.[28] Insofar as a culture war paradigm leads us to imagine evangelicals as monolithically conservative, this distorts the real situation in which evangelicals range across the far right, center-right, and center-left parts of a culture war spectrum.

Scholars and journalists also underestimate the ongoing strength of moderate to liberal Protestants in mainline denominations. As noted above, some scholars frame the core conflict as religious conservatism versus secular liberalism; in effect they have no category for religious liberals except as an anomaly. Others see liberal churches declining toward irrelevance; such scholars have so deeply internalized the story of a complacent establishment losing members and being unmasked for exaggerating its power, that they have swung the pendulum to the opposite extreme and overstress mainline weakness. In Chapter 6 we will discuss how NCR leaders imagine themselves to be more persecuted than they really are because they focus on the gap between their power today and the inflated power they hope to wield in the future. Liberals focus on a related gap – except it is between their current struggles and the exaggerated influence that they imagined wielding in the 1950s. Highlighting such a gap leads people to feel that the mainline has fallen further than it really has. Although such a perception may deflate morale and create self-fulfilling prophecies, it distorts the current situation.

Notwithstanding evangelical growth, mainline Protestants maintain enough historical momentum and ongoing strength that they still enjoy a rough parity of power with evangelicals, at least outside of Washington, DC. The center of gravity for them, as well as liberal Catholics and many moderate evangelicals, is a tolerant style that scholars call Golden Rule Christianity.[29] Such Christians interpret the Bible using historical methods and are fairly uninterested in doctrinal disputes. Rather than born-again conversion and conservative values they stress building communities that nurture compassionate and loving everyday lives. Golden Rule Christians are broadly pluralistic. Although they tend to be apolitical compared with the NCR and left-wing activists, they tilt toward peacemaking, compassion for the poor, and cultural inclusivity. Their leaders have largely supported moderate civil rights activism, second-wave feminism, and so on.[30] Alongside programs for youth they often sponsor community arts events and social services for needy people. Golden Rule Christianity is the leading form of suburban religion, especially if we count its Catholic and evangelical variants along with its mainline Protestant center of gravity. It is not merely a watered-down form of evangelicalism, but a distinctive practice that has solid future prospects and needs to be understood on its own terms.

Why have Golden Rule Protestants, as well as a smaller group of activist churches to their left, lost market share to evangelicals? Some scholars argue that liberal clergy have steered too far to the left, thus alienating core constituents, and have become vacuous and undemanding in the name of inclusivity, thus attracting half-committed 'free riders.' According to this line of thought, evangelical growth results from mainline laity voting with their feet and shifting to congregations that are more conservative politically, as well as stronger institutionally because they demand higher commitments.[31] However, at best this explanation is a half-truth; around eighty per cent of the difference between liberal and conservative growth is a result of lower liberal birthrates. (To understand this dynamic, imagine that half of all babies born to church-going parents join churches when they grow up. If so, each family needs four children to maintain a steady number of church members in the next generation; a couple with two children will only provide one member in the next generation for a fifty per cent decline.) Most of the remaining difference is due to evangelicals retaining a higher percentage of youth. This might be explained partly by the free rider dynamic, but it also raises the question of what motivates people to leave – and brings us to the interesting point that (counter-intuitively given the growth trends) the long-term historical pattern is for more evangelicals to switch toward mainline churches than vice versa.[32] This pattern is becoming less pronounced, most likely because evangelicals are defining themselves more loosely, thus retaining more people who earlier might have moved toward the mainline. For example, it is now easier for upwardly mobile Pentecostals to remain in the same denomination, rather than switching to more upscale Methodist churches as often happened in earlier years. Switchers often join evangelical megachurches with programs that cater to many lifestyle niches. These are among the country's fastest growing churches – and the ones that recruit free riders most aggressively.[33] In other words, some evangelical growth reflects 'voting with one's feet' not by shifting toward the right, but rather from conservative evangelicalism toward more moderate evangelicalism.

Meanwhile, most people who leave mainline churches do not join conservative churches. Enough do to create the half-truth effect mentioned above, but most drift toward the left or into a half-engaged religious limbo. In one study, only six per cent of Presbyterians confirmed in the 1960s converted to fundamentalism, while half drifted toward an apathetic or hostile stance, with the most liberal people being the most likely to leave.[34] The best political analogy is not switching from Democratic to Republican, but joining the ranks of Democrats who do not vote because they see no candidates for whom they care to vote. Mainline denominations are between a rock and a hard place because anything they do alienates either their right or left wing. If they move in any direction except to the right – even if they follow a middle-of-the-road Golden Rule path – conservatives will question their Christian credentials and they will alienate members who donate disproportionate amounts of money. However, if they continue backpedaling to avoid alienating the right, they will lose many of their brightest youth.

Thus, we might compare questions about the future of liberal Christianity to questions about the future of the Democratic Party. Can Democrats become a vehicle for addressing concerns of working people, women, and racial minorities? The issue is not whether any given Democratic politician will do so, but whether pockets within the party can work effectively with more radical movements. Similarly, can we imagine spaces in mainline denominations that capture the energies of left-liberal youth? This would require presupposing women's equality, engaging with creative parts of popular culture, and (for the activist-minded) providing opportunities to work for peace, economic justice, and equal rights for racial and sexual minorities. The question is not whether this is possible – it clearly is – nor whether any given congregation will do so, but whether such practices can thrive in mainline networks. If mainline leaders continue a least common denominator approach that tries not to alienate conservatives – the religious version of centrist Democrats wooing political moderates – this is likely to sustain Golden Rule churches in many places but it seems unlikely to change the demographic trends of low birthrates and high apathy among upcoming generations. Should disaffected liberals reconsider the virtues of Golden Rule churches? Should they leave their churches to atrophy, somewhat like political radicals write off Democrats? Should they build activist churches as a counterweight to the NCR? Such are the debates among left-liberal Christians at the beginning of the twenty-first century.

Trends among Other Key Players

None of the groups introduced above disappeared in the second half of the century. Nor did they remain static. The explosive growth of Mormons and Pentecostals is worth recalling in this connection. Although neither group was new, in this era each achieved an unambiguous status as a national and international player. Forthright secularists also emerged as an increasingly important player within the overall map. To a greater extent than any time since the 1700s, it became culturally acceptable to claim no significant religious interest. Although the number of people who claimed no religious preference remained low compared with other industrialized societies – somewhere in the ten to twenty per cent range depending on how questions are framed – by late in the century there was little stigma attached to such a stance, especially in the national media and large cities. Also, the numbers seemed to be creeping upward. Only three per cent of the population told pollsters that their 'religious preference' was 'none' in 1957, but fourteen per cent did by 2000. Weekly church attendance (which is notoriously hard to estimate because people often exaggerate it) probably dropped from the forty per cent to twenty per cent range.[35]

After World War II, Jews continued to blend into the suburban middle class, with sizeable new communities developing in Los Angeles and Miami. A growing concern among Jewish leaders was intermarriage with Gentiles. As late as the mid-1960s the intermarriage rate stood around ten per cent, but by 1990 it had risen above fifty per cent. We have seen that Reform Jews, and to a lesser degree also Conservatives, distinguished between Jewishness (the general culture) and Judaism (the focused religious commitment). True, this line becomes blurry when we consider how religion has historically defined Jewish identity; from this perspective we might compare how – for both Jews and Native Americans – it can be hard to distinguish religious heritage from a larger way of life. Nevertheless, such a distinction did become important in Judaism. The original purpose of this distinction for Reform Jews was to hold fast to essential Jewish religious practices amid an overall desire to assimilate. However, since it created a religious Judaism that one could abstract from a larger Jewish culture, in the long run this distinction also enabled the growth of 'secular Jews' – that is, people from Jewish families who participate in certain forms of Jewish community life, but with limited interest in such things as attending worship at synagogues, observing Sabbath rituals at home, studying Jewish scriptures, or following the dietary laws. This secular group may now be the largest one in the Jewish community, although this depends on where one sets a minimal threshold to qualify as a religious Jew.[36]

Orthodox Jews remained a minority compared with Reform and Conservative Jews, but continued to thrive into the twenty-first century. Some scholars believe that the fastest growing parts of the Jewish community are secular and Orthodox Jews, both gaining at the expense of centrist groups. There were two key sources of Orthodox strength. One was continuing immigration after World War II, largely from

Russia, that continued to feed ethnic enclaves. The other was the growth of a 'Modern Orthodox' group that lived relatively assimilated suburban lives but remained ritually observant. Ultra-Orthodox Hasidic Jews who have maintained close-knit ethnic enclaves over many generations comprise a small percentage of the Orthodox. What Amish and Old Order Mennonites represent for Christians – a pious separatist community with distinctive dress and strong resistance to many aspects of modernity – the Hasidim represent for Jews. Despite their small numbers they are the best-known Orthodox group because of novels like Chaim Potok's *The Chosen* and their tensions with African-American neighbors in Brooklyn which boiled over into a riot in the summer of 1991.[37]

Until the 1970s most US Jews were solidly left-liberal in politics; they voted for Democrats or groups further left and were pillars of support for left-liberal causes. This still tends to hold true. However, one post-war development was the growth of neo-conservative Jews. Key Jewish leaders such as the intellectuals associated with *Commentary* magazine, who had begun as anti-Stalinist socialists and/or New Dealers before World War II, took a sharp right turn by the 1970s. They put special emphasis on fighting the Cold War, defending Israel against its enemies, and asserting conservative moral values against what they considered the excessive individualism and divisiveness of the post-1960s left. Probably this shift was due partly to affluent Jews voting their pocketbooks. Undoubtedly two factors were tensions with people who criticized Israeli policies toward Palestinians (since neo-conservatives stressed a convergence between support for Israel, the Cold War, and the 'global war on terror') and the break-up of the historic black–Jewish alliance on issues of civil rights for minorities – an alliance that became strained in the late 1960s as blacks turned toward separatist strategies while Jews remained committed to integration and questioned affirmative action. By the 1980s neo-conservative Jews had become partners in many conservative coalitions with two groups that Jews historically opposed and still mistrusted: traditional business conservatives and the NCR. Although by no means all neo-conservatives were Jewish and it bears repeating that most Jews remained liberal, Jews did have disproportionate influence among neo-conservative leaders.[38]

We have seen how suburban Catholics became part of Golden Rule Christianity and how Catholics engaged in a culture war somewhat like the Protestant one. However, key aspects of Catholic experience were distinctive. They maintained emphases that we have already noted:

sacramental and communal sensibilities; ethnic traditions; stress on Catholic education; and defensiveness toward Protestant hegemony. At mid-century they were more working-class compared to Protestants or Jews – today they are similar to Protestants – and white Catholics were slower to move from close-knit urban neighborhoods toward the suburbs. Above all, they are distinctive because nearly half their members are Latino/as, and there are also Catholics from Vietnam and the Philippines. Thus, they continue to engage with concerns of impoverished recent immigrants whose first language is not English, as well as the institutional racism that confronts long-established Latino/a communities. Latino/a popular devotions remain very important.

Near the rightward pole of a culture war spectrum, Catholics tend to base their arguments more on natural law (ultimately ordained by God but accessible to all) and church authority, as opposed to Protestant appeals to revelation (from God to specific believers) and the Bible. Compared with Protestants, conservative Catholics put more stress on fighting abortion and less on celebrating free market capitalism. Their leaders are more highbrow, interested in dialogue with neo-conservative intellectuals rather than fundamentalists.[39] In general Catholic relations with Protestants in the NCR are tense given the historic tendency of fundamentalists to deny that Catholics are Christian. Meanwhile, in the leftward parts of the culture war, Catholics tend to be more interested in Latin America than Protestants, more conflicted about abortion, and more likely to approach social issues with a communitarian as opposed to individualist sensibility. (On this issue Jews emphasize civil liberties; Protestants swing both ways.) In center-left parts of the spectrum, a paradigmatic approach among Protestants is to transmute earlier missionary sensibilities into global famine relief; Catholics are more likely to emphasize 'seamless garment' approaches that oppose abortion, militarism, and the death penalty in similar terms.

Until the 1950s, US Catholic leaders carried forward the defensive posture that they inherited from the defeat of Americanist bishops. However, pressure for change was building both from laity and inside church leadership ranks. We might imagine the situation as a dammed-up stream, with water mounting behind the dam and people working from within to open a channel. On this analogy, the moment when the floodgates opened was the Second Vatican Council, or Vatican II. This was a 1962–5 meeting convened by Pope John XXIII that brought together church leaders from throughout the world. The Pope spoke about opening the windows to let in some fresh air on the question of how Catholics should relate to modernity. Vatican II brought major changes both in church policies and underlying conceptions of what it meant to be Catholic. Bishops came around to adopting the classic Americanist position on the permissibility – indeed desirability – of decoupling Catholics from the state and embracing religious freedom. They moved toward a greater sense of co-operation and dialogue with people of other religions – especially Protestants and Jews – as opposed to judging and trying to convert them. They encouraged Catholic schools to engage more deeply with modern secular thought. Most importantly, they moved to a more lay-centered, participatory, and democratic sense of how to be Catholic – as opposed to a clergy-centered, authoritarian, and top-down sense. The most vivid symbol was switching the language of the mass from Latin to local vernaculars – along with other changes in worship such as seating people in the round, encouraging lay participation, and playing folk music on guitars. Nuns tried out new roles and began to dress like the laity rather than wearing severe black outfits called habits. Teachers put less stress on rote memorization and more on discerning the signs of the times – thus making the church seem less monolithic and more open to diverse spiritual paths.

Since 1965 Catholic history has been a tug of war between people who moved eagerly through the floodgates opened at Vatican II – for example, those who expected a democratic church to ordain women and give married Catholics a voice in its policy toward contraception – and conservatives who immediately began to worry about the flood raging out of control. For example, Catholics had to endure much mediocre folk music and priests who were too quick to dismiss deeply rooted devotional practices; for traditionalists the remedy was not finding better music and more thoughtful priests, but returning to the Latin Mass while blasting liturgical reform as a slippery slope toward Protestantism. Others simply felt that excessive openness to modern individualism was eroding core Catholic identities and that clear lines of authority that had helped the Church survive for centuries were becoming blurred. John Paul II, who was Pope from 1977 to 2005, was a harsher critic of capitalism and militarism than most US Democrats – but partly due to his experience in Poland under Communist rule he was even more hostile to socialism. When Latin American bishops (especially from Brazil and Central America) rethought their traditional alliance with conservative elites and joined popular anti-imperialist movements – thus threatening not merely to align Catholics with socialists but even to promote class struggle inside the Church – the Pope moved to block them and systematically replaced radical bishops with conservatives. This power struggle spilled over into the US. Moreover, Pope John Paul had little sympathy for women's equality, especially inside the Church – on such issues he was more conservative than most US Republicans. The current Pope, Benedict XVI, headed the Vatican's office for enforcing orthodoxy during John Paul's papacy. So far he has largely followed in John Paul's footsteps, with an accent on its more conservative side.[40]

In 1968 the encyclical *Humanae Vitae* decreed on the basis of natural law that Catholics could not use contraceptives under any circumstances – sex was only permitted between married people who were open to conceiving a child (bishops have rejected the use of condoms even by couples in which one partner has HIV). Laity in the US were incredulous toward this rule and largely ignored it, but they had less room to maneuver when the Vatican took similar hard lines against ordaining women, making celibacy optional for priests, and rethinking the teaching that any abortion under any circumstance after conception constitutes murder – and thus should be criminalized as a matter of state policy even for people who deny that it is murder. True, just as Catholic women can buy contraceptives, they can still (as I write) obtain legal abortions if they judge this to be a lesser evil in light of their personal circumstances and the difference between a zygote and a late-term fetus. Likewise they can experiment with new roles for nuns and laywomen in their parishes. They can – and do – lobby to change church teachings about these matters. But bishops have been able to fire (or otherwise punish) Catholics who question their teachings about reproduction and to maintain a hard line on ordination policy.

Many young church leaders who poured through the floodgates of Vatican II and pursued liberal reforms – only to hear the hierarchy calling them back – kept on going rather than heeding the call to return. Some gravitated toward the Catholic left and exist today in various degrees of revolt against conservative bishops; others renounced their vows and left the Church. Today there is a severe shortage of priests, and many orders of nuns are unlikely to survive because women who formerly might have joined them are choosing secular careers, becoming Catholic lay professionals, or seeking ordination in other branches of Christianity.

The problem of recruiting priests recently went from bad to worse as people learned about pervasive sexual abuse by priests. According to a church-commissioned study, 4,000 priests – four per cent of the total – were accused of sexually molesting minors (largely teenaged boys) between 1950 and 2000. Equally damning were revelations of systematic cover-ups by leading bishops; the resulting lawsuits had cost the Church more than a billion dollars by 2005.[41] It will be difficult for the priesthood to recover from this blow to its reputation. Currently the top strategies are importing foreign priests (often conservative), shifting responsibilities to lay professionals (often liberal women), and trumpeting a policy of keeping gays out of seminaries (a risky strategy since a substantial proportion of priests in the past have been gay). Given its huge numbers, historical momentum, and global strength, Catholicism will no doubt remain a major player for a long time to come. However, it enters the new century with deep internal conflicts and a leadership crisis.

A religious tendency that grew from older roots to become a key player after mid-century was the New Age movement. In part, New Agers revitalized and extended nineteenth-century religions like Spiritualism and New Thought. In part they experimented with Asian and Native American spirituality as an alternative or supplement to Christian and Jewish religion that they found boring and/or oppressive. The search for alternative spiritualities was especially prevalent in the 1960s counter-culture, where it was often linked to experiments with psychedelic drugs. Subsequently it evolved in many directions, mainly among white and middle-class people.

It is hard to identify a center of gravity for the New Age. Some scholars stress how it updates specific metaphysical movements such as Theosophy and/or promotes 'harmonial' correspondence between various levels of reality. Others stress its dialogue between Asian philosophies of the self, on one side, and Western theories like Jungian psychology and quantum physics on the other. Debunkers paint it as the mere commercialization and trivialization of the 1960s counter-culture. There are various spins on whether common New Age practices – for example, channeling spirit guides from other dimensions of reality, seeking esoteric wisdom that was taught by Theosophists and other occult groups in earlier generations, assuming that the depths of the self encompass all reality, seeking spiritual healing, or trying to spark wider cultural change through expanding the consciousness of a few New Age elites – are defining aspects of the movement or merely optional themes within it. Searching for the movement's intellectual heart, one scholar defines it as the popular name for 'a constellation of ideas ...

related to paradigmatic cultural changes in the last third of the twentieth century.' These changes include 'the resacralization of the cosmos; the interconnectedness of all things; change or process, rather than statis, as the nature of reality; the emergence of a planetary culture; and the reintegration of such dualisms as spirit and matter, emotion and reason, and science and religion.'[42] A sense of breaking with the past and moving toward a new stage of history is reflected both in the term 'New Age' and the related term 'Age of Aquarius' that was popular in the 1960s. Since New Agers do not worry much about finding agreement among these overlapping approaches, it is best not to seek one rigid definition, but simply to associate the term 'New Age' with a reasonable number of the above themes coming together. In the long run we may need new terminology, since one of the most common traits of New Agers as we have defined them is to disavow the New Age label.

It is no easier to identify an outside boundary for the New Age than to find its center. We could point to many groups which are sometimes mapped outside it, with their own distinct identities, and sometimes treated as sub-groups under its umbrella. Among these groups the most important is Wicca, which seeks to revive pre-Christian nature religions of Europe. Many Wiccans practice individually while others form small groups called covens; some stress the complementarity of men and women while others form women-only covens focused on worshipping the Goddess. (Wiccans may also be called witches or neo-pagans, if we are clear that their witchcraft has nothing to do with stereotypes about casting evil spells or worshipping Satan and that Wicca is only one approach within a wider category of neo-paganism.) Other groups often considered New Agers include several organized around belief in UFOs, including the Raelians who promote the teachings of a four-foot tall extra-terrestrial named Yahweh and are actively trying to clone a human, the Heaven's Gate group which committed mass suicide in the expectation that they would rescued by a spaceship and then the earth would be recycled, and the Ashtar Command which expects Jesus to return alongside Commander Ashtar and Lady Athena leading a fleet of UFOs. Also near the boundaries of the New Age – but shading off toward the suburban mainstream instead of the radicalism of UFO religions – are people who seek spiritual depth through communing with nature, sometimes in dialogue with aspects of Native American religion. Each of these three groups – Wiccans, UFO believers, and do-it-yourself nature mystics – may take offense at being associated with the other two groups and/or consider suburban New Age spirituality to be shallow and over-commercialized.

Moreover, many people whose core religious practice is centered outside the New Age – perhaps in Buddhism, Vodou, or Christianity – share selected New Age behavior such as using holistic medicine, identifying gods and goddesses within, or entertaining the hypothesis that bodhisattvas, UFOs, angels, African spirits, and channeling are all complementary sources of wisdom. In fact, even though New Agers and evangelicals are often mapped as polar opposites, they have overlapping interests in spiritual healing, communication with supernatural beings, direct experience of the divine, and prophecies about the world as we know it coming to an end. Anyone who is open to the New Age claim that a global shift in consciousness is underway might well ask whether the parallel growth of the counter-culture and Pentecostalism are the left and right wings of such a shift. In general, if we adopt an inclusive definition of the New Age, the movement appears both as a key player in its own right and a diffuse trend that inflects the experience of other groups. One scholar estimates that twelve million people participate in New Age activities, spending $10 billion dollars a year on alternative healing, channeling, and self-help businesses associated with the movement.[43]

This is by no means an exhaustive list of significant players within post-war religion. We could offer more examples in any category mentioned above – movements led by Hindu gurus, emerging Christian movements, aspects of Latino/a religion, and so on. Indeed, we could extend our list indefinitely if we lowered our threshold for what counts as a key player. There are hundreds of alternative religions in the US today. For example, we could explore the Unification Church, with its claim that the Reverend Sun Myung Moon is the second coming of Christ, its rituals in which hundreds of devotees are married en masse to partners selected by Moon, and its extreme right-wing politics expressed partly through its control of a major US newspaper, the *Washington Times*. Studying Moon might draw our attention to an evangelical movement that kidnaps members of so-called 'cults' (Moon's and many others) and tries to 'deprogram' them from what the kidnappers consider brainwashing. Alternatively, we might explore the Rastafarian beliefs of Jamaican immigrants, the South Asian religion of Sikhs, the indigenous practices of Hmong refugees from Laos, the racist forms of Christianity associated with right-wing militias, or the interplay of Buddhist, Christian and indigenous religion in Hawaii.[44]

However, the whole idea of identifying key players requires us to stop before we are overwhelmed by diversity and lose our ability to keep patterns in perspective. Therefore, let us bring this chapter to a close by recalling the key players that we have met so far: the foundational set introduced in Chapter 1 (with its many varieties of red, white, and black); immigrants (Jewish, Catholic, Orthodox); emerging Protestant groups ('Of Christs,' 'Of Gods,' Mormons); and a growing set of others (nineteenth-century new religions, positive thinkers, Afro-Caribbean religions, Muslims, Hindus, Buddhists, secularists, and New Agers.) Then, let us agree that we could put an exclamation point on the dazzling diversity of US religion by gathering an additional set of religions with enough combined weight to count as another key player. It is safe to predict that at least one such group will gain media attention every year – perhaps because a stockpile of guns at an apocalyptic commune leads to a standoff with police, or a movie star hypes a psycho-religious therapy like Scientology, or a Satanist gang commits serial murder – even if we cannot predict which group will gain its fifteen minutes of fame.

Notes

1 Overviews include Manning Marable, *Race, Reform, and Rebellion: the Second Reconstruction in Black America, 1945–1982* (Jackson: University Press of Mississippi, 1984) and Lincoln and Mamiya, *Black Church in the African American Experience*. See also citations in Chapter 6.

2 James Olson and Raymond Wilson, *Native Americans in the Twentieth Century* (Urbana: University of Illinois, 1984). Vine Deloria, *Custer Died for Your Sins* (New York: Macmillan, 1969); M. Annette Jaimes, ed., *The State of Native America* (Boston: South End Press, 1992); Paul Chaat Smith and Robert Allen Warrior, *Like a Hurricane: the Indian Movement from Alcatraz to Wounded Knee* (New York: New Press, 1996).

3 Richard Etulain, *Cesar Chavez: a Biography with Documents* (New York: Palgrave Macmillan, 2002); Manuel Vasquez and Marie Marquardt, *Globalizing the Sacred: Religion Across the Americas* (New Brunswick: Rutgers University Press, 2003); David Badillo, *Latinos and the New Immigrant Church* (Baltimore: Johns Hopkins University Press, 2006).

4 Figures cited by Manuel Vasquez on National Public Radio, *Speaking of Faith*, 1/19/06.

5 Laderman and León, *Religion and American Cultures*, 177–204; Thomas Tweed, *Our Lady of the Exile: Diasporic Religion at a Cuban Catholic Shrine in Miami* (New York: Oxford University Press, 1997); symposium on Latino/a religion in *Journal of the American Academy of Religion* vol. 67, no. 3 (1999), 541–635. On how Latino/a history fits in wider historical narratives, see Maffly-Kipp, 'Eastward ho,' Ronald Takaki, *A Different Mirror: a History of Multicultural America* (Boston: Little, Brown, 1993); Ramón Gutiérrez, 'Community, patriarchy and individualism: the politics of Chicano history and the dream of equality,' in Maddox, *Locating American Studies*,

353–84; Janice Radway, 'What's in a name?' in *Futures of American Studies*, Robyn Wiegman and Donald Pease, eds, (Durham: Duke University Press, 2002), 45–75.

6 David Wills, *Christianity in the United States: a Historical Survey and Interpretation* (South Bend: Notre Dame University, 2005), 76–7; Gurinder Singh Mann et al., *Buddhists, Hindus, and Sikhs in America* (New York: Oxford University Press, 2000), 64–6; Philip Jenkins, 'New religious America,' *First Things* (August 2002), 25–8.

7 R. Stephen Warner, 'Coming to America,' *Christian Century*, 2/10/04, 22; Warner, 'Religion and new (post-1965) immigrants: some principles drawn from field research,' *American Studies* vol. 41 , no. 2/3 (2000), 267–86.

8 Jenkins, 'New religious America,' 25–8.

9 Warner, 'Coming to America,' 21.

10 Jane Smith, *Islam in America* (New York: Columbia University Press, 1999); Yvonne Yazbeck Haddad, 'Make room for the Muslims?' in *Religious Diversity and American Religious History: Studies in Traditions and Cultures*, Walter Conser and Sumner Twiss, eds (Athens: University of Georgia Press, 1997), 218–61.

11 Melani McAlister, 'One black Allah: the Middle East in the cultural politics of African American liberation, 1955–1970,' *American Quarterly* vol. 51, no. 3 (1999), 622–56; Moustafa Bayoumi, 'Moorish science: the secret history of African American Islam,' *Transition* vol. 8, no. 4 (2000), 100–19.

12 Gaustad and Schmidt, *Religious History of America*, 420. For more citations see Chapter 7.

13 Mann et al., *Buddhists, Hindus, and Sikhs in America*; Thomas Tweed, *The American Encounter with Buddhism 1844–1912* (Bloomington: Indiana University Press, 1992); Diana Eck, *A New Religious America* (San Francisco: HarperCollins, 2001).

14 Surveys that mesh well with this book are John Esposito, Darrell Fasching, and Todd Lewis, *World Religions Today* (New York: Oxford University Press, 2002) and Jacob Neusner, ed., *World Religions in America* (2nd edn) (Louisville: Westminster Press, 2000).

15 Stephen Batchelor cited in Richard Hughes Seager, *Buddhism in America* (New York: Columbia University Press, 2000), 234.

16 On these issues see Eck, *New Religious America*, 148–218.

17 Swami Vivekanada, 'Remarks at the World's Parliament of Religions,' in Laderman and León, *Religion and American Cultures*, 794–800. See also Diana Eck, *Encountering God: a Spiritual Journey from Bozeman to Benares* (Boston: Beacon Press, 1993), 22–44.

18 For an overview of US Buddhism see Seager, *Buddhism in America*. See also Mann et al., *Buddhists, Hindus, and Sikhs* and citations in Chapter 7.

19 Gaustad and Schmidt, *Religious History of America*, 415–16.

20 George Lipsitz, *The Possessive Investment in Whiteness: How White People Profit from Identity Politics* (Philadephia: Temple University Press, 1998)

21 Godfrey Hodgson, *America in Our Time* (New York: Vintage, 1976); Fraser and Gerstle, *Rise and Fall of the New Deal Order*.

22 Wuthnow, *Restructuring of American Religion*; see also James Davison Hunter, *Culture Wars: the Struggle to Define America* (New York: Basic Books, 1991).

23 Mark Chaves, *Congregations in America* (Cambridge: Harvard University Press, 2004), 33; Grant Wacker, 'Searching for Norman Rockwell,' *Piety and Politics*, Richard John Neuhaus and Michael Cromartie, eds (Lanham: Ethics and Public

Policy Center, 1987), 330–1; Kirk Hadaway and David Roozen, eds, *Church and Denominational Growth: What Does (and What Does Not) Cause Growth and Decline* (Nashville: Abingdon Press, 1993).

24 William Hutchison, 'Past imperfect: history and the prospect for liberalism,' in *Liberal Protestantism: Realities and Possibilities*, Robert Michaelsen and Wade Clark Roof, eds (New York: Pilgrim Press, 1986), 65–84.

25 See Joel Carpenter, *Revive Us Again: the Reawakening of American Fundamentalism* (New York: Oxford University Press, 1997) and books by George Marsden cited above.

26 On counting evangelicals see the website of the Institute for the Study of Evangelicals at Wheaton College, *http://www.wheaton.edu/isae/defining_evangelicalism. html*; on the NCR's core constituents *vis-à-vis* its target constituencies see Wilcox, *Onward Christian Soldiers*.

27 Mark Silk and John Green, 'The new religion gap,' *Religious Studies News*, March 2005), 8, 21; Alan Cooperman, 'Liberal Christians challenge "Values Vote",' *Washington Post*, 10/10/04, A07; Marcus Baram, 'Losing faith in the GOP,' *ABC News*, 11/7/06, accessed at *http://abcnews.go.com*.

28 Jason Bivins, *The Fracture of Good Order: Christian Anti-Liberalism and the Challenge to American Politics* (Chapel Hill: University of North Carolina Press, 2003).

29 Nancy Ammerman, 'Golden Rule Christianity: lived religion in the American mainstream,' in *Lived Religion in America: Toward a History of Practice*, David Hall, ed., (Princeton: Princeton University Press, 1997), 196–216. A more ambitious study supporting these conclusions is Ammerman, *Pillars of Faith*.

30 If we include mainline laity the picture is murkier, since they vote Republican more than their clergy do, due partly to a long-term historic alliance with Republicans and partly to voting their pocketbooks. However, the converse is also true – evangelical laypeople vote Democratic more than their leaders, also due partly to voting their pocketbooks. On both sides, it is hard to weigh religious versus non-religious motives. See James Reichley, 'Faith in politics,' in *Religion Returns to the Public Square: Faith and Policy in America*, Hugh Heclo and Wilfred McClay, eds (Baltimore: Johns Hopkins University Press, 2003), p. 184

31 Dean Kelley, *Why Conservative Churches are Growing* (New York: Harper and Row, 1972); see also Finke and Stark, *Churching of America*.

32 Chaves, *Congregations in America*, 33; Kirk Hadaway, 'Denominational defection: recent research on religious disaffiliation in America,' in *The Mainstream Protestant 'Decline'*, Milton Coalter, John Mulder, and Louis Weeks, eds (Louisville: Westminster Press, 1990), 102–22.

33 For more on megachurches see Chapter 7. They address the free rider issue in various ways. Typically they put little pressure on so-called seekers, although some demand tithes and/or small group participation. Most are evangelical but some are in mainline denominations and their politics range from conservative to centrist. They make a distinctive contribution to muddled statistics on US religion because they often advertise themselves as independent and non-denominational; pollsters may count them as evangelical, as Christian but neither Protestant nor Catholic, or in 'none of the above' categories that unwary scholars use as evidence of Protestant decline.

34 Dean Hoge, Benton Johnson, and Donald Luidens, *Vanishing Boundaries: the Religion of Mainline Protestant Baby Boomers* (Louisville: Westminster Press, 1994). See also Mark Massé, *Inspired to Serve: Today's Faith Activists* (Bloomington: Indiana

University Press, 2004).

35 Chaves, *Congregations in America*, 3.

36 Riv-Ellen Prell, *Prayer and Community: the Havurah in American Judaism* (Detroit: Wayne State University Press, 1989); Deborah Dash Moore, *To the Golden Cities: Pursuing the American Jewish Dream in Miami and L.A.* (New York: Free Press, 1994); Jonathan Sarna, 'American Jews in the new millennium,' in Haddad, *Religion and Immigration*, 117–27.

37 Chaim Potok, *The Chosen: a Novel* (New York: Simon and Schuster, 1967); Lis Harris, *Holy Days: the World of a Hasidic Family* (New York: Summit, 1985); Stephen Bloom, *Postville: a Clash of Cultures in Heartland America* (New York: Harcourt, 2000).

38 Gary Dorrien, *The Neoconservative Mind* (Philadelphia: Temple University Press, 1993).

39 An example is Richard John Neuhaus of *First Things* magazine. See also Mary Jo Weaver and Scott Appleby, *Being Right: Conservative Catholics in America* (Bloomington: Indiana University Press, 1995). On issues of this section see, in addition to books cited above, Peter Steinfels, *A People Adrift: the Crisis of the Roman Catholic Church in America* (New York: Simon and Schuster, 2003), Mary Jo Weaver, 'American Catholics in the twentieth century,' in Williams, *Perspectives on American Religion and Culture*, 154–68; and Weaver, ed., *What's Left: Liberal American Catholics* (Bloomington: Indiana University Press, 1999).

40 Peter Boyer, 'A hard faith: how the new Pope and his predecessor redefined Vatican II,' *New Yorker* 5/16/05, 54–65.

41 Rachel Zoll, '4392 priests accused on sex abuse,' Associated Press report accessed 2/27/2004 at *http://salon.com/news/wire/2004/02/26/priests/index.html*; Associated Press, 'Catholic Church's costs pass $1 billion in abuse cases,' accessed 6/11/06 at *http://nytimes.com*.

42 Mary Farrell Bednarowski, 'New Age Movement,' in Boyer, *Oxford Companion to US History*, 545. See also James Lewis and Gordon Melton, eds, *Perspectives on the New Age* (Albany: SUNY Press, 1992); Sarah Pike, *New Age and Neopagan Religions in America* (New York: Columbia University Press, 2004); and Adam Possamai, *In Search of New Age Spiritualities* (Burlington, VT: Ashgate, 2005).

43 Sarah Pike, 'New Age,' in Laderman and León, *Religion and American Cultures*, 233. On issues of this paragraph see Cynthia Eller, *Living in the Lap of the Goddess* (Boston: Beacon, 1995); Margot Adler, *Drawing Down the Moon: Witches, Druids, Goddess-Worshippers and Other Pagans in America Today* (Boston: Beacon, 1979), Daniel Wojcik, *The End of the World as We Know It: Faith, Fatalism, and Apocalypse in America* (New York University Press, 1997); John Saliba, 'The study of UFO religions,' *Nova Religio* vol. 10, no. 2 (2006), 103–23; and Catherine Albanese, *Nature Religion in America From the Algonkian Indians to the New Age* (Chicago: University of Chicago, 1990.)

44 On Moon and deprogrammers see Sean McCloud, *Making the American Religious Fringe: Exotics, Subversives, and Journalists 1955–1993* (Chapel Hill: University of North Carolina Press, 2004), 127–59. See also Laderman and León, *Religion and American Cultures* and R. Stephen Warner and Judith Wittner, eds. *Gatherings in Diaspora: Religious Communities and the New Immigration* (Philadelphia: Temple University Press, 1998).

CHAPTER 6

Religion and Evolving Social Conflicts from World War II to the Present

Once again, as in Chapters 3 and 4, our goal in this chapter is not to survey every important dimension of religion and post-1945 sociopolitical conflict. Nor will Chapter 7 attempt to treat every significant aspect of religion and culture. Rather we will select a few cases – midday breaks and evening stopovers on our whirlwind tour – that provide texture to our overview chapters while rounding out our trip in a reasonably representative way.

Faces of African-American Religion and Politics

Chapter 1 stressed that whites did not simply displace disappearing Native Americans nor exploit the labor of a black population that we can treat as marginal. On the contrary, the foundation of US history was constituted by the interplay of red, white, and black. Of course, whites seized by far the most power as the three groups built on this foundation. They took over and/or trashed most parts of the house that Native Americans had built – including parts that were still inhabited by the remnant of Native people who had not died in epidemics. They confined blacks to the servant quarters while relying heavily on black labor. Especially in the 1800s, waves of immigration were overlain on this foundation, so that divides among European-Americans became the main activities in much of the house. Immigrants built such large additions on the house that we might imagine them changing the contours of the foundation.

Nevertheless, although white people have taken center stage during much of our study, we must not forget that blacks have been present all along as part of the foundation. Even if we have not highlighted the point, they have been actors in strikes, producers of popular culture, founders of denominations, and so on. Many observations that we made in passing would be worth expanding in this evening stopover devoted to

African-American religion. For example, we noted the black contribution to Pentecostalism, but we could spend this entire section expanding on issues like William Seymour's career, Pentecostal contributions to popular music, or the interplay of blacks, Latino/as, and Asians in global Pentecostalism. We touched on how blacks related to the labor movement, social gospel, and New Deal (all of which largely excluded them) and how black women's clubs in some ways mirrored organizations like the WCTU while working with a different context and set of priorities. Both issues would be worth exploring further. We treated the KKK in relation to nativism and the push-pull dynamic of immigrants who debated whether to assimilate or maintain a more defensive posture – but obviously the anti-black aspects of the KKK and black forms of this dynamic are no less important.[1]

At least we were able to touch on the above points; in other cases we simply left out observations about race in the interest of brevity. For example, we discussed how Tennessee's white Baptists attacked evolution without considering how its black Baptists perceived the issue. Social Darwinism justified white supremacy, and it is interesting to explore how blacks divided over the Scopes Trial, unsure whether they had more to fear from southern fundamentalists or northern Darwinists. We discussed film censorship – but it is difficult to overestimate the centrality of race to Hollywood in light of films such as *Birth of a Nation* (a celebration of the KKK that was the paradigmatic feature-length film), *The Jazz Singer* (a celebration of minstrelsy and Jewish assimilation that was the first talking film) and *Gone With the Wind* (a nostalgic look at slavery that was the most popular film in Hollywood's classic era) – plus hundreds of Westerns based on whites subjugating dark-skinned savages.[2] In general, we have not given African-American art the attention it would reward, neither during the Harlem Renaissance when artists like Langston Hughes and Louis Armstrong spearheaded a flowering of black urban culture, nor in later years when works like James Baldwin's *The Fire Next Time*, John Coltrane's *A Love Supreme* and Alice Walker's *The Color Purple* had a huge impact on the nation's religious discourse.[3] Most of the groups we have discussed (missionaries, Populists, Buddhists, etc.) have black minorities and most social issues (consumerism, war, feminism, etc.) affected blacks in distinctive ways.

For the rest of this section, let us concentrate on the role of religion in the civil rights movement and the diversity of African-American religion. We noted how black Baptist and Methodist churches entered the century as major social institutions of their communities. They moved to cities like Chicago and Detroit with African-Americans during the Great Migration of the early twentieth century, joined by Holiness and Pentecostal churches that often operated out of urban storefronts. Although we should not imagine that all churches were politically engaged – some were otherworldly and/or complacent – nevertheless, leaders based in churches helped to spearhead the push for equal rights. Once again, we could spend this entire section discussing figures in this story, such as Adam Clayton Powell, Jr., who led Harlem's Abyssinian Baptist Church and was a long-time Congressman, or C. L. Franklin who led Detroit's New Hope Baptist Church and was the father of singer Aretha Franklin. We could retell famous episodes such as Martin Luther King, Jr. emerging as a leader of the Montgomery Bus Boycott or the Birmingham police turning fire-hoses and attack dogs on non-violent protesters.[4]

It is hard to overstress the centrality of the black freedom movement to post-war cultural politics. Whether in the North or South, blacks suffered from poverty and discrimination that they found increasingly intolerable in light of New Deal reforms and economic growth that were lifting other groups into the middle class. Blacks had a toehold in the New Deal coalition; although they were junior partners they reaped some benefit from its policies, they played key roles in the urban networks that formed the cultural matrix for the left, and (at least in the North) their votes counted. During World War II they appealed to the stated US war goals – defending a society that respected democratic rights from a racist enemy – and pointed out that the army fighting for these goals was segregated, that blacks lacked voting rights in the South, and that lynching and other forms of violent intimidation were widespread. Such 'ironies' (as pundits described them) became a headache for US elites because they were an embarrassment for Cold War propaganda in Africa and Asia, and this provided an opening for blacks to win changes that had earlier been beaten back.[5]

Three components must come together for a social movement to succeed: grievances that provide a motive to mobilize; enough organizational strength to give a reasonable chance of success; and the insurgent consciousness to imagine change and provide the morale to pursue it.[6] Of course blacks have never lacked a sense of grievance, but organizational weakness has often made rebellion risky if not suicidal. Martin Luther King, Jr., knew that he was risking his life when stepped forward as leader of the Montgomery Bus Boycott – and indeed, his house was firebombed and he was later murdered. However, King's network of support is a good example of how black organizational strength was growing; blacks built autonomous urban organizations (such as King's church) and forged alliances in the New Deal coalition (such as King's relationships with northern clergy and the White House) at the same time that the southern cotton economy was becoming less important. Still, even given both a motive to mobilize and the strength to succeed, a movement cannot get off the ground without insurgent consciousness – especially when sticking one's neck out is risky. Progressive churches were keys to black mobilization both as organizational resources in their own right and as spaces to nurture counter-hegemonic visions – expressed broadly through sermons, music, education, funerals, and so on. Although churches were not always pillars of strength and not every strong church nurtured insurgent consciousness – for instance, top leaders of the National Baptist Convention saw King as too radical and he had to form a splinter organization – progressive churches were usually in the mix when all three components came together.

The civil rights movement was led by predominantly black organiza-tions – politically active churches, unions, grassroots organizations, and pressure groups like the National Association for the Advancement of Colored People – in a sometimes tense alliance with white liberal groups that were often led by Jews and mainline Protestant clergy. Although the Democratic Party was always uncertain whether to tilt toward southern whites or blacks and their white liberal allies, increasingly it supported a moderate civil rights agenda. White clergy played significant roles in the protests and political bargaining that led to the Civil Rights and Voting Rights Acts of 1964 and 1965, backing up black activists on the front lines of the struggle. It must be said, however, that church-based resistance to civil rights was also strong. White Southerners rallied behind the 'southern way of life' and 'law and order' (that is, the status quo order, not equal rights for all under the law) and deplored the politicization of preachers (that is, black and liberal preachers). Much of the effort that grew into the current network of private evangelical schools began as an alternative to the desegregation of public schools. Northern working-class Catholics resisted desegregating their neighborhoods and schools on the grounds that this would destroy their communities and property values.[7]

Largely in response to the Democrats' support for civil rights, white Southerners increasingly voted Republican. This was a key to the electoral strategy that brought Richard Nixon, Ronald Reagan, George Bush,

Sr., and George W. Bush to power. Ever since Nixon's 1972 victory, Democratic politicians such as Bill Clinton have assumed that to succeed they must lean toward the right to co-opt swing voters; this has allowed Republicans to move the political center steadily rightward. We have seen that there was a related dynamic in mainstream churches; moderates put the brakes on social activists to avoid alienating conservatives. In both political and religious circles, the result was decreasing anti-racist commitment. Activists were seen as especially divisive if they pursued black nationalist strategies that stressed autonomous self-organization in light of the limitations of civil rights approaches.

By the 1990s, fewer scholars were writing about African-American *religion* (meaning Christianity) as opposed to *varieties* of African-American religion – including various forms of Christianity, orthodox and heterodox Islam, Afro-Caribbean religion, and others including lodges, alternative communities like Father Divine's Peace Mission, positive thinkers, and secularists.[8] Black Christianity by itself is diverse. Most majority-white denominations – Lutherans, Presbyterians, and so on – have a few black members and are trying to recruit more. (Catholics are the most important, especially in places like New Orleans where entire black neighborhoods were historically organized into Catholic parishes.) Although black members of such denominations share in these groups' standard practices, they often retain distinctive styles and priorities. By the 1960s black leaders in mainstream denominations, although small in number, played key strategic roles in educating and organizing whites on racial issues – as well as popularizing music and theology that originated in black churches.

Pundits often note that few blacks worship with whites and lament that Sunday morning is the most segregated hour of the week. However, there can be a disturbing undertone to such comments – as if separate black churches are like 'separate but equal' public schools that can be upgraded through consolidation with 'normal' churches. Of course, blacks do not appreciate being told (overtly or subtly) that they are unwelcome in white churches; however, most are happy with their own churches and have no desire to give up their autonomy.

Theologically and denominationally, most blacks are evangelicals. Although they do not stress Biblical literalism as much as white evangelicals, nor do they have the same tradition of splitting spiritual and social equality into separate compartments, they often have conservative instincts about doctrine and social mores – especially on issues of feminism and homosexuality. Therefore, although most black churches are stand-offish toward the NCR because of its alliance with the Republicans and history of opposing civil rights, some high-profile black clergy such as T. J. Jakes and Creflo Dollar have cast their lot with the NCR. Republicans have actively recruited black conservatives, not least through offering them funding through the Faith-Based Initiatives program. NCR leaders commonly claim that no one who supported Martin Luther King, Jr., has any right to oppose their activism. In 2006, when the NCR was lobbying for Samuel Alito's appointment to the Supreme Court, a black church in Philadelphia hosted a NCR rally called Justice Sunday, complete with one of King's nieces singing 'We Shall Overcome' for a national audience watching via satellite.[9]

Therefore, just as we stressed that white evangelicals are largely conservative but include a spectrum of positions, something similar is true of black churches. It remains fair to map them as largely liberal – especially in their voting patterns and stance toward race and class issues – but a minority is conservative. Since the same black Christian might stress born-again conversion, conservative gender roles, fighting racism, and redistributing wealth, the question arises whether such a person fits on a conventional culture war spectrum at all, or whether we should reserve this map for white religion.

As we have seen, black religion has included an Islamic presence since slavery days. Today most African-American Muslims are affiliated with orthodox mosques that have organized since the 1960s. However, such Muslims build on earlier movements that sought to recover or reinvent Islamic practice in twentieth-century US cities – notably the Moorish Science Temple which was founded by Noble Drew Ali in the 1910s, and the Nation of Islam (NOI), which was founded by W. D. Fard in the 1930s and built by Elijah Muhammad, who became Malcolm X's teacher. Both groups stressed the African Muslim roots of the black community, organized along lines of strict racial separation, and taught unorthodox doctrines that were politically provocative – notably a NOI mythology which held that whites were a race of devils, thus inverting Christian claims that blacks were cursed by God to be 'hewers of wood and drawers of water' (Joshua 9:21). Both made claims that outraged orthodox Muslims, such as the NOI's teaching that Fard was Allah incarnate. (One might compare how orthodox Christians responded when Sun Myung Moon declared himself the second coming of Christ.) Neither Moorish Science nor the NOI was politicized in the sense of promoting activist causes, but at the level of culture they had significant political effects through their teaching of economic self-reliance, black pride, and self-defense 'by any means necessary.'[10] It is instructive to imagine the NOI as a black variation on Zionism: how would attacks on Malcolm X's self-defense sound if transposed into criticisms of Jewish self-defense; conversely, how would calls for Jewish self-determination sound if transposed into X's voice calling for black power?

The NOI became the best-known US group claiming Islamic identity, due largely to Malcolm X and his most famous convert – Muhammad Ali, the world heavyweight boxing champion and outspoken critic of the Vietnam War (when Ali was drafted, the US denied his claim to conscientious objector status because it was based not on pacifism, but rather on Ali's refusal to fight unjust wars). However, after Elijah Muhammad died in 1975, his son Warith Deen Muhammad led the NOI on a path toward orthodox Islam somewhat like Malcolm X had earlier traveled. He largely dissolved the NOI's organization, repudiated its separatism, brought its ritual practice in line with orthodoxy, and encouraged its members to join local mosques.

Complicating this picture is the fact that the NOI still exists. Indeed, it garners more attention than the far larger group of orthodox African-American Muslims – who, let us recall, account for a third of US Muslims. Louis Farrakhan, a long-time follower of Elijah Muhammad, revived the original NOI in response to Warith Deen Muhammad's reforms. (In recent years, Farrakhan has sometimes appeared to be leading his followers toward orthodoxy, following the path blazed by Malcolm X; however, Farrakhan continues to give mixed signals.) In 1995 Farrakhan organized a demonstration called the Million Man March in co-operation with a wide spectrum of black leaders; it may have been the largest African-American protest rally in US history. Although most marchers were not NOI members and the rally's goals were vague – a show of strength linked to a call for grassroots community-building and anti-racist organizing – such efforts kept the separatist traditions of Malcolm X, the NOI, and kindred groups near the center of African-American religious dialogues. Important hip-hop musicians have been associated with the NOI and/or an offshoot called the Five Percenters.[11]

Due to immigration and increasing respect for African and Latino/a cultures, Afro-Caribbean religions such as Santería and Vodou have also grown since mid-century, starting with immigration from Puerto Rico after World War II and Cuba after its 1960 revolution. Although most

Caribbean immigrants have been Christian (mainly Catholic), many of them also brought a relatively unbroken extension of traditional African religions, blended with Christianity to a greater or lesser degree. Religious practices that were largely stamped out by the US slave system, or at best forced underground and practiced in fragmented ways, returned to the US from places where African traditions had remained stronger. These were mainly practiced by immigrants – especially Cubans and Haitians – but also attracted some interest from longer-established African-Americans, as well as whites who explored alternatives to Christianity and/or religious dimensions of music from New Orleans, Cuba, and Jamaica.

Communities that practice Santería and Vodou are often structured like extended families. They gather around priests or priestesses who build reputations for spiritual knowledge and the ability to lead powerful ceremonies. Devotees form relationships with supernatural beings known as *orishas* in Santería and *loa* in Vodou. These beings take standard forms such as (in Vodou) the snake Danbala, the trickster Papa Gede and the mother Ezili Danto. They also shade off in two directions from place to place: toward veneration of ancestor spirits and toward devotions that merge with popular Christianity (*orishas* and *loa* are often considered the African forms of the same spiritual powers that Christians call saints). Individuals may approach priests or priestesses for divination or healing. Near the center of the religion, however, are communal ceremonies. In the context of feasting, animal sacrifice, other gifts to the spirits, and ceremonial drumming, the spirits communicate with devotees in the most dramatic way – by taking over their bodies as they enter ecstatic trances. For example, Papa Gede might possess a priestess, who then speaks in Gede's voice to other people in attendance.[12]

Vodou has a reputation as exotic and dangerous; horror films popularize sensationalistic misinformation about its dark side. Although medicines and spells in Vodou (like its less systematized cousin, conjure) can in fact be used for negative goals, its blend of the positive and negative is more like Christianity – in which one might, after all, invoke death on one's enemies by praying for victory in a war – than unlike it. The main focus of Afro-Caribbean religion is on similar kinds of community-building, respect for spiritual mysteries, and searches for healing and wisdom that are stressed by other religions. In 1993 the Supreme Court overturned a Florida law that forbade Santeros to sacrifice animals in a ritual context.[13]

By the century's end, it was harder to identify the central actors in black religion and their political priorities than it had been at mid-century. One reason was rising religious diversity; another was post-1965 immigration and an increase in mixed-race marriages that made it increasingly misleading to approach US race relations as a binary black–white system. Perhaps most important, however, was a change in discourses about race after the breakthrough of the civil rights movement.

The racial discourse inherited from slavery and extended by Jim Crow segregation stressed rigid hierarchical separation of the races. Any racial ambiguity was polarized into two separate and unequal categories. For example, because masters sought to maintain the children of slaves in servitude even if one parent (typically the master himself) was free, laws declared that even one drop of African blood in a person's genealogy made him/her legally black. People of mixed-race parentage were lumped into the category of blackness, although the lightest-skinned among them could illegally pass as white. To maintain an ideology of racial purity and to discourage sexual attraction from eroding racial boundaries, there were powerful taboos against inter-racial sex (with an exception for master–slave 'breeding'). After emancipation and continuing far into the twentieth century, whites lynched black men accused of transgressing these taboos. In 1955, fourteen-year-old Emmett Till was murdered in Mississippi because he whistled at a white woman, even though (as a visitor from the North) he did not even realize he was doing anything considered inappropriate. Although the popular image of lynching presents it as small-scale and spontaneous vigilante justice – perhaps to save a white virgin from violation – lynchings were often public events complete with newspaper advertising, souvenir postcards, and spectators who rode excursion trains to the spectacle.[14]

By the 1980s there was change on this front, related to the rise of a discourse celebrating racial inclusivity and the success of the civil rights movement in removing barriers to blacks rising into professions and middle-class enclaves. True, some conservatives maintained overtly degrading and segregationist ideas. More importantly, aspects of white supremacist common sense remained embedded in subtler parts of the culture; many whites associate black behavior with moral decline rather than positive and enriching pluralism, and many whites who give lip service to respecting black culture actually treat it as irrelevant to their lives in white suburban enclaves. Nevertheless, the mindset that enjoyed watching blackface films or found Emmett Till's murder logical now seems significantly outdated, even if many entertainers still engage in neo-minstrelsy and the prison system carries forward many aspects of institutional racism. Who is scandalized today because a film screens an inter-racial kiss or Elvis Presley's music seems 'too black?' A liberal paradigm that accents how all people are the same under the skin and celebrates cultural blending has become hegemonic. While this is a real gain, it brings new problems into view. To understand why, it is helpful to introduce the concept of racial formations – the idea that race (or more precisely racialization, the projection of largely arbitrary racial categories onto reality) is not static, but takes fluid forms in different contexts. In this perspective, before we can identify the key forms of racism to attack, we must clarify how particular hegemonic discourses – racial formations – function to maintain unjust power relations between racialized groups. If we do so, we find that the major form of US racism since the 1960s has not been the maintenance of strict racial hierarchies – such that pursuing race-blind integration is the main challenge – but rather a racial formation that *discounts* the ongoing structuring of society in racialized ways, for example, through residential segregation or differential enforcement of laws.[15]

At its best, a vision of religious–racial equality – King's American Dream – was an insurgent consciousness well matched to overcoming segregation and barriers to upward mobility for middle-class blacks. However, this vision is less satisfying insofar as black people experience US society more as a nightmare than a dream. The hegemonic idea can mislead people into believing that the US is steadily achieving multicultural equity, and in this regard King's approach can be a form of false consciousness – looking at a nightmare through rose-colored classes and seeing a utopian dream. The prophet Jeremiah complained of people who 'heal the wound of my people lightly, saying "Peace, peace" when there is no peace' (Jeremiah 6:14). Likewise, liberal multiculturalism heals ongoing legacies of racism too lightly. Thus, some people suggest that a better motto for anti-racism is 'No justice, no peace' – that is, without justice there cannot be peace. Either Christians or non-Christians can sound this theme; their stress may be demanding equality or respecting diversity, and their strategy may be engagement with mainstream society or autonomous self-organization. In any case, as long as racialized injustices persist in the US – and they show every sign of being an ongoing structural component – variations on this theme will remain a basic feature of US religion.

More on the Culture War

There were worlds within the world of mainstream religious politics in the post-war era, and it would take far longer than one evening stopover to introduce them all with the texture that we are aiming for. If we had more time, it would be useful to introduce many activists from the NCR and the religious left and to treat their projects in depth. At best we can speak briefly about trends, starting on the rightward parts of a culture war spectrum and moving to the left.

The revitalized NCR that became a pillar of the Republican coalition did not emerge from nowhere in the 1970s. Anyone who bothered to look could have found evangelicals making significant cultural-political interventions all along.[16] Their top leader from the 1940s to the 1970s, Billy Graham, was famous for socializing with Presidents Eisenhower and Nixon and preaching televised sermons with understated but unmistakable political overtones. As noted above, the revivals that launched Graham's career fused concerns about saving souls and fighting Communists. In the 1960 election, evangelicals lobbied against John Kennedy, although their tactics backfired and scholars often cite this episode – perhaps somewhat wishfully – as the last gasp of anti-Catholicism in mainstream US politics. In the 1970s Graham preached at the White House and sponsored a national rally called Honor America Day. In support of Nixon's claim to represent a silent majority, Graham invited Nixon to speak at one of his televised revivals on the campus of the University of Tennessee shortly after the National Guard killed anti-war protestors at Kent State University, which had made it nearly impossible for Nixon to appear on college campuses without massive counter-demonstrations.

Before the 1970s scholars and pundits discounted such activities as marginal and fading. Certain aspects of evangelicalism reinforced this interpretation. Evangelicals nursed a sense of marginality that led them to stress otherworldly themes and teach that the fallen world of politics was no place for serious Christians. This was especially true of old-time separatist fundamentalists, and somewhat less common but still significant among neo-evangelicals aligned with Graham. Nevertheless, despite the otherworldly self-understanding of conservative Protestants, scholars exaggerate the political disengagement of even the most uncompromising fundamentalists before the 1970s. For example, when Falwell preached a 1965 sermon that accused Martin Luther King, Jr. of meddling in politics and failing to proclaim the gospel, his sermon had a clear political thrust.[17] Given the strong overlap between hegemonic practices and evangelical mores – not only their stances toward race but also toward gender, wealth and poverty, and foreign policy – evangelicals played an implicit political role simply through stressing personal spirituality and obedience to authority. In this sense most evangelicals formed part of the post-war liberal consensus, even though some of them supported far-right groups like the KKK and the John Birch Society.

Evangelical political mobilization moved to a higher level of self-consciousness and intensity after the mid-1970s. The world of the NCR became diverse. The most powerful and visible NCR power brokers are fundamentalists – so much so that some people use 'NCR' as a shorthand term for such people alone. However, Christians who are highly politicized and allied with Republicans include conservative Catholics, neo-conservatives in Protestant circles, and conservative evangelicals in mainline denominations. Some people in this group focus on single issues such as criminalizing abortion, building fundamentalist schools, policing Hollywood, teaching creationism, or promoting sexual abstinence. Others press for a multi-issue agenda in alliance with secular politicians or simply attempt to take over the Republican Party. By 2002 the NCR dominated the Republican organizations of eighteen states and controlled at least a quarter of Republican committees in forty-four states.[18] As one NCR leader said, 'We've gone way beyond the point where we need a seat at the table … We're in a position to offer others a seat at the table, because we really are the heart of the party.'[19]

In the 1970s and 1980s, Falwell was the NCR's most visible leader. He played a key role in prodding fundamentalists toward overt activism. His organization, the Moral Majority, worked with secular operatives of the Reagan Administration. In the late 1980s and 1990s, the NCR leadership shifted to the Christian Coalition organized by televangelist Pat Robertson and his lieutenant Ralph Reed; this was a more autonomous organization with greater grassroots strength. In recent years the top NCR power brokers have included James Dobson's radio empire called Focus on the Family (which has its own zip code in Colorado Springs) and its allied lobbying arm, the Family Research Council.

Falwell revealed core NCR assumptions two days after the terrorist attacks of 11 September 2001, when he stated on Robertson's television show that 'the pagans, and the abortionists, and the feminists, and the gays and the lesbians … [and groups like the ACLU] who have tried to secularize America' were partly responsible for the attacks. He said, 'I point the finger in their face and say "you helped this happen."' This was so because they undermined the essential nature of the US as a Christian nation, which had prospered due to a covenant with God that could be traced back to the Puritans. God would protect the nation if it fulfilled its mission, but if not, 'God will be not mocked.' The NCR perceives a huge gap between its current influence and the power it needs to uphold this covenant. Falwell's supposed apology for his comments was premised on such gap; he expressed regret that he had included only liberals on his list of sinners, and claimed that his comment would have been unobjectionable 'if I had added the church as one of the offenders – a sleeping church that is not praying enough.'[20]

Not all NCR projects involved pressing for changes in public policy; some focused on strengthening and policing the boundaries of their communities. Especially important in this regard were Christian schools and media, as well as efforts to purge liberals from churches. After an NCR faction took over the Southern Baptist Convention (SBC) in the 1980s and carried out such a purge – which included rolling back support for women's ordination – conservatives in other denominations attempted related strategies, with generous funding from neo-conservative foundations. The result in denominations like the Presbyterians and Lutherans was a stalemate rather than an NCR victory. However, this was enough to block many liberal goals in these denominations, so that the two main options on the national stage became the hard-right policies of the NCR and a center-left but largely paralyzed mainstream. As we have seen, a growing group of evangelicals fell between these poles. For example, moderate Baptists unhappy with the SBC purges built alternative institutions such as the Cooperate Baptist Fellowship; one turning point in their efforts to gain support was the SBC's 1998 policy declaration that 'A wife is to submit herself graciously to the servant leadership of her husband even as the church willingly submits to the headship of Christ.'[21]

The claim that evangelicals are persecuted outsiders fighting for seats at tables of power, carried forward as standard rhetoric since the 1920s, made less and less sense as the years passed. No doubt the idea remained pervasive; NCR leaders exhorted their followers to see themselves as underdogs battling for survival against secular elites who dominated the media, universities, and (non-military) government agencies. Granted, it made sense for evangelicals to feel defensive in cultural niches such as university English departments or parts of Hollywood. However, with Republicans controlling all three branches of government by 2004 and conservatives dominating the news media, it became difficult to give evangelicals the benefit of doubt when they claimed to feel like underdogs. If sincere, the claim seemed to be a gross misperception of their situation, akin to the rich executive posited in our Introduction who felt oppressed because he was shy and left-handed. Or was the claim a mere debating tactic of cynical NCR leaders? The best way to give the NCR the benefit of doubt for sincerity was disturbing to most other people; it was to posit that the NCR 'normally' expected not only to control huge slices of demographic pie, political muscle, and cultural influence (as it already did) but to control preponderant power across the society. In short, NCR leaders expected to exercise hegemony, and when they did not do so they felt oppressed even when they constituted one of the nation's strongest power blocs.

The point is not that the NCR sought a total monopoly of power or a theocracy that ended the separation of church and state. True, end-times novels did imagine such a monopoly as a long-term utopian vision, and radical members of an NCR movement called Reconstructionism hoped to replace the Constitution with Biblical laws, including stoning for adultery. However, most NCR people felt misunderstood and insulted if liberals accused them of such goals. What they actually sought was less dramatic, although nearly as ambitious: it was to undo the damage they perceived as arising from the moral anarchy of the 1960s and their cultural disestablishment earlier in the century, whether through turning back the clock or moving into a new era. Without envisioning bloody purges of secularists and religious minorities, NCR leaders hoped to convert most opponents in the long run – and meanwhile to block them from corrupting a faithful Christian majority. Without plotting to take over the state, they felt entitled to a routine overlap between their priorities and the decisions of politicians.

We have seen that Golden Rule Christians remained strong (if sometimes neglected) during the years when the NCR mobilized on its right. Still deserving more attention, however, is a network of loosely allied movements on its left. Recall how liberals entered the 1950s presupposing Reinhold Niebuhr's Christian realist approach. Although the Niebuhrians' stress on God's prophets keeping pride in check made them suspicious of activists whom they considered too socialist or pacifist, they did carry forward commitments from the social gospel era. They enthusiastically supported social goals that they deemed realistic, which in practice meant those that dovetailed with the New Deal and

Cold War. After the mid-1950s, whenever greater space for 'responsible' cultural–political critique opened in mainstream public opinion, people from the rising generation in Niebuhr's tradition – professors, clergy, and ecumenical leaders – moved into this space. They were increasingly joined by Catholics who carried forward traditions of Catholic social thought in relation to the spirit of Vatican II. Often they worked with liberal rabbis to forge Protestant–Catholic–Jewish alliances, especially before the 1970s when such alliances became strained over the Israel–Palestine conflict.[22]

Such activists were not radically opposed to government polices before the mid-1960s; they remained New Dealers who broadly supported John Kennedy and Lyndon Johnson. Still, their changes from a 1940s Niebuhrian baseline were not trivial. Around 1960 they began to rethink their justification of US nuclear policy, and by the 1980s such questions ripened into major statements against the arms race by Catholic and Methodist bishops, as well as widespread support for activism to slow down Reagan's arms build-up. Although not all liberal clergy supported all forms of civil rights activism – King's famed 'Letter from Birmingham City Jail' was a response to liberal clergy who used Niebuhrian-style logic to question his methods – nevertheless, by the 1960s they strongly supported the movement. Many white activists joined blacks who were jailed, beaten, or even killed in the struggle.[23] In the mid-1960s liberal clergy broke with a Cold War mindset and joined older pacifist groups like the Catholic Worker Movement in opposing the Vietnam War. They organized a peace group called Clergy and Laity Concerned about Vietnam, or CALCAV, which was a key bridge between the radical student left and middle America. King gave a major speech in 1967 against the war under CALCAV's umbrella.[24] Meanwhile a Jesuit priest named Daniel Berrigan caused a furor by breaking into a selective service office and burning draft files with homemade napalm. At his trial he uttered the famous words 'Apologies, good friends, for this fracture of good order, the burning of paper instead of children.'[25]

As people in this network moved toward radical critiques of US Vietnam policy, their wider thinking about foreign relations moved in related directions. Increasingly they forged alliances with anti-imperialist movements in Latin America, Asia, and Africa, especially if they knew colleagues from these places through missionary and ecumenical networks. They qualified their support for capitalist development strategies and came to insist that it was ideological mystification to use free market theory to posit equal relationships of trade in which former colonies could freely chose strategies of comparative economic advantage. On the contrary, market choices in every nation were shaped by political factors such as tax incentives, labor law, corporate welfare, and government investment in road-building and arms production. Global economics involved unequal relationships of dependency, in which strong parties took advantage of weak ones through various means, from pillage and slavery in the colonial era to neo-colonial arrangements like the politics of international debt in the present.

By the 1970s left church networks strongly supported revolutionary coalitions in Central America. These movements, which included strong grassroots religious participation, overthrew a US-backed dictator in Nicaragua and began prolonged class struggles against US-backed fascist elites in Guatemala and El Salvador. Many US church people (both white clergy and Latino/a immigrants) had personal friends among the revolutionaries, so when their friends began to be tortured and killed by soldiers whom the US government had armed – for example, when Archbishop Oscar Romero was assassinated and four US nuns were raped and murdered in El Salvador – this had a powerful galvanizing impact. A network of US Christians smuggled refugees from these wars into their communities, offering them sanctuary in their churches. (At this time the US government refused asylum to such refugees because it denied that it supported human rights abuses.) Such civil disobedience personalized the transnational religious solidarities that were being forged. In many places this network was the backbone of organizing against US Central America policy; it was enough of a brake on Reagan's plans that he ordered extensive illegal surveillance of churches.[26] Let us pause to consider how this dramatizes an abstract point from our Introduction – that religion takes both hegemonic and counter-hegemonic forms. In this case, anti-imperialist activism flowered within the same institutions and theological traditions that had earlier sponsored colonial missions and justified scenarios for nuclear war as a lesser evil. Recall how the journal, *Christianity and Crisis*, was created to support US efforts in World War II and US post-war global planning. By the 1970s this journal had evolved into a forum for anti-imperialist solidarity activists and an alternative source of news about Latin America to countervail against the spin of mainstream news sources.

William Slone Coffin was among the best-known leaders in this network. He was born into an upper-class family (his uncle was the head of Union Theological Seminary and friend of many New York elites) and his youth included adventures working for the Central Intelligence Agency during the 1940s and 1950s. He became the chaplain of Yale University in the 1960s, the head of New York's influential Riverside Church in the 1970s and 1980s, and president of the anti-nuclear group SANE/Freeze thereafter. Coffin crafted sermons informed by a prophetic liberal theology, dealt skillfully with the media, and acted boldly in the public sphere. While at Yale he risked his life as a Freedom Rider (that is, as part of an inter-racial group that desegregated interstate buses through direct action), traveled to Vietnam with a CALCAV group, and helped to lead the draft resistance movement. At Riverside Church he sponsored an influential disarmament program, visited US hostages in Iran, and supported the push for gay and lesbian equality that embroiled churches late in the century.[27]

Among the many forms of left religious activism that rose between the 1950s and 1970s, feminist versions were the slowest to pick up momentum, but they sustained the most power by century's end. This was true largely because (unlike calls for solidarity with Nicaragua) they harnessed the self-interest of a large group of young clergy, as well as the ongoing female majority of church members who were coming to expect equal opportunities in the non-religious parts of their lives. (By the 1990s even NCR leaders had cut back on their talk about women's place being in the home because their wives and daughters were pursuing careers – for example, one of Jerry Falwell's daughters is a surgeon – although they still held up domesticity as an ideal.[28]) Recall that before the 1950s only a handful of women had been ordained outside the Holiness–Pentecostal tradition. However, after the breakthrough of second-wave feminism, mainstream churches increasingly took for granted a moderate commitment to women's equality. Methodists and Presbyterians dropped barriers to ordination in 1956 and Lutherans did so in 1970 (Reform and Conservative Jews followed in 1972 and 1985). In 1974 dissident Episcopal bishops ordained eleven women, arguing that the authority of the Holy Spirit allowed them to do so even though the denomination had prohibited it.

This set the stage for women to be ordained on a large scale for the first time in the 1970s. Student bodies at seminaries of liberal Protestantism and mainstream Judaism were rapidly transformed. No longer were they overwhelmingly male, with a few women pursuing degrees in religious education; now male/female ratios approached parity and women pursued the same careers as men.[29] To say the least, these were not settled issues for evangelicals or Catholics. Moreover, many mainline churches resisted changes taken for granted in liberal seminaries, such as creating gender-inclusive translations of the Bible. (To dramatize the need for such changes, one satire imagined a liturgy focusing not on God the Father and the brotherhood of Man, but rather on God the Mother and the sisterhood of Woman – a sisterhood 'which includes men, of course'.[30]) Because many denominations resisted women's ordination, the overall percentage of female clergy remained in the twenty-five to thirty per cent range at the end of the century, and women did not always have access to the best jobs. Nevertheless, most moderate-to-liberal Christians agreed that women's ordination was a good idea; Protestants enacted it directly and Catholics experimented with new roles for nuns and female church professionals while lobbying for change at higher levels of the Church.

Along with increased women's leadership came feminist approaches to issues of gender and sexuality. Religious feminists divided in complex ways, along lines that included advocates of radical change versus moderate reform, those who incorporated concerns about race and class versus those who were mainly worried about opportunities for middle-class women, and those who stressed issues of pornography and sexual abuse (with a default assumption that explicit sexual images were associated with objectification and rape) versus those who were more 'sex-positive' and interested in unleashing erotic energies repressed by patriarchal culture. Radical feminists raised in Christian and Jewish circles repudiated their traditions entirely. For example, Mary Daly began her career in the 1960s advocating women's equality in Catholicism; however, she soon concluded that a woman seeking gender equality in the Church was 'comparable to a black person's demanding equality in the Ku Klux Klan.'[31] In 1971 when she was invited to give the first sermon by a woman at Harvard's Memorial Church, she used the opportunity to exhort women to abandon Christianity and led a 'women's exodus' out of the door. Some religious feminists embraced Daly's philosophical critiques and/or experimented with female Wiccan groups. However, most religious feminists built on traditions of nineteenth-century activism (purged of Victorian assumptions and expanded through multiculturalism and feminist theory) to build spaces in mainstream congregations that presupposed women's equality and functioned as networks for change.

By the 1970s, activist clergy like Coffin and theologians rooted in the feminist and black freedom movements joined Third World leaders like El Salvador's Romero and South Africa's Archbishop Desmond Tutu in developing liberation theologies that correlated radical activism with Christian discipleship and hegemonic policies with sin and oppression.[32] Such ideas became staples in liberal seminary curricula and sermons. When neo-conservatives objected to this theology and exhorted churches to stand in judgment on all ideologies, Dorothee Soelle responded that neoconservatives would do better to ask why people were turning toward radical positions. 'Wouldn't it be thinkable that this has do with some major events in this century – say Auschwitz?' asked Soelle. 'A spirituality that is stripped of human need, or any desire, becomes blood-less.'[33] For Soelle, the practice of faith was a struggle against cynicism, exploitation, and the flattening of human relationships into commodities. Contrary to classic Marxian analysis, religion was not false conscious-ness; rather, losing sight of utopian dimensions of religion was just what capitalism *wanted* people to do. As Soelle confronted the defeats of the left after the 1960s, her writing represented an effort to sustain hope, even in the seeming absence of objective foundations for it. This was the heart of religion as she understood it.

Thinking about the End of the World with Conservative Protestants

At least three things are clear about evangelical end-times speculation. One is that it is a major phenomenon. During the 1970s, Hal Lindsey's *The Late Great Planet Earth* sold twenty-eight million copies, making it the top-selling non-fiction book of the decade – yet its success was dwarfed by the twelve-volume, multi-media juggernaut of the *Left Behind* series, written by Jerry Jenkins and NCR leader Tim LaHaye. Dozens of variations on the same plot are available as films, novels, sermons, and Bible study tapes; some of these break through to mainstream theaters and marketing behemoths like Wal-Mart, while others circulate through churches and Christian bookstores. One scholar tried to estimate the number of Christians who are 'deeply preoccupied' with the end-times, 'place [this] at the center' of their worldview, and believe that God has 'a specific, detailed, plan for history's last days.' By this definition, he found eight million prophecy believers out of an evangelical sub-culture of fifty million.[34] However, this leaves aside people who are concerned about the end-times as just one interest among others within a broad evangelical worldview. We might define prophecy belief so that it blends seamlessly into US culture at large. Where does it end when twenty-five per cent of US citizens think that the Bible predicted the attacks of 9/11, sixty-two per cent have no doubt that Jesus will return, and eighty-five per cent accept the Bible as divinely inspired? Can interest in films like *Matrix Revolutions* (2003) and *End of Days* (1999) – both with apocalyptic scenarios and heroes who are crucified somewhat like Christ – be disentangled from end-times prophecy belief?

Second, certain basics about the tradition are straightforward. End-times belief is part of the evangelical sub-culture. It stands in a long tradition of interpreting apocalyptic texts of the Hebrew Bible like the book of Daniel and similar Christian texts such as the book of Revelation and the thirteenth chapter of Mark. Christians have commented on these texts throughout history; for example, Puritans drew on this tradition when they spoke about building a Kingdom of God in America. In the nineteenth century, writers like Cyrus Scofield (author of the *Scofield Reference Bible*) reworked the tradition into the theory of dispensational premillennialism. As discussed above, dispensationalists interpret the Bible by breaking it into stages, including current and future stages that they see as foretold in prophecy. Premillennialists believe that Jesus will return before a thousand-year period at the end of time called the millennium, which they expect to begin soon in the context of a global crisis. End-times believers map standard plot elements from apocalyptic texts – for example, the rapture of believers and rise of an anti-Christ with marks like the number 666 – onto current events. Whereas most scholars see apocalyptic texts as comments on struggles during the years when they were written – especially persecution of Jews and Christians by Greeks and Romans – end-times believers see these texts as predicting the future and seek one-to-one correspondences with current political events. For example, a mysterious enemy called Gog in the book of Ezekiel became associated with scenarios of the Soviet Union attacking Israel, and one Biblical literalist managed to translate the Hebrew word for 'bow and arrow' as 'missile launcher.'[35]

All of the following people have been identified as the anti-Christ in end-times discourse: King George III, several Popes, Adolph Hitler, John Kennedy, Henry Kissinger, Sun Myung Moon, and Ronald Reagan. Marks of the Beast include the Stamp Act during the Revolutionary War, the blue eagle logo of the National Recovery Administration in the New Deal era, and a birthmark on the face of Soviet leader Mikhail

Gorbachev during the Cold War. In every generation since the book of Daniel was written, prophecy writers have piled up evidence that their interpretive scenarios have flawlessly predicted all events up the moment when they are writing – then concluded with an appeal to readers to trust them about the future.[36] Through such methods, believers comment on current events and express their hopes and fears about the future. For example, they currently worry that the anti-Christ is planning a global system to control people using implanted computer bar codes. Since 1948 they have often voiced concern about Israel – both support for Israeli policy and the expectation that most Jews will be punished for rejecting Christ. One evangelist used a computer analysis of the Bible to discern that Palestinian leader Yasser Arafat was in league with the anti-Christ. Coded messages could be uncovered if, for example, one read the book of Daniel backward and counted every seventh letter. Through such a method, the preacher discovered the words 'Arafat shake hands'; he felt that this revealed the futility of peace negotiations that were underway at the time.[37]

A third feature of end-times discourse is implicit in what we have already said – it includes a sense of embattlement or persecution that focuses the discontent of ordinary people against people they perceive as enemies. It can mobilize dissent toward many political ends. Even the elite authors of end-times novels are examples of this phenomenon when their fears of the anti-Christ merge with fears of corporate globalization or domination by secular liberals. However, we can discover a wider range of dissent if we expand the discussion. Rastafarian musician Bob Marley might be considered an end-times prophecy believer, and much hip-hop is bursting with apocalyptic images.[38] More important for US evangelicals is the blend of end-times ideas and populism. For example, let us return to Huey Long. As discussed above, Long deserves some of his reputation as anti-democratic; after all, he was a successful Louisiana politician during an era when there was no route to power that did not involve corruption and ruthless political tactics. In this context, Long used Biblical rhetoric to focus the anger of his working-class supporters against southern elites, rather than against the northern elites and local blacks who were often targets of kindred politicians. The 1995 film *Kingfish* captures some of the complexities. Overall, this film reflects the common interpretation of Long as little more than a proto-fascist demagogue. However, in one scene he presents his plan to increase taxes on the rich as an example of 'God's law' and denounces his enemies by quoting a prophetic text: 'Break up the concentration of wealth in this country and redistribute it according to the Lord's plan. For if you do not, listen: "Go to now, ye rich men. Weep and howl for the miseries that shall come upon you"!'[39]

With these three points to orient our discussion, the point to underscore is the ambiguity of end-times politics. Scholars disagree whether the discourse encourages fatalism. Many argue that it breeds cynicism and complacency about efforts at social reform. Premillennialists tend to be downbeat about the prospects for humans doing God's will on earth, at least compared with those who expect progress toward the millennium within history; they feel that modern society is more like a Babylon to shun than a kingdom of God to build. In this view, Jesus needs to come back and clean up the mess made by humans before the kingdom of God can come. Trying to reform Babylon makes no sense. What does make sense is to flee, preferably to a place with a nice view of God destroying one's enemies.

However, many scholars overstress this fatalistic interpretation. There is no contradiction – in fact there are logical affinities – between actively working toward one's goals and believing that God is fighting on one's side to guarantee an inevitable victory. The rise of Dominion theology dramatizes the worldliness of many prophecy believers. Radical Dominionists want to reconstruct US law along strict Biblical lines (thus their other name, Reconstructionists); some of them literally stockpile arms that they expect to use in a coming war with the anti-Christ. Moderate Dominionists (including many NCR leaders) shift their stress away from a goal of separating from Babylon toward a goal of redeeming it; one of their mottos is the Bible verse, 'Occupy Until I Come.'[40] Either way, they attack premillennialists for timidity and otherworldliness. One measure of their growing strength is the behavior of heroes in end-times novels since the 1970s. Earlier heroes were often passive victims awaiting rescue by God, whereas today's heroes (such as the fighters in *Left Behind*'s Tribulation Force) are bold, confident, and technologically savvy. Moreover, even classic forms of premillennialism have optimistic aspects. One scholar speaks of a contrast between liberal Protestant optimism that is like a flashlight dimly illuminating a future landscape, and premillennial optimism that concentrates its utopian hopes on a vision of heaven, like a flashlight held close to a page.[41]

Whether end-times beliefs focus dissent in fatalistic or optimistic ways, their political impact remains fluid. Suppose that a passenger sitting next to you on a plane is reading *Left Behind*. Suppose she notices you reading this book and says to you conspiratorially, 'The Bible teaches that we must fight God's enemies – don't you agree?' What does she mean? Clearly there is room for alarm about what this question might imply for people in the network of militias, paramilitary cells, and churches of the far right. *The Turner Diaries* was a favorite book of Timothy McVeigh, the Christian terrorist who bombed the Oklahoma City Federal Building. It describes how a disciplined group can (as McVeigh did) blow up a building with a truck bomb using agricultural fertilizer. This is among the milder episodes in the book, which reads as a how-to manual for starting your own terrorist cell. Its heroes escalate the conflict to nuclear war using bombs they obtain by taking over a military base. Their plans are guided by 'The Book,' which assures them that 'We are truly the instruments of God in the fulfillment of His Grand Design.' In their liberated zone they lynch 55,000 race traitors, including many identified as 'faculty members from the nearby UCLA campus.' The hero comments: 'As the war of extermination [that is, the clean-up operations after the nuclear attack] wore on, millions of soft, city-bred, brainwashed, Whites gradually began reclaiming their manhood. The rest died.'[42]

The Turner Diaries takes its vision of establishing order and rolling back gains of the civil rights movement to cartooonish extremes. Often it returns to images of black rapists who threaten white sexual purity; the book opens with an attack that at first seems to be an example of this threat, although it turns out to be a government goon squad confiscating white people's guns (in this version of reality blacks collude with the police and are never harassed by them). The heroes execute 'pulpit prostitutes' who compromise with Republican leaders; they complain that 'the Jewish takeover of the Christian churches ... [is] virtually complete.' That is, they condemn NCR leaders for inadequate commitment to Dominion theology and excessive support for Israel. Such support is anathema for the splinter of the far right called the Christian Identity movement, which teaches that the true identity of the Bible's chosen people is Anglo-Saxon and that Jews are the 'spawn of Satan.'[43]

Almost everyone would consider such ideas noxious. However, it is equally clear that other forms of end-times belief are fairly innocuous. One preacher saw a rise in overdue library books as a sign of Christ's imminent return. Your airline companion may be reading *Left Behind* with no more political agenda than passengers who are reading Stephen King novels or watching *The X-Files* as their in-flight movie. Consider the end-times believers who watched *The PTL Club*, a television show hosted by Jim and Tammy Faye Bakker in the 1980s. PTL stands for 'Praise the Lord' and 'People That Love.' The Bakkers' show was a Christian version of *Oprah*, and their empire included an amusement park called Heritage USA that was a Christian version of Disneyland. Like many of their viewers, Jim and Tammy were raised in a Pentecostal sub-culture that taught them to shun 'the world' – not attend movies, not to use make-up, and so on. However, by their heyday they modeled for their viewers how to use Pentecostal teachings about God's blessing to blend seamlessly into a world of middle-class consumerism. They represent a classic case of what we earlier called Pentecostal pragmatism as opposed to primitivism. Jim told his viewers not simply to ask God for a Cadillac, but to tell God the exact color it should be.[44]

Unfortunately PTL took this to such extremes – for example, using donations to buy an air-conditioned doghouse, a yacht, and a pet giraffe – that it provoked a backlash. Like many other evangelists, Bakker used a seed-faith fundraising approach. That is, he taught that anyone who made a gift to God could expect this seed to grow into a yield of material blessings. In effect, donating to PTL was partly like offering a hopeful prayer, but also like investing in a lucrative stock. Bakker pushed this model so hard that the lines blurred between asking viewers to support a program they valued (as National Public Radio does during pledge drives), inviting viewers to invest in PTL through seed-faith gifts, and making fraudulent guarantees of future vacations at Heritage USA in apartments that PTL promised to build with the donations. We might compare his vision to the promises of future growth made – on a larger scale – by Enron Corporation. Just as Enron's financial house of cards collapsed, so did PTL's, and the question arose whose fault it was – the company's for making promises it could not keep or investors' for believing these promises. Jim Bakker wound up in jail, and today Tammy Faye is better known among college students for appearing on an MTV reality show than for her work on PTL. One of the few people who benefited from PTL's debacle was Falwell. He gained control of PTL by presenting himself as a father figure who could put its house in order, and wound up appropriating its communications satellite.

The point we must grasp is that both Tammy Faye and Timothy McVeigh are part of end-times discourse. When Tammy appeared on television after PTL's collapse and sang, 'When Life Gives You a Lemon, Start Making Lemonade,' her song included a line about 'being pruned by

God's blade.'[45] Fans could recognize this line as Biblical prophetic motif and recall how PTL had talked about Christ's return along with vacations at Heritage USA. But in this case, if end-times theology is supposed to be otherworldly and defined by a sense of fighting God's enemies – then exactly what did PTL viewers fight, other than a sense that they were not yet as comfortable as Tammy in the world of consumerism? If an evangelical sub-culture is supposed to be defined by its distance from and embattlement with dominant culture, doesn't the boundary of the PTL sub-culture appear less like the perimeter of a paramilitary compound and more like a wave that ripples off and disappears somewhere near a shopping mall?

In light of this range of meanings, the question arises: where do the heavy-hitters of end-times discourse like LaHaye and Robertson fall on this continuum, and how do ordinary readers in pews and airplanes interpret them? To begin, it is clear that some sectors of the NCR shade into the less radical parts of the extreme right. This does not mean that *The Turner Diaries* reveals the pure essence of prophecy that will naturally ripen into action for serious believers; NCR leaders worked hard to distance themselves from it. Nevertheless – approaching this question from the far right looking toward the center – the same far-right network that produced McVeigh also produced the former KKK leader David Duke, who won the Republican nomination and fifty-five per cent of the white vote for governor of Louisiana in the 1990s. Approaching from the NCR establishment looking right, Robertson's book, *The New World Order*, recycled key arguments from the *Protocols of the Elders of Zion*, albeit with fewer Jews and more New Agers in its conspiracy. Written shortly after the fall of the Soviet Union when George Bush, Sr., spoke about building a new world order, Robertson stated that Bush's participation in the Trilateral Commission and his co-operation with the United Nations in the Persian Gulf War were part of a Satanic conspiracy to institute 'an occult-inspired world socialist dictatorship.' For his part, LaHaye is a major NCR leader who has stated that public schools teach youth to be 'anti-God, anti-moral, anti-family, anti-free enterprise, and anti-American'; he blames ruling 'educrats' controlled by a web that includes the National Endowment for the Humanities, the Trilateral Commission, and the Illuminati.[46]

It is also clear that prophetic scenarios reinforce isolationism and unilateralism – as well as nationalism, although only insofar as government leaders are seen as Biblically sound. In books like *Left Behind*, when US leaders capitulate to the anti-Christ, the duty of believers is to disobey them, even to the extent of treason and armed resistance. In Robertson's *End of the Age* – a book that restated the themes of *New World Order* in a novel with a similar plot – a heroic Christian general lies to the President and secedes from the US with several nuclear bases. With God's help, he battles a world government headquartered in Iraq that worships the Hindu 'demon' Shiva.[47] End-times books teach that cosmic history depends on faithful disciples – especially, although not exclusively from the US – refusing to co-operate with the United Nations. As one scholar summarizes, within end-times discourse 'treaties, alliances, and participation in the UN all pave the way for the coming of the anti-Christ ... [who] unites the world to form a One World Government.'[48] He promises peace – thus duping ignorant people like the head of a seminary portrayed in *End of the Age* who says that the anti-Christ represents everything that liberal Christians had expected in the Messiah. However, once the anti-Christ gains power, he tries to kill everyone who will not worship him. In most versions of the plot, believers escape the tribulation by being raptured before it starts. However, *Left Behind* is an exception to this rule, and we have seen how believers debate whether to stockpile arms for fighting in the tribulation. The plot always ends with Jesus returning to win a cosmic battle, either by turning the tide in a war fought by Christians or fighting the war himself.

It is difficult to assess the political impact of end-times prophecy compared with other factors. Clearly it plays some role in shaping public attitudes. At a minimum it inflects the climate of discussion and helps to block roads not taken, especially in US policies toward Israel. At times it has been part of high-level discussions. Reagan's end-times beliefs were a factor in his ideas about the Cold War and the support he garnered from the NCR. Robertson is prominent in Republican politics. George W. Bush has made many religiously inflected comments about the Iraq war. He spoke of a crusade against radical Islam after the attacks of 11 September 2001, and he continues to speak about a global war between good and evil in a way that implies a contrast between Western Christian values and much of the Muslim world. Whether or not Bush actually stated that 'God told me to strike at al-Qaeda and I struck them, and then he instructed me to strike at Saddam, which I did' (either this report or Bush's denial of it is a lie) he made it clear to advisors that he felt 'God put me here' to pursue his Middle East policies.[49]

Bush's comments are in dialogue with the sixty per cent per cent of

US citizens who say that they expect Biblical prophecies to come true and the twenty-five per cent who say that the Bible predicted the attacks of 9/11.[50] Recall how we discussed the relation between the Puritan ethic and the rise of capitalism; neither caused the other, but the two reinforced each other. Likewise, end-times belief – with its nationalism, self-righteousness, dualism, and possible fatalism – does not shape US foreign policy by itself. Nor is it merely a reflection of deeper processes in US policies, for example, in the anti-Christs it targets in any given year. The point is that together they form a mutually reinforcing world-view that powerfully motivates believers and is difficult to refute in conventional rational terms.

A key interpretive problem, however, is that the continuum of end-times belief does not simply run from McVeigh through Robertson to Bush – it keeps running to the center and all the way through Huey Long to Bob Marley on the left. Moreover, people traveling this route can get sidetracked at the mall with Tammy Faye anywhere along the way. End-times beliefs can be compartmentalized, fade into the mix of other concerns, or become diluted. We have noted that apocalyptic theology dovetailed with anti-Communism in Billy Graham's sermons. At the same time as we take Graham's melding of the Cold War and the Bible with the utmost seriousness – if Graham made people more fatalistic about the question of whether nuclear war was inevitable, what issue could be more weighty? – we might also notice that by the 1980s the super-market tabloid *Weekly World News* published a story about Graham's end-times book, *Approaching Hoofbeats*. Although this story was full of easily corroborated facts about the book, it ran it alongside another story about an asteroid that (according to the tabloid's 'reporter') was the literal location of hell and would probably crash into the earth in the year 2000. Another article in the same issue, receiving equal billing with Graham, was entitled 'Shoplifter Stuffs 4-lb. Frozen Chicken Down Her Bra ... Then Passes Out from the Cold.'[51]

The point I am trying to accent is that end-times believers fight God's enemies in many ways, from the chillingly political to the utterly trivial and many points in between. Most evangelical sermons are closer to Tammy Faye than to Timothy McVeigh, especially by the time that they filter down to supermarket lines. What we don't know, and can't know without case-by-case investigation, is how this plays out in the inter-play between authors like LaHaye and his readers. To what extent does imagining oneself fighting God's enemies represent a utopian critique of capitalism, to what extent a distraction from social issues, and to what extent a death wish? What would it mean to someone who watched *Left Behind* during the same week that she also watched *The Matrix*, worked at a minimum wage job, talked to her lesbian cousin, was sexually harassed, took offense when her pastor said that her Pakistani co-worker was going to hell, and danced to R.E.M.'s song, 'It's the end of the world as we know it, and I feel fine'? How would this all fit together, pull apart, or co-exist in separate compartments? We do not have good answers to such questions. We need to inquire further about this issue.

Notes

1 Ralph Luker, *The Social Gospel in Black and White* (Chapel Hill: University of North Carolina Press, 1991); Evelyn Brooks Higginbotham, *Righteous Discontent: the Women's Movement in the Black Baptist Church, 1880–1920* (Cambridge, MA: Harvard University Press, 1993); Michael Rogin, *Ronald Reagan, the Movie and Other Episodes in Political Demonology* (Berkeley: University of California Press, 1987).

2 Jeffrey Moran, 'Reading race into the Scopes Trial: African American elites, science, and fundamentalism,' *Journal of American History* vol. 90, no. 3 (2003), 891–911; Michael Rogin, *Blackface, White Noise: Jewish Immigrants in the Hollywood Melting Pot* (Berkeley: University of California Press, 1996); Tom Engelhardt, *The End of Victory Culture: Cold War America and the Disillusioning of a Generation* (2nd edn) (Amherst: University of Massachusetts Press, 1998).

3 George Hutchinson, *The Harlem Renaissance in Black and White* (Cambridge, MA: Harvard University Press, 1996); James Baldwin, *The Fire Next Time* (New York: Dell, 1964); John Coltrane, *A Love Supreme* (Impulse Records 1964); Alice Walker, *The Color Purple* (New York: Simon and Schuster, 1982).

4 In addition to texts already cited see Gayraud Wilmore, *Black Religion and Black Radicalism* (2nd edn) (Maryknoll: Orbis, 1984); John Hope Franklin and August Meier, eds, *Black Leaders of the Twentieth Century* (Urbana: University of Illinois Press, 1982); Taylor Branch, *Parting the Waters: America in the King Years, 1954–63* (New York: Simon and Schuster, 1988).

5 Brenda Gayle Plummer, ed., *Window on Freedom: Race, Civil Rights, and Foreign Affairs, 1945–1988* (Chapel Hill: University of North Carolina Press, 2003).

6 Doug McAdam, *Political Process and the Development of Black Insurgency, 1930–1970* (Chicago: University of Chicago Press, 1982).

7 Charles Marsh, *God's Long Summer: Stories of Faith and Civil Rights* (Princeton: Princeton University Press, 1997); Michael Friedland, *Lift Up Your Voice Like a Trumpet: White Clergy and the Civil Rights and Antiwar Movements* (Chapel Hill: University of North Carolina Press, 1998); John McGreevy, *Parish Boundaries: the Catholic Encounter with Race in the Twentieth Century Urban North* (Chicago: University of Chicago Press, 1996).

8 Hans Baer and Merrill Singer, *African-American Religion in the Twentieth Century: Varieties of Protest and Accommodation* (Knoxville: University of Tennessee Press, 1992); Anthony Pinn, *Varieties of Black Religious Experience* (Minneapolis: Fortress Press, 1998).

9 Michelle Goldberg, 'We shall overcome ... liberals,' accessed 1/9/06, at http://salon.com/news/feature/2006/01/09/justice_sunday/.

10 Malcolm X with Alex Haley, *Autobiography of Malcolm X* (New York: Ballantine, 1999); Sonsyrea Tate, *Little X: Growing Up in the Nation of Islam* (Knoxville: University of Tennessee Press, 2004); William Van Deburg, *New Day in Babylon: the Black Power Movement and American Culture, 1965–1975* (Chicago: University of Chicago Press, 1992); Joe Wood, ed., *Malcolm X in Our Own Image* (New York: St. Martin's Press, 1992).

11 Henry Louis Gates, Jr., 'Farrakhan speaks: a conversation with Louis Farrakhan,' *Transition*, 70 (1996), 140–67; Felicia Miyakawa, *Five Percenter Rap: God Hop's Music, Message, and Black Muslim Mission* (Bloomington: Indiana University Press, 2005).

12 Murphy, *Santería*: Karen McCarthy Brown, *Mama Lola: a Vodou Priestess in New York* (Berkeley: University of California Press, 1991); George Brandon, 'Sacrificial practices in Santería,' in Holloway, *Africanisms in American Culture*, 119–47.

13 This ruling established a weak precedent because it held that laws restricting religious freedom were permissible if they applied equally to all citizens; thus a new law could criminalize any slaughter of animals except in licensed facilities. In a related decision noted above, the court permitted the firing of Native Americans who failed a drug test after they used peyote in prayer ceremonies, since the purpose of anti-drug laws was not to target religion. See Robert Drinan and Jennifer Huffman, 'Religious freedom and the *Oregon v. Smith* and *Hialeah* cases,' *Journal of Church and State* no. 35 (1993), 19–35.

14 Hilton Als et al., *Without Sanctuary: Lynching Photography in America* (Santa Fe: Twin Palms Publishers, 2000).

15 Michael Omi and Howard Winant, *Racial Formation in the United States from the 1960s to the 1980s* (2nd edn) (New York: Routledge, 1992); Lipsitz, *Possessive Investment in Whiteness*.

16 Diamond, *Roads to Dominion*; George Marsden, ed., *Evangelicalism and Modern America* (Grand Rapids: Eerdmans, 1984); Carpenter, *Revive Us Again*; William McLoughlin, *Billy Graham: Revivalist in a Secular Age* (New York: Ronald Press, 1960).

17 Discussed in Susan Harding, *The Book of Jerry Falwell: Fundamentalist Language and Politics* (Princeton: Princeton University Press, 2000) – a book that nevertheless is an example of overplaying the contrast between evangelical political engagement before and after the 1970s.

18 Figures from Esther Kaplan, *With God on Their Side: George W. Bush and the Christian Right* (New York: New Press, 2005), 73. On the evangelical political spectrum see Robert Booth Fowler, *A New Engagement: Evangelical Political Thought, 1966–1976* (Grand Rapids: Eerdmans, 1982). On the NCR see Wilcox, *Onward Christian Soldiers* and Linda Kintz and Julia Lesage, eds, *Media, Culture, and the Religious Right* (Minneapolis: University of Minnesota Press, 1998).

19 Gary Bauer speaking on religious television in 2003, cited in Kaplan, *With God on Our Side*, 75.

20 Cited in Bruce Lincoln, *Holy Terrors: Thinking About Religion After September 11* (Chicago: University of Chicago Press, 2003), 104–7; Peter Carlson, 'Falwell: I misspoke' *Knoxville News Sentinel*, 11/24/01, C1.

21 'SBC approves family statement' *Christian Century*, 6/1/7/98, 602. For context

see Nancy Ammerman, *Baptist Battles: Social Change and Religious Conflict in the Southern Baptist Convention* (New Brunswick: Rutgers University Press, 1990) and Bill Leonard, 'A crumbling empire,' in *Religion in the Contemporary South*, Corrie Norman and Don Armentrout, eds (Knoxville: University of Tennessee Press, 2005), 75–88.

22 Hulsether, *Building a Protestant Left*, 135–40. On later developments see Cornel West and Michael Lerner, *Jews and Blacks: a Dialogue of Race, Religion, and Culture in America* (New York: Plume Books, 1996); Lerner, *The Left Hand of God: Taking Back our Country From the Religious Right* (San Francisco: HarperSanFrancisco, 2006); Laura Levitt, *Jews and Feminism: the Ambivalent Search for Home* (New York: Routledge, 1997).

23 King, 'Letter from Birmingham City Jail,' in *Testament of Hope: the Essential Writings of Martin Luther King, Jr.*, James Washington, ed. (New York: Harper and Row, 1986), 289–302. See also James Findlay, *Church People in the Struggle: the National Council of Churches and the Black Freedom Movement* (New York: Oxford University Press, 1993).

24 Mitchell Hall, 'CALCAV and religious opposition to the Vietnam War,' in *Give Peace a Chance: Exploring the Vietnam Antiwar Movement*, Melvin Small and William Hoover, eds (Syracuse: Syracuse University Press, 1992), 35–52.

25 Later Berrigan entered a nuclear weapons plant and damaged a missile's nose cone with a sledgehammer, thus symbolically beating swords into plowshares. He considered this act analogous to sabotaging a Nazi death camp and tried to use his trial as a forum to declare the arms race criminal under international law. Berrigan often worked with his brother Phillip on such projects; see William Van Etten Casey, ed., *The Berrigans* (New York: Avon, 1971), who cites the poem, 60, and Phillip Berrigan, *Fighting the Lamb's War: Skirmishes with the American Empire* (Monroe: Common Courage Press, 1996).

26 Christian Smith, *Resisting Reagan: The U.S. Central America Peace Movement* (Chicago: University of Chicago Press, 1996).

27 Warren Goldstein, *William Sloane Coffin: a Holy Impatience* (New Haven: Yale University Press, 2004).

28 Among many worthy 'evening stopover' topics that did not make it into our tour, one of the most interesting is gender contestation among evangelicals in recent years. Some of the evangelical stress on male headship in the family functions as a fig leaf covering male egos as they make a *de facto* retreat to presupposing rough gender equity in economic power and decision-making. A classic locus for analyzing this issue is the men's movement called Promise Keepers; see Donna Minkowitz, 'In the name of the Father,' *Ms.* (November/December 1995), 64–71 and Dane Claussen, ed., *Standing on the Promises: the Promise Keepers and the Revival of Manhood* (Cleveland: Pilgrim Press, 2000). See also Sally Gallagher, *Evangelical Identity and Gendered Family Life* (New Brunswick: Rutgers Universty Press, 2003), R. Marie Griffith, *God's Daughters: Evangelical Women and the Power of Submission* (Berkeley: University of California Press, 2000) and Judith Stacey and Susan Elizabeth Gerard, 'We are not doormats: the influence of feminism on contemporary Evangelicals,' in *Uncertain Terms: Negotiating Gender in American Culture*, Faye Ginsburg and Anna Lowenhaupt Tsing, eds (Boston: Beacon Press, 1990), 98–117.

29 Jackson Carroll et al., *Women of the Cloth: a New Opportunity for Churches* (San Francisco: Harper and Row, 1981); Conrad Cherry, *Hurrying Toward Zion: Univer-*

sities, Divinity Schools, and American Protestantism (Bloomington: Indiana University Press, 1995), 250–3.

30 Theodora Wells, 'Woman – which includes men, of course,' photocopy in author's possession, ca. 1980.

31 Daly, *The Church and the Second Sex* (2nd edn) (New York: Harper and Row, 1975), 6. A concise introduction to Daly's work is her 'Sin Big,' *New Yorker*, 11/26/96, 76–88.

32 For a range of approaches see Rebecca Alpert, ed., *Voices of the Religious Left: A Contemporary Sourcebook* (Philadephia: Temple University Press, 2000); Marc Ellis and Otto Maduro, eds, *Expanding the View: Gustavo Gutierrez and the Future of Liberation Theology* (Maryknoll: Orbis, 1990); Rebecca Chopp and Sheila Greeve Davaney, eds, *Horizons in Feminist Theology: Identity, Tradition, and Norms* (Minneapolis: Fortress Press, 1997). Good introductions are Cornel West, *Democracy Matters: Winning the Fight Against Imperialism* (New York: Penguin, 2004) and Dorothee Soelle, *Thinking About God* (Philadelphia: Trinity Press International, 1990).

33 Soelle, 'Continuing the discussion: a politicized Christ' *C&C*, 3/19/79, 50, 51–2.

34 Paul Boyer, *When Time Shall Be No More: Prophecy Belief in Modern American Culture* (Cambridge: Harvard University Press, 1992), ix. Some paragraphs in this section are adapted from my review essay on Boyer, 'It's the end of the world as we know it,' *American Quarterly* vol. 48, no. 2 (1996), 375–84. See also Bruce Forbes and Jeanne Kilde eds, *Rapture, Revelation and the End Times* (New York: Palgrave Macmillan, 2004).

35 Boyer, *When Time Shall Be No More*, 133.

36 Boyer, *When Time Shall Be No More*; Dwight Wilson, *Armageddon Now! The Premillennarian Response to Russia and Israel Since 1917* (Grand Rapids: Baker Book House, 1977).

37 Local religious broadcast on channel 99, Knoxville, Tennessee cable television, 3/16/97.

38 On alternative uses of apocalyptic see Peter Linebaugh, 'Jubilating: or, how the Atlantic working class used the Biblical jubilee against capitalism, with some success,' *Radical History Review* no. 50 (1991), 143–82 and Wojcik, *End of the World as We Know It*.

39 *Kingfish: the Story of Huey Long* (Turner Pictures Worldwide, 1995.) For Long's own words, see his 1934 pamphlet, *Share Our Wealth* (Indian Mills, WV, 1980).

40 Diamond, *Roads to Dominion*. The text quoted is Luke 19:13 (King James Version). The context for these words is a story about a master – typically interpreted as Jesus – who gives his servants money and a command with a disputed meaning; the *New Revised Standard Version* translates it as 'Do business with these until I come back.'

41 Boyer, *When Time Shall Be No More*, 319; Heather Hendershott, *Shaking the World for Jesus: Media and Conservative Evangelical Culture* (Chicago: University of Chicago Press, 2004), 176–209.

42 Andrew MacDonald, *The Turner Diaries* (2nd edn) (copyright William Pierce, 1978; Hillsboro, WV: National Vanguard Books, 1995), 71, 160–1, 207.

43 MacDonald, *Turner Diaries*, 64. For more on these issues see Michael Barkun, *Religion and the Racist Right* (revised edn) (Chapel Hill: University of North Carolina Press, 1997).

44 Frances Fitzgerald, 'Jim and Tammy,' *New Yorker*, 4/23/90, 45–87. For more in

this vein see Carol Flake, *Redemptorama: Culture, Politics, and the New Evangelicalism* (New York: Penguin, 1984).

45 Tammy Faye Messner (her name after remarriage) on *The Shirley Show*, video recording in author's possession, n/d, ca. 1994.

46 Pat Robertson, *The New World Order* (Dallas: Word Publishing, 1991), 92; for a critique see Michael Lind, 'Rev. Robertson's Grand International Conspiracy Theory,' *New York Review of Books* (2/2/95), 21–5. LaHaye quoted in Bivins, *Fracture of Good Order*, 95.

47 Pat Robertson, *The End of the Age: a Novel* (Dallas: Word Publishing, 1996). His conflation of Muslims and Hindus, like a related conflation of New Agers and secular rationalists in *New World Order*, is an extreme example of the evangelical tendency to divide the world into two basic camps – Christians versus everyone else.

48 Amy Johnson Frykholm, in Forbes and Kilde, *Rapture, Revelation and the End Times*, 169.

49 Melani McAlister, *Epic Encounters: Culture, Media, and US Interests in the Middle East, 1945–2000* (Berkeley: University of California Press, 2001). See also Garry Wills, *Reagan's America* (New York, Penguin: 1988) and Rogin, *Ronald Reagan, the Movie*. Bush quote reported by Mahmoud Abbas and cited in Kaplan, *With God on Their Side*, 9; Seymour Hersh, 'Up in the Air,' *New Yorker* 12/5/05, 43. Bush later distanced himself from the crusade remark, since it worked at cross-purposes with a stress on universal values of freedom that can be shared by Muslims who support global capitalism and Western-style democracy.

50 2002 Time/CNN poll cited in Bill Moyers, 'Environmental Armageddon,' accessed at *http://www.beliefnet.com/story/161/story_16143_1.html*.

51 Graham, *Approaching Hoofbeats: the Four Horsemen of the Apocalypse* (New York: Avon, 1985); *Weekly World News*, 4/15/79, 2–3, 8–9, and 21.

CHAPTER 7

Cultural Aspects of Religion from World War II to the Present

As we near the end of our trip, many goals compete for a dwindling amount of time. We have loose ends to tie up from earlier discussions, cruel choices among many worthwhile issues we could explore in our last mid-day breaks, and a need for closure. Accordingly, this chapter is divided into short sections so that we can address more issues before running out of space. We begin with two cases of Christians responding to changes of the late twentieth century, then continue with cases that touch on several groups – including Buddhists, Muslims, New Agers, Native Americans, and Christians – responding to consumer culture, racial issues, and culture war.

Creationism and the Emergence of a Postmodern Evangelicalism

Evangelicals wrestled with change in many ways besides their political activities discussed above; a fascinating example is their ongoing debate with evolutionists.[1] When we last left this story, fundamentalists were widely seen as having lost this battle at the Scopes Trial. Yet these 'primates from the upland valleys of the Cumberland' largely won their war with evolutionists – or at least negotiated a truce they could live with – by pressuring textbook publishers to touch lightly on evolution. This truce depended on creationists teaching that each 'day' in the Genesis story referred to a long age of biological change (day-age creationism) or that there was a gap between the beginning of time and the creation of Adam and Eve. If so, fundamentalists did not have to reject all evidence about the earth's age; they could grant that evolutionary theories made sense of evidence such as fossils, mutating strains of the flu, or changes within species such as dogs. Moreover, many neo-evangelicals came to agree with their modernist adversaries about theistic evolution, or the idea that God works through the evolutionary process.[2]

If we count theistic evolution, there were actually three camps in this war: strict creationists who deny the validity of evolutionary theory; scientists who deny the validity of creationism; and people in the middle who defend forms of religion that are consistent with science. Consider how science can make true statements describing human bodies in terms of DNA while artists can make true statements in a language of poetry. Likewise, religions can do so with languages of theology and ritual. The point is not that they describe different phenomena – science treating bodies and religion treating supernatural phenomena – but that they approach the same embodied life in complementary ways. Insofar as people think about God in ways consistent with evolution – for example, if they understand 'God' as a term for creative forces immanent within natural processes – and do not attempt to replace evolution with theology in science classrooms, the war between religion and evolution dissolves.

For creationists who rejected this compromise as too liberal, the truce with Darwinism fell apart in the 1960s and war resumed. Textbooks began to present evolution forthrightly – thus ensuring a prominent place for science alongside school prayer, desegregation, and secularism in NCR complaints about public education. In West Virginia one conflict about teaching evolution rose to the level of armed resistance. Meanwhile, many fundamentalists repudiated day-age creationism and adopted a strict theory of young earth creationism (YEC) which held that the Genesis account of God creating the earth less than 10,000 years ago was literally true, that the fossil record could be explained by the story of Noah and the flood, and that Noah carried baby dinosaurs on the ark. YEC is widely taught in evangelical schools and has given rise to a network of touring speakers, think thanks, and creationist museums.

Creationists amazed and infuriated scientists by winning the battle for public opinion. Today forty-five per cent of citizens believe that 'God created man pretty much in his present form at one time during the past 10,000 years,' and forty per cent more believe that God guided an evolutionary process. Only thirteen per cent embrace natural selection without any role for God. George W. Bush has called on schools to teach creationism, and a third of citizens tell pollsters that they want it taught instead of evolution in science classes.[3] However, YEC has been utterly unconvincing to scientists and judges, who have struck down a succession of efforts to teach it in public schools – in Arkansas (1968), Louisiana (1987), Kansas (1999), and Pennsylvania (2005) among others.

In an attempt to move beyond YEC's political and intellectual impasse, the intelligent design (ID) movement arose as a more sophisticated form of creationism. ID revisits classic philosophical arguments for God's existence, highlights limits to the forms of knowledge that science can find, and holds that certain forms of life cannot be explained by evolution, but only by hypothesizing an intelligent designer. Most proponents of ID are evangelicals who assume that this designer is the Christian God; they would be outraged if their children were taught Raelian theories of creation by extra-terrestrials or NOI theories of an evil scientist breeding a race of white devils. However, they propose to remain agnostic about the identity of the designer in school curricula. To maintain this supposed neutrality and some academic plausibility, their theories are quite abstract, sometimes shading off toward theistic evolution.

Scientists overwhelmingly agree not only that YEC is bankrupt as a theory to account for biological and geological evidence, but also that ID fails as an explanation for scientific evidence, even at its most sophisticated. Many perceive ID as a Trojan horse to smuggle YEC into classrooms. Thus, courts have so far rejected the teaching of both YEC and ID in biology and anthropology classes. Introducing ID's philosophical arguments alongside other approaches in classes on comparative religion, cultural history, or philosophy of science might be a different matter. However, such classes would probably become *de facto* evangelical catechism sessions in many schools, and if so they will face constitutional challenges.

Although both YEC and ID are equally unsuitable for science classrooms, they have major differences as religious stances. ID rejects two of the doctrines that Bryan was most concerned to defend at the Scopes Trial – the literal truth of Genesis (since ID assumes an ancient earth and focuses on things like God designing a bacterial flagellum early in the evolutionary process, rather than God creating Adam from dust) and the need to oppose evolutionary models of thinking (since ID combs the scientific literature in an effort to find chinks in its armor, with the result that it presupposes much of the scientific common wisdom). Thus, it is both surprising and revealing that the friction between YEC and ID has been limited so far. The ID movement faces a dilemma: its political muscle comes from people who value it as a Trojan horse for YEC, but its scholarly credibility depends on breaking unambiguously with YEC and highlighting the parts of ID theory that overlap with sophisticated forms of theistic evolution.

Either way, ID unsettles the stereotype of evangelicals as backward-looking anti-modernists who refuse to engage with emerging trends.

Whereas the Scopes Trial involved creationists who criminalized the teaching of evolution outright, creationists now *presuppose* the teaching of evolution and seek equal time for alternative theories. Proponents of ID use postmodern theory to question the adequacy of modern universalism and expand the range of valid scientific paradigms. They propose that different discourses – including fundamentalist ones – can be equally valid for different communities that work with different sets of evidence. We might compare how alternative systems of medicine challenge orthodox doctors' monopoly on knowledge about the body; they assume that many valid theories of healing can coexist.

Note that one could accept this general framework of thinking but still refuse to grant that ID mounts persuasive arguments within the framework. After all, there are many forms of alternative medicine, from discredited theories of bloodletting to sophisticated theories of acupuncture. Evolution may be 'just a theory,' but it has explanatory power comparable to the theory of gravity, whereas ID has been unproductive as a paradigm to generate new scientific knowledge. One ramification of the push to teach creationism on an equal basis with evolution is to erode an already embattled distinction between facts in a so-called reality-based community, on the one hand, as opposed to 'facts' that are fabricated for political reasons on the other hand. For example, many NCR leaders deny the evidence of global warming. Scientists point to a mountain of evidence about a crisis that can hardly be underestimated, and the NCR responds, 'Well, it's only a theory; we have a different theory.' To the alarm of scientists, NCR activists in the Bush administration have worked – with considerable success – not only to block environmental initiatives but also to promote abstinence-only sex education, defund research on HIV, restrict access to emergency contraception, throw away surplus embryonic stem cells that are urgently needed for research, and manipulate decisions of science advisory boards.[4]

Whatever the fate of ID, evangelicals have come a long way since the Scopes Trial. Ethnographer Susan Harding's visit to a creationist museum at Falwell's Liberty University dramatizes the transformation. At first the museum stuck her as an 'oxymoronic beast with the body of the fossil record and the head of the Book of Genesis.' It 'seemed willfully amateurish,' but at least it left 'the impression that creation scientists literally believe what they say they believe.' However, this was before Harding noticed a display that parodied scientific arguments of all kinds – both mainstream and creationist – with such items as a 'bird's nest containing a fragment of Noah's diary (*Birdis Nestialis Noahinsis*)' and bones sticking out of plaster of paris which purported to show two dinosaurs, a chicken, a human, an eel, and other creatures being trampled in a rush to board Noah's ark. Harding alluded to a famous anthropologist who pondered how an observer could tell whether someone is twitching, winking, practicing a wink, or parodying a wink. She wrote: 'Midway through [the display] about animals "trampled on the way to the ark," the museum winked at me. Or did it blink? Or, God forbid, was it a parody of a wink? ... I was no longer absolutely certain that these fundamentalists simply believed what they said they believed.' Harding relates this insight to a larger analysis of how Falwell's rhetoric drew people into his worldview. However far-fetched his ideas seemed to secularists, he persuaded his followers to enter a discursive world that was less anti-modern than post-modern: 'multistoried, code-switching ... playful, and confident.'[5]

Debates about Accepting Gay and Lesbian People

We have discussed how religious people debated about gender as they came to terms with the growing equality of women. NCR leaders typically resisted these changes or made only the minimal adjustments that they could not avoid, such as muting their opposition to women entering the paid workforce. Often the NCR became obsessed with blocking female ordination, resisting feminists, and promoting 'Biblical values' that they saw as requiring heterosexual nuclear families with male heads. Meanwhile, liberal churches and synagogues increasingly took the gains of second-wave feminism for granted. Although these denominations exhibited more than enough inertia to frustrate feminists – especially when they spent more effort placating neo-conservatives than moving forward with liberal agendas – they largely embraced women's ordination and moved toward other forms of gender equality.

Whereas these were becoming settled patterns by the turn of the century, issues related to equal treatment of gays, lesbians, bisexuals, and transgendered (GLBT) people – both in the larger society and within religious institutions – remained unsettled. A vague awareness of closeted gay people had lurked near the margins of mainstream consciousness for years, but the movement to bring GLBT issues unapologetically out of the closet, combat hate crimes, and repeal discriminatory laws brought much homophobic discomfort to the surface. Even in denominations that had long ordained women, efforts to ordain openly gay people or support gay marriage led to firestorms of controversy. Neo-conservatives and most evangelicals held that the Bible condemned homosexuality as impure, that marriage required heterosexuality because God ordained it to produce children, and that only heterosexuality was natural while all other forms of sexual desire were sinful. Whether such sin involved a willful choice to indulge a perverse form of lust or was more like being born with a chronic disease, they felt that Christians must keep their teaching clear – the Bible must judge human moral codes and theories about 'normal' sexuality, not vice versa. Positions ranged all the way from calls to institute a death penalty for gays, through 'ex-gay' ministries that used prayer and psychological therapy to 'heal' gays (or at least help them keep their temptations in check like alcoholics use Alcoholics Anonymous), to the gentler stance of 'hating the sin but loving the sinner.' The latter approach, popular among moderates, welcomed GLBT people on the sole condition of acknowledging that their queer sins were on a par with straight sins like sloth, greed, and heterosexual lust. The NCR seized upon GLBT issues as a wedge issue to split blacks and Catholics from Democrats – it trumpeted the idea that anti-discrimination laws (framed as 'special rights' for gays) and gay marriage represented an assault on the family and collapse of moral standards.[6]

At the end of the century, religious liberals were tired of debating these issues. They perceived that arguments against ordaining gays paralleled earlier arguments against ordaining women (because the Bible was seen to demand a subordinate place for both in a patriarchal system) and divorced people (because the Bible condemns divorce more clearly than homosexuality and both were seen as unsuitable role models). They were also tired of GLBT controversies crowding out other priorities. However, conservatives remained agitated. It did not seem to matter whether liberals were blasé or militant about the issue – either response enraged the NCR. GLBT issues split mainline denominations down the middle and became a major topic of discussion, even overshadowing the Iraq war and the gap between the rich and the poor. Early in the new century Methodists, Lutherans, and Presbyterians were mired in seemingly insoluble negotiations about gay marriage and ordination, and Episcopalians were near schism over the appointment of an openly gay bishop.

Let us consider how the magazine *Christianity and Crisis* (*C&C*) treated these issues, since it was a key arena for emerging discussions on the religious left and since it was more open to GLBT and feminist concerns than most kindred journals – the evangelical left *Sojourners* and the liberal Catholic *Commonweal* were both less supportive on this front despite similar perspectives on race, class, and empire. Until the 1970s *C&C* rarely addressed GLBT issues overtly, and homophobia often lurked below the surface. One example is the status of GLBT issues in a 1960s debate about the so-called 'new morality' – that is, changing stances toward premarital sex in light of the sexual revolution and its associated changes such as easier access to contraceptives and co-educational dormitories. Along with other liberal clergy, *C&C* editors engaged in a tug-of-war between their inherited logic of prophets judging sinful license and an emerging logic of celebrating embodied sexuality. Eventually they concluded that youth would ignore church teachings that were too legalistic and that it no longer made sense to insist that all sexual acts between puberty (when many people married in Biblical times) and the end of higher education (seen as a typical time for contemporary marriages) were sinful. The test of whether a sex act was moral was not the presence of a wedding ring: sex inside marriage could be coercive or alienating while sex outside it could (at its best) build up relationships in creative, responsible, and life-affirming ways. Although the guideline for permissible sex did not dissolve into 'anything goes,' it did become rather vague: the issue was whether sex would 'express and encourage the responsible behavior of the whole person' or conversely whether it 'involved exploitation.'[7] This reframed sex from mainly being a sin unless it produced children to mainly being a gift from God unless it was destructive or exploitative.

This guideline seemed to apply equally to straights and gays. *C&C* writers did say this, but they talked far less about gay sex than straight sex, with more discomfort. Before the 1970s *C&C* was typically silent about homosexuality or treated it like a disease – one that was not too debilitating and should inspire compassion rather than quarantine. By the mid-1970s, however, *C&C* was writing about GLBT movements in roughly the same terms as black power and feminism. One writer compared the founding of a gay denomination called the Metropolitan Community Church to the founding of independent black churches in the nineteenth century. In both cases, people broke with established churches because of discrimination, and in both cases they felt Jesus was in solidarity with them.[8]

Scholars defended GLBT relationships in various ways. A common argument was that natural law ethics should support GLBT rights: God had created many people gay, and 'for homosexuals it is entirely natural to love and to act homosexually.' Ethicist James Nelson argued that the actual sin in the Bible's leading proof-text for condemning gays – the story of Sodom and Gomorrah – was inhospitality to strangers and homosexual *rape*. (If it were about heterosexual rape, would people use it to condemn all straight people?) Nelson also argued that Biblical writers had no concept, either that some people had fixed same-sex orientations or that both male sperm and female eggs contributed to procreation. Consider the implication: whereas conservatives saw the Bible rejecting homosexuality in a sweeping way, Biblical writers may have seen themselves condemning willful *promiscuity* by people who were basically straight and rejecting *all* forms of non-procreative sex – including male masturbation – because they saw the waste of sperm as the murder of fully developed human seeds, somewhat like contemporary pro-lifers view abortions. The assumption that all gay sex was promiscuous dissolved, along with the assumption that masturbation was akin to murder, if one presupposed the best contemporary understandings. There was no obstacle to revising these understandings, continued Nelson, because the 'Protestant principle' of reforming traditions had led Christians to change other teachings: they had not maintained a Biblical assumption that the sun moved around the earth, nor Biblical justifications of polygamy, nor Biblical prohibitions against eating shellfish.[9]

There was a tension in Nelson's article between his appeal to fixed GLBT orientations that he took as givens and his appeal to changing cultural constructions of sexuality – continually being reshaped by the 'Protestant principle' in his formulation, or capable of being performed in many ways as explained by queer theorists. Theologian Carter Heyward addressed this tension explicitly. She highlighted the constructedness of the 'boxes' in which people perform sex/gender roles, including the categories 'gay' and 'straight.' Yet she insisted, 'These categories – boxes – are real. We live in them.' She argued that it made sense, at least for some people including herself, to identify as lesbian feminists. Being forced into a straight box short-circuited the creative power of passion and its associated drive for mutuality, which refused to flow in the directions where hegemonic sex/gender roles tried to channel it. Feminism in general, and lesbian feminism in particular, was a creative place for Heyward to situate herself as a Christian because of the way it destabilized sexism and maximized mutuality.[10]

Because such ideas were so embattled in the churches, *C&C* often reported on GLBT ordination battles. John Cobb attacked Methodist pretensions to be upholding Biblical values with a rule (mainly designed to exclude gays) that required clergy to promise 'fidelity in marriage and celibacy in singleness.' Cobb reviewed the Bible's many models for sexuality, 'from the multiple wives and concubines of the patriarchs and kings of Israel to the lifelong chastity that seems to have been favored by Jesus and Paul.' He could not find where 'the exact pattern now being proposed [including tolerance of divorce] is reflected.' Cobb asked Methodist bishops if they were sure they wanted to condemn pre-marital sex for engaged couples – which many Methodists accepted as a normal practice – and if not, whether they wanted a double standard for clergy. Did their rule reflect a lingering assumption that sex is sinful except for procreation? Did they really want a policy that could 'make no distinction between long-term faithful relationships and utter promiscuity?'[11]

For liberal Christians by the 1970s, 'the real theological problem … [was not] reconciling acceptance of homosexuality with the scriptural passages that appear to condemn it, but rather how to reconcile the condemnation of homosexuals with the criteria of morality that are truly central to the Christian message.' One writer described a friend who was dying of AIDS but could not find a sense of peace because he believed that God hated him. 'I am an atheist to the God he feared,' said the writer. 'I believe that kind of a God is a fraud [but] if that God turns out to be real, let the sucker burn me.' However, his friend saw angels at the foot of his bed – a signal that at least God, if not most US churches, had compassion for GLBT people.[12]

Religion in an Age of Consumerism

Few forms of religion were untouched as late twentieth-century US culture placed ever-higher emphasis on consumer choice and electronic communication. In some ways this trend reduced diversity, since information became more centralized and homogenized, with decisions about which ideas to promote and which to suppress shaped by corporate conglomerates. However, in other ways the situation became more decentralized and responsive to consumer desires. Products were segmented into brands catering to every market niche. For example, there were enough on-line sources of news and music that people with computers could largely choose, if they wished, to bypass mainstream sources. Similarly, a neo-pagan who felt isolated in a conservative part of the country (or who wished to remain anonymous) could participate in on-line Wiccan communities.

According to some critics, the idea that growing consumer choice creates greater diversity was actually a symptom of a deeper problem, which was that too many cultural priorities were being determined through the logic of consumerism. Critics noted that this way of determining priorities did not take place on a level playing field, but rather a field tilted toward corporate elites, white majorities, and individualistic lifestyles. Such critics could easily be tempted to despair, since they had little hope of reaching their audience except through bookstores and media outlets that entangled them in the net of commercialization they feared. According to the logic of their own arguments, any critique that gained widespread attention would be dead on arrival, already fatally compromised at the moment it reached an audience. Could there be any such thing as counter-hegemonic consumer democracy, or did the very idea of consumer democracy presuppose a consumer mentality that undermined democracy?

Both religious critics of consumerism on the right (who stressed the market's secular and hedonist logic) and the left (who stressed its corporate, individualistic, and racist logic) faced versions of this problem. Leftist critics did a better job of diagnosing the problem and (sometimes) creating pockets of community that countervailed against it though teaching simple living and working for the common good. Critics on the right were at least as vehement. They fulminated against the decadence and narcissism of baby boomers, and they also (sometimes) made efforts to countervail against it through home schooling, sheltering their children from television, and so on. However, they were less willing to consider that the free market capitalism they loved was at the root of the problem.

A scholar who surveyed the rise of commercialized religion declared New Agers 'the reigning champions of religious salesmanship.' For example, consider the lucrative market for products that promise authentic Native American wisdom. Popular books described journeys with feminist shamans or more generic hippie-style shamans, and a Vermont woman declared herself the 'keeper of the sacred Cherokee crystals' – crystals that originated on Atlantis and now have healing powers. In the world of New Age channeling, J. Z. Knight, the teacher of actress Shirley MacLaine and star of the film *What the Bleep Do We Know?* (2004), became famous as the medium for an enlightened being named Ramtha (who incidentally was MacLaine's brother in Atlantis in a past life). A judge once asked Knight to channel Ramtha in a divorce court to determine whether Ramtha was 'a god, a spirit, or a fake.'[13]

Meanwhile, in the world of Hindu gurus with counter-cultural disciples, Bhagwan Sri Rajneesh became famous for his fleet of Rolls-Royces and the permissive conception of what it meant to be a 'renouncer' in his movement. He formed an ashram in rural Oregon and tried to take over the local government before legal troubles forced him out of the country. Maharishi Mahesh Yogi, who taught a form of yogic trance called Transcendental Meditation (TM), became the guru of the world-famous musicians, The Beatles. TM built on the less commercialized Self-Realization Fellowship founded by Paramahansa Yogananda in the 1920s, which pioneered the teaching of yoga in the US through a blend of minimal Hindu devotionalism and maximal emphasis on yoga's scientific benefits. Yogananda met with President Calvin Coolidge at the White House and still has influential followers such as the head of Def Jam Records. Whatever insight and health that these gurus brought and whatever the sincerity of their disciples – matters that we should not prejudge or trivialize – their practices largely conformed to an individualized model that was more in line with personal self-actualization than with forming communities that worked against the grain of a consumer society.[14]

If Christians wanted to nominate a contender to wrest the religious salesmanship title from New Agers, one possibility is the PTL Club. 'We have a better product than soap or automobiles,' Jim Bakker stated. 'We have eternal life.' There are, however, many worthy challengers; as one scholar puts it, 'religion is everywhere' but it 'has become an ordinary commodity … Jim Bakker is Velveeta; Norman Vincent Peale is sliced Swiss in plastic wrap; Reinhold Niebuhr is Brie.'[15] Evangelical megachurches offer programs catering to every lifestyle niche: childcare centers, schools, bookstores, aerobics classes, coffeehouses, health clinics, sports leagues, television studios, soccer fields, tattoo parlors, retirement homes, and mortuaries. In Houston, a predominantly black megachurch has its own McDonald's restaurant, complete with a drive-through window and golden arches; meanwhile a white televangelist bought an auditorium formerly used by Houston's professional basketball team and spent $95 million to renovate it for his 30,000 weekly worshippers (more than the membership of the second largest branch of US Buddhism).[16] A pioneering Chicago megachurch called Willow Creek has 7,500 associated churches in twenty-five countries; if this loose network organized as a denomination it would be as large as the Episcopal Church.

Evangelicals often express themselves through such products as T-shirts based on the Coca-Cola logo that say, 'Christ, the Real Thing' or prayers that sing 'Thank You, Thank You, Jesus' to the tune of the heavy-metal anthem 'We Will Rock You.' One disaffected former evangelical set himself the challenge of creating a jingle that would be considered too over-the-top to use for such a purpose, but without being overtly crass and disrespectful in the manner of certain heavy metal songs or the satirical website that markets thong underwear with the logo 'What Would Jesus Do?' He finally settled on a lyric sung to the tune of 'Rudolph the Red-Nosed Reindeer' entitled 'Jesus, My Lord, Come Reign Here' – but, even so, he wondered if people would take the spoof seriously. If a rapper can market $50,000 diamond-encrusted pendants in the shape of Jesus's head, why not put Jesus in a song about Santa's reindeer?[17]

Such examples return us to a question posed in Chapter 4: is there anything more to this trend than religion being swallowed up by secularism in the form of religious individualism? Can religious leaders fight fire with fire in consumer markets, or do they face a lose–lose choice between trivialization (if they engage with consumerism) and irrelevance (if they do not engage with it)? Let us reflect on this question by tying up the loose ends of our story about Hollywood censorship. The system described above unraveled in the 1960s. One factor was the rise of television; another was increased free speech protection for films. Inside the censorship apparatus, priests influenced by Vatican II took over the reins at the Legion of Decency and introduced new rating categories for adults. Mainly the system collapsed under its own weight as lightweight trash based on sexual innuendo was approved while acclaimed films tackling social problems such as *The Bicycle Thief* (1948) and *The Pawnbroker* (1965) were condemned for trivial reasons. In 1966 the system was scrapped for the current rating system. This happened at the same time that Hollywood's classic studio system gave way to a decentralized distribution network and became more open to independent producers. Later, the rise of home video further decentralized the system and made effective censorship hard to imagine.

According to one study of blockbusters from 1946 to 1990, the demise of censorship had a negative effect on treatments of religion.[18] Hollywood's portrayal of religion became less sympathetic and there were fewer plots in which religious characters successfully achieved their goals. However, it is not entirely clear whether we should interpret such trends as a defeat for religion and a gain for secularization. Because the early films in this study's sample were produced under the Code, they banned unfavorable portrayals of religion outright. Thus, the ratio of positive clergy to negative ones was a perfect 100 per cent to zero per cent. Should clergy really be alarmed that after 1976 they were heroes only fifty per cent of the time? Perhaps they should be pleased that they remained heroes or mixed characters two-thirds of the time – about the same as other characters – without help from censors. Religious characters remained more likely to be good guys than other characters, and nearly as likely to succeed.

Moreover, the criteria used to generate this data were none too subtle. Some declines in religious prestige were straightforward, such as a change from *The Bells of St. Mary* (1946) featuring Bing Crosby as a saintly priest to *The Witches of Eastwick* (1987) featuring Jack Nicholson as a glamorous Satan. However, *Samson and Delilah* (1949), a dubious artistic success with a notably sexist plot, was counted as a positive portrayal of religion because it supposedly promoted Biblical literacy and taught that success comes from obeying God's will. Despite the mixed messages of *The Exorcist* (1974) – it features priests who not only help a demon-possessed girl after secular professionals fail, but even sacrifice their lives in a battle for her soul – it was counted as an unambiguously negative portrayal. Implicit in such judgments is a conservative moral: if evil is shown as getting out of control, or if good is mixed with evil, this is a step backward for 'religion.' The Code's demise opened the way for a wider range of ideas about good and evil to be screened. It also opened space for films that questioned authority.

To some degree we might interpret this story as support for the commodification approach to popular religion introduced in Chapter 4. Amid the range of films produced in any period, we could easily select examples (such as *Bells of St. Mary* and *Witches of Eastwick*) that fit this paradigm. Armed with such selections, the NCR carries forward an ideal of censorship, albeit without much power to enforce its recommendations. NCR leaders complain about Hollywood's hostility to religion and wax nostalgic for an era when Hollywood's religious characters were invariably good and usually successful.[19] However, on balance it is more illuminating to adopt an approach that showcases how films interact with religion in diverse ways and how changing standards of morality relate to struggles for hegemony. In every period some films have challenged hegemonic religious values while others have reinforced them: for example, both *Duel in the Sun* and *Keys to the Kingdom* in the 1940s, and both *Kinsey* and *The Passion of the Christ* in 2004.

Importantly, the Code was a mixed blessing for the filmed portrayal of religion in the long run. Its legacy helps to explain a backlash against religion by many films since the 1960s, the tendency of filmmakers to be cool toward religion, and the gap between Hollywood's sophisticated skills at evoking romance compared with its underdeveloped traditions for conveying spirituality. The flat-footed behavior required of religious characters under the Code still haunts the screening of religion, so that films that portray complex religious characters such as *The Apostle* (1997) and *Little Buddha* (1993) remain less influential than satires like *Life of Brian* (1979). Clergy are often portrayed as repressed killjoys, and films that paint a picture of ordinary citizens often pay more attention to schools, workplaces, and nightclubs than to churches that are equally important in real life. No doubt there are various reasons for this, but Hollywood's history of conflict with religious pressure groups is surely one of them.

At the same time, momentum remains from Hollywood's tradition of dramatizing sharp lines between good and evil and assuming that religion is on the side of the good. Such momentum is easy to see if we focus on underlying themes that many films take for granted. *Star Wars* (1977) and its invocation of 'the Force' is a classic example. We might also note the complexities of a film that conservatives loved to hate, *Leap of Faith* (1993). Although this film lampoons a corrupt faith healer, it judges him against standards of Christian virtue and *true* faith healing that are the film's core presuppositions. Although it teaches skepticism about televangelists, it assumes that sincere religion is a good thing, echoes arguments from the Bible's prophetic tradition, and redeems most of its characters.

All of this suggests the value of understanding the fate of religion in Hollywood – and by extension in other forms of entertainment – less as a story of religion being swallowed by secularization, and more as story of ongoing negotiation between many people, all of whom used media to promote their values with results that we must explore case by case. If we had more time we could introduce other cases, including examples that dramatize how counter-hegemonic religious ideas can circulate through the media. As one socially-conscious rapper comments, 'I've heard it said the revolution won't be televised/But in this land of milk and honey there's a date you've got to sell it by.' He also notes that 'I speak in schools a lot because they say that I'm intelligent/No, it's 'cause I'm dope/If I was wack I'd be irrelevant.'[20] Without giving up on communicating through the media, popular musicians of the early twenty-first century have made strong contributions to debates about politics and spirituality; their best interventions are among the most probing and critical available anywhere in the culture.

Faces of the Buddhist Sangha in America

We have noted the difficulty of generalizing about US Buddhists, given the complexity of world Buddhism and the divisions between immigrant Buddhists and converts who are largely middle -class whites.[21] Buddhism began as an offshoot of Hinduism and evolved in complex ways as it spread throughout Asia. Its Mahayana branch, which became dominant in China and Japan, introduced innovations that distinguish it from the Theravada branch that dominates in Southeast Asia. There is also a third branch (sometimes mapped as part of Mahayana) called Vajrayana or Tibetan Buddhism. It is famous for its charismatic leader, the Dalai Lama, its meditation practices that include visualization of celestial Buddhas, and its tradition of tantric yoga that includes sexual positions. Although all three branches are present in the US, two forms of Japanese Mahayana (Pure Land and Zen) arrived first and have special historic importance.[22] The upshot is a tug-of-war between three root images for 'normal' US Buddhism: immigrant forms of Pure Land; convert forms of Zen; and classic forms of Theravada monasticism that are stressed in religion textbooks but not practiced much in the US. If we combine all three into one composite image the likely result is confusion, like throwing together a classical violinist, jazz drummer, and accordionist who plays polkas. Such a threesome might jell as a group if they are all skilled musicians, but the first step is to sort out their differences.

Siddhartha Gautama, the original Buddha or enlightened one, gave a sermon summarizing the Four Noble Truths of Buddhism. He taught that life in samsara (the cycle of deaths and rebirths) is inevitably tinged by suffering and dissatisfaction, and that this suffering is caused by a craving or grasping that makes people try to hold onto things that are impermanent. Release from samsara into a state of transcendent bliss called nirvana is possible through extinguishing such craving, and Buddhist practice shows the way to accomplish this. This requires moving beyond a false sense of self, in ways somewhat similar to the Hindu goal of realizing that the Absolute is ultimately the same as the individual soul. However, Buddhists stress that no permanent immutable soul or stable divine Absolute exists; all existence is marked by change, impermanence, and a sense of 'no-self' or 'emptiness.' The world is a giant web of interconnections in which everything is related and nothing stays the same.

All Buddhists trace their history to Siddhartha's enlightenment, and all speak of taking refuge in the Buddha, the Dharma (Buddhist teaching), and the Sangha (the community of those who follow the dharma). Theravada Buddhism grew from the monastic community formed by Siddhartha's disciples, who sought to follow in the Buddha's footsteps and become monks who achieve nirvana – either in this lifetime or a later rebirth. This is the classic form of the sangha, and its ideal of solitary meditating monks (supported by local laity) anchors popular images of Buddhism.

Mahayana Buddhists made large changes in these ideals; they saw themselves drawing out the implications of earlier dharma and improving Buddhism. With respect to taking refuge in the Buddha, they taught that Siddartha did not leave the wheel of samsara after one lifetime. When he was enlightened he became identified with deeper reality, sometimes called Buddha-nature. He did not really die, and devotees have continuing access to his power and insight. Moreover, the deep truth about all beings – not only humans but even grasses and trees – is that they already have a perfect Buddha-nature. They only need to wake up to this truth. Thus, rather than one historical Buddha, there are many Buddhas. Anyone can be (and in a sense already is) a Buddha.

With respect to taking refuge in the dharma, Mayahana proposed a different ideal role model. Seeking nirvana on an individual basis was, in their view, too selfish to be consistent with the Buddha's teachings about compassion and the interdependence of all beings. The new ideal was the vow of a bodhisattva, or Buddha-to-be, to help all beings achieve enlightenment. Great bodhisattvas fulfill such vows over many lifetimes without (selfishly) leaving samsara; in the process they build up huge stores of merit that they can use to help people who ask for assistance. Thus, celestial bodhisattvas such as Amida Buddha can become God-like saviors, in some ways comparable to Jesus's role in atoning for sins in Christianity or to Hindu gods whose devotees call on them for help in bhakti. This expands the meaning of taking refuge in the Sangha beyond its classic meaning of becoming a monk. If all beings already have the Buddha-nature and ordinary people can call on bodhisattvas for help, this creates a sangha that is far more open to laity, both men and women.

These were the central teachings of the first large group of Buddhists who came to the US on a permanent basis, the Japanese Pure Land Buddhists who arrived in Hawaii and California between the late 1800s and the 1920s.[23] Pure Land traces its roots to the thirteenth-century reformer, Shinran, who felt that history had entered a stage of decline in which human self-power was inadequate for attaining nirvana. Somewhat like Luther taught that Christians could not be saved through their own works but had to rely on God's grace, Shinran taught Buddhists to call on the 'other-power' of celestial Buddhas. In particular, Amida had vowed to create a beautiful heaven in which spiritual progress was easier than on earth. People could be reborn there, no matter how bad their karma, simply by asking Amida for help. All it took was saying a prayer called the *nembutsu*. Thus, the distinction between monks and laity largely dropped away. Shinran left the monastery and married a former nun, and Pure Land developed congregational forms of worship. In time the tradition came to stress funerals and ceremonies at the graves of ancestors. Above all, it stressed faith, gratitude to Amida, and recitation of the *nembutsu*.

Pure Land temples were major community institutions for Japanese immigrants who had been recruited to provide cheap agricultural labor. They provided places not only for worship but also education and social events; often temples sponsored programs such as sports leagues and Young Men's Buddhist Associations. Along with typical concerns of first generation immigrants, such temples also faced severe racism. This reached a peak during World War II, when Japanese-Americans were rounded up and sent to concentration camps, supposedly because of doubts about their loyalty (although German and Italian immigrants did not suffer such treatment). The first Japanese arrested were Pure Land priests because of their role as community leaders. Often people were forced to sell their businesses and other property on short notice for a fraction of its value, and/or their homes and temples were vandalized.

The camps pressured diverse Japanese religious groups – Pure Land, other Buddhists, and Christians – to co-operate in ways that otherwise might not have happened. The camps also raised the push–pull dynamic of immigration to an extreme. Naturally being imprisoned made people rally behind their community and question their place in US culture, but it also increased pressure for assimilation. It disrupted traditions of generational deference because the US government did not negotiate with elders from the first immigrant generation, but rather with their sons who had been offered citizenship (unlike their parents), spoke better English, and were more open to assimilation. In the camps, Pure Land leaders decided to change their name to the Buddhist Churches of America (BCA), to call their priests reverend, and to move toward a worship style modeled on Protestantism, complete with pews, homilies, and hymns such as 'Buddha Loves Me, This I Know.' The BCA maintains links to its founding institutions in Japan; it sponsors activities like Taiko drumming and traditional festivals like *Obon* to honor ancestors. Nevertheless, it has largely assimilated into US suburban life. In recent years it has experienced membership declines somewhat like those in mainline Protestantism.

The BCA holds little appeal for whites who are interested in Buddhism because they want an alternative to Christianity that is exotic, atheistic, and focused on meditation. However, whites flocked to another form of Japanese Buddhism called Zen.[24] The roots of Zen are entwined with the rise of samurai warriors and their associated military disciplines during the Kamakura Period that corresponds loosely to the era of European feudalism. Zen monasteries stressed courage and self-discipline, and there are Zen arts of swordsmanship and archery. In general, whereas Pure Land stressed the other-power of bodhisattvas, Zen focused on harnessing self-power toward the goal of breaking through a false sense of self and reaching a state of *satori*. Although Zen evolved in multifaceted ways (like Pure Land, its temples in Japan often stress funeral rites), monastic practice was near its heart. Monasteries were male-dominated, with a stress on lineages of mind-to-mind transmission of wisdom from teachers (or *roshis*) to students. One branch stressed wrestling with conceptual puzzles called *koans*, such as 'What is the sound of one hand clapping?' Another branch stressed seated meditation.

A Zen monk spoke at the World's Parliament of Religion and one of his students named D. T. Suzuki wrote influential books that placed Zen ideas in dialogue with Western philosophy. Other writers also popularized Zen ideas; the most famous (albeit with the least claim to authority in Zen institutions) were the Beat Poets of the 1950s, especially Jack Kerouac.[25] These precursors of the 1960s counter-culture used selected Zen ideas to critique middle-class conformity. They stressed affinities between Zen and jazz – especially insofar as both stress creativity, spontaneity, and forms of concentration beyond ordinary consciousness that Zen calls 'no-mind' and athletes and musicians call 'being in a zone.' One beat poet imagined a bodhisattva taking the form of Smokey the

Bear and promoting a consciousness that would 'save the planet Earth from total oil slick,' protect anyone 'threatened by advertising, air pollution, television, or the police' and ensure that people 'will always have ripened blackberries to eat and a sunny spot under a pine tree to sit at.'[26] Such writing set the stage for Zen to become a key interest of countercultural and ecological movements after the 1960s.

By the 1950s a handful of Zen monks had come to the US as missionaries, primarily to work with Japanese-Americans. They were surprised to discover that, while few Asian immigrants were interested in meditation or monastic practice, growing numbers of whites wanted to move beyond reading about Zen to practicing meditation under their guidance. They founded Zen centers in Los Angeles, San Francisco, and eventually many other places. Students of these teachers, and later these students' own dharma heirs, formed much of the leadership cadre that built the network of Buddhist centers, journals, and other organizations mentioned above. We could tell related stories about Buddhist traditions besides Zen.

The Zen of white converts is quite different from Japanese Zen. It builds on the improvisational and jazz-inflected sensibility of the Beats, in contrast to the quasi-military discipline and veneration for ancestors in Japanese institutions. Its students are eclectic: they may dabble in yoga, depth psychology, and shamanism along with Zen. Importantly, whereas Japanese Zen is largely a male world, the US Zen community includes many women, including many leaders of major Zen centers.[27] In some cases this has led to contentious sexual politics when teachers and students became lovers. Other innovations of US Zen also push the envelope of what Buddhism can be. For example, in 1979 a former aerospace engineer named Bernard Glassman, a dharma heir of the founder of the Zen Center of Los Angeles, became the head of the Zen Center of New York. A benefactor gave his center a mansion near the Hudson River, and people expected Glassman to lead weekend retreats there. This is a typical way that US Buddhist leaders sustain themselves, given the lack of endowed institutions and day-to-day support from laity that Asian monks rely upon. However, Glassman chafed at this lifestyle. He wanted full-time monastic practice, and he wanted to shatter preconceptions about how Zen relates to US culture. So he started a catering business, and later a commercial bakery, to make his center self-sufficient. His students helped staff the bakery on the model of work commitments in Asian monasteries. Later he started a homeless shelter and employed some of its residents at the bakery. Still later, he founded the Zen Peacemaker Order, which has held retreats on the streets with homeless people and sponsored rituals at Auschwitz. In general, he told an interviewer, 'All the things that people say are not Zen are the things that I want to get involved with.'[28]

Who speaks for US Buddhism? What are the models for going for refuge to the Buddha, the dharma, and the sangha in the US? How can we tell if someone is stretching these models so far that they are not 'truly Buddhist' anymore? Obviously the classic Theravada sangha, with its full-time monks seeking nirvana in a symbiotic relationship with supportive laity, is a valid form of Buddhism. This model is also taking root in the US, although more among Southeast Asian immigrants than followers of Japanese traditions. However, forms of Buddhism very different from this model, such as Glassman's Zen bakery or Japanese-Americans who do not meditate but do sing 'Buddha Loves Me, This I Know' in Protestant-style churches, reflect decisions by the duly empowered leaders of major US Buddhist organizations. They have the right to tell non-Buddhists what 'real US Buddhists' are like, rather than vice versa. In any case, the diversity of US Buddhism dramatizes the dynamism and fluidity of Asian religions in the US. If we had more space, we could extend this exploration in many directions.

Race and Religious Tradition in an Era of Cultural Hybridity

Many of the interactions between mainstream US culture and racialized groups – Latino/as, Muslims, Native Americans, and so on – involve straightforward institutional racism and cultural disrespect from the white side, coupled with attempts by minorities to defend themselves against attacks or break through barriers to grow and thrive. However, these interactions also include complex forms of sharing, dialogue, and cultural cross-pollination. Although we must not ignore factors of power when thinking about these issues, not every case reduces to a simple power struggle between racial blocs.

Questions about racial dialogue and hybridity appear in many forms. One example returns us to the Italian-American *festa* in Harlem. After mid-century, Italians struggled to sustain their *festa* as people moved out of their old neighborhood. There was much hostility – expressed partly through the *festa* – between Italians and the Puerto Ricans who replaced them in East Harlem. In this conflict, Italians found an unexpected ally in Haitian immigrants from Brooklyn. Haitians traveled across New York to their church because it is dedicated to the same form of Mary that is venerated in Haiti – where it is also associated with the Vodou goddess Ezili Danto. As we have seen, many Haitians blend prayers to saints and *loa*, considering them manifestations of the same spiritual powers. Thus, they bring incense and offerings for Ezili Danto to the *festa*. In a striking example of the plasticity of US racial discourse, Italians disparaged Puerto Ricans as members of an inferior dark race who were not good Christians – even though the Puerto Ricans' skin tone and loyalty to Catholicism were the same as the Italians' – while simultaneously claiming that the Haitians were not really black (since they spoke a French dialect) and were not practicing Vodou at the *festa*. In other words, fluid racial–religious boundaries simultaneously increased and decreased group conflict, in ways that would be almost impossible to explain through an appeal to fixed racial essences.[29]

Another example of cross-pollination is the dialogue among immigrant Muslims, African-American Muslims, and Christians about the proper form of Islamic practice in the US. A basic aspect of the contemporary world, viewed from Muslim perspectives, is the nexus between modernity, colonialism, racism, and the Christian defeat of the Islamic empire. George W. Bush escalated such concerns when he spoke of his policies as a crusade, imprisoned US Muslim citizens under the Patriot Act, and subjected Muslims to interrogation that is illegal under international law, including torture and the desecration of the Qur'an. NCR leaders often make inflammatory anti-Muslim statements. Franklin Graham, the son and heir-apparent of Billy Graham, called Islam 'evil and wicked'; a former president of the Southern Baptist Convention stated that 'Christianity was founded by the virgin-born son of God, Jesus Christ. Islam was founded by Muhammad, a demon-possessed pedophile ... Jehovah's not going to turn you into a terrorist.'[30] When Muslims – as well as other Asian immigrants – seek to build mosques and temples, they often face protests, the use of zoning laws to block their plans, and vandalism.

Muslim responses to such hostility unfold in complex patterns, some of which lead Muslims to work with white Christian allies. One such pattern is combating stereotypes about fanatical Muslims. Both Muslims and their non-Muslim allies stress that Islam promotes peace and that the term 'jihad' does not ordinarily imply engaging in war, but rather struggling to do God's will (one might compare how Christians talk of 'fighting the good fight' despite their overall principles of seeking peace and justifying war only as a last resort). Another pattern is aligning Muslims behind US traditions of religious freedom and civil liberty; this is not a difficult stretch since many Muslims came to the US to escape religious persecution in their homelands. Yet another pattern is sharing in opposition to Islamists like Osama bin Laden, who is condemned by almost all US Muslims both because he attacked their country and because they see his targeting of non-combatants as an affront to Muslim values. (We might compare how mainstream Christians responded to the Christian terrorists who bombed the Oklahoma City Federal Building.) Of course, this does not prevent Muslims from lobbying alongside other citizens against US policies that they see tilting dangerously toward Israel.

Another understandable response to anti-Islamic pressures is for Muslims to rally behind their racial–religious communities in ways that carry forward certain anti-Western aspects of world Islam and/or the separatism of groups like the NOI. In part this is simply a variation on standard defensive responses of first-generation immigrants. Beyond this, however, Muslims are not always sure whether they can embrace aspects of the modern world such as women's rights and consumer capitalism without falling prey to individualism, injustice, and imperial conquest. They wonder if they can voice principled critiques of bin Laden without appearing to endorse US foreign policy.

Some disputed questions concern cultural style. Should Muslims have distinctive forms of dress, especially for women? How standoffish should they be toward US popular culture? Is it appropriate to promote Muslim popular music, roughly analogous to contemporary Christian music? Other questions concern ritual practice. Can Muslims harmonize mainstream lifestyles with a commitment to pray five times daily, maintain Friday as a day of prayer, and observe Islamic holidays? Should they embrace the US pattern of ending gender-segregated worship? Still other questions are political or legal. Should Muslims support interfaith dialogue and the separation of mosque and state, both in the US and in countries where the US wields influence? Should they organize their own schools? Should they enforce traditional prohibitions of alcohol and lending money at interest? Should they expand on Islamic traditions that support women's equality (Muslim women originally had more rights than in most other religions including Christianity) to forge alliances with Christian feminists, or should they join forces with the NCR to defend patriarchal power and resist sexual liberation? Should they carry forward traditions such as men receiving larger inheritances and enjoying advantages over women in cases of divorce, or should they use their tradition of prenuptial contracts to create forms of marriage similar to mainstream ones?[31] Variations on these debates are ongoing in forms that defy easy mapping – between converts and immigrants, immigrants from different countries and generations, men and women, and the overall Muslim community and the Christian mainstream. The future of US Islam hinges on how upcoming generations address such issues.[32]

Things were equally complicated in Native American communities. In addition to factors we have already introduced – urbanization, historic differences among tribes, diverse attitudes toward AIM activism and tribal governments, and so on – another factor was the flood of white seekers who approached Native people with their hunger for Cherokee crystals, New Age shamans, and authentic healing ceremonies. Sometimes such seekers were mere sources of amusement in Indian country, but at other times their romanticized spirituality threatened to push the religious ideas and political priorities of native people to the margins. White artists and scholars, steeped in English-language sources or a sense of personal calling, felt entitled to speak for native culture, especially if they assumed that true native culture was part of the past. Insofar as their books and museums taught young Indians about their culture, whites inserted themselves within the transmission of tradition across generations. In effect they declared themselves elders and hijacked native traditions for their own purposes. Such whites often focused on the noble but doomed ways of disappearing Indians, thus enabling themselves to discuss victims of colonialism without paying much attention to colonialism – or if questions about it did arise, they could focus on past defeats (lamented as tragic) rather than ongoing resistance (treated as irrelevant to their spiritual concerns). This dynamic allows people who are complicit in ongoing conquest to transform their guilty consciences into self-congratulation about their liberal sensitivity. Few Indian people were impressed. As one commented, 'any of you who are prompted by *Dances With Wolves* [a pro-Indian Western film of 1990] to make a trip out to Indian country to get in touch with the earth should go soon, before your destination of choice is contaminated by a tribally-owned toxic waste dump.'[33]

Further complicating this situation, centuries of intermarriage and cultural cross-pollination led to a situation in which the majority religion of contemporary Native America is Christianity.[34] Although this disappoints whites who prefer exotic Indians who go down in flames and nobly disappear, in fact a Hopi becoming Catholic or a Cherokee becoming Baptist makes as much sense as an African-American becoming Baptist. That is, it may or may not make sense (given that people were conquered in the name of a Christian God) depending on whether native Christians can control their own institutions and use them to address their needs. Most native communities include a spectrum of debate about such matters. At one pole are traditionalists who maintain older languages and rituals relatively unchanged and keep them secret, as well as AIM activists (often urban and pan-tribal) who argue somewhat like Malcolm X about the need for autonomy and separation from white society. At another pole are Indians who turn away from tradition and embrace forms of Christianity that they consider superior to the pagan ways of their ancestors. (Here we might recall the people who feel that 'real Norwegian religion' can advance beyond its Viking stage.) People at both poles assume a zero-sum choice between Christianity and tribal tradition.

Most native people fall between such extremes. They both embrace Christianity – Catholics, Protestants, and Mormons are all strong – and continue at least limited traditional practices. Often they do this on parallel tracks, somewhat like one could play both jazz music and basketball but not at the same time. Thus, they may attend sweat lodge ceremonies on Saturday and mass on Sunday.[35] Other times they fuse traditions, just as one could develop a musical style that blends jazz and country. Thus, they may bring sacred pipes into churches, pray to Jesus in sweat lodges, treat native spiritual powers as equivalent to angels or saints, and blend the Sun Dance's rituals of sacrifice with Christian theology. Some clergy promote such blending based on their belief that Christianity is a universal truth that can perfect and harmonize local traditions, somewhat like Christians see themselves completing Jewish teachings or Vivekananda saw himself taking up Christian truths into a higher Hindu synthesis. Other people reject this approach; they see themselves exploring an overlap between two equally powerful traditions or grounding Christianity in deeper forms of wisdom. Indian intellectuals vigorously deny the premise (hidden in much Western thought) that embodied relationships between communities and sacred landscapes are less important than (purportedly universal) conceptual abstractions.[36]

Some whites fear that if they take too much interest in native culture, they will fall into the role of New Agers who hijack native tradition and generally get in the way – yet if they do *not* pursue such interests they risk complicity in racist traditions that neither grasp the importance of native culture nor address ongoing power dynamics between the two communities. Either horn of this dilemma may be decisive from case to case. In some ways this is a lose–lose proposition for whites – a mild inversion of the lose–lose choice historically faced by Indians, who risked losing their culture if they fell into a melting pot that sought to remake them, yet risked military annihilation if they stayed aloof from it. However, it is also a win–win proposition for whites who are serious about becoming informed allies of Indian people, because whichever horn of the dilemma they select, they can find native allies. The issue shifts to choosing allies wisely in particular cases.

Not all attempts at solidarity are equally constructive. US culture continues to stereotype Indian people, and many books about native issues do more harm than good. Moreover, anyone who remains grounded in an individualistic mindset and uninvolved in native communities is likely to misunderstand these communities. One must start somewhere, and as long as a seeker is not damaging a native group, then learning more is usually better than knowing less – even if one is not contributing to the community. However, in the long run establishing relationships with a community and contributing to its well-being are not merely desirable on their own terms, but essential for anyone who claims to speak for Native Americans. From a native standpoint, such relationships determine which aspects of native culture are worth learning and which should be kept secret – seeking additional knowledge 'for its own sake' is pointless and borderline racist, like procuring a powerful Hopi *kachina* doll and letting it gather dust on a shelf. One Mohawk gave these instructions to seekers who asked to participate in a ceremony: invite people to a feast you prepare, listen to their problems and advice, and then repeat the process three more times. 'That's it! You've done an Indian ceremony!' The point is that one cannot 'prepare to participate in a ceremony ... other than by becoming a member of the community enacting the ceremony.'[37]

There is no simple recipe for becoming a trusted ally of a community, but one rule of thumb is to notice how much of US society remains constituted by the interplay of red and white. At this level everyone who lives in the US is part of a dialogue – implicit or explicit – with native culture. Another rule of thumb is to uphold the integrity of native traditions as they interact with emerging challenges, and to contribute to the community's health and survival. For example, if the top priority on a given reservation is blocking a toxic waste dump, this may require an alliance of traditionalists, native churches, AIM activists, New Age environmentalists, and nearby Lutheran ranchers. This is not merely hypothetical: such a 'Cowboy and Indian Alliance' blocked the testing of missiles in the Black Hills in the 1980s.[38]

Mainstream Culture Warriors Respond to Rising Pluralism

For Protestants who nursed hopes of rebounding from their disestablishment of the 1920s, the flowering of diversity after 1965 was a challenge at best and a nightmare at worst. However, liberals and conservatives approached the issue differently. Liberals took pluralism more or less in stride, since they supported civil rights and moderate feminism, had long made peace with the modern world, and were interested in comparing insights with other religions. Nevertheless, some liberals feared that the US might lose the minimal cohesiveness it needed to thrive if it tolerated too much activism by feminists and racial minorities, as well as too much raw cultural difference from unassimilated immigrants and incompatible religions. Liberals worried less about maintaining overt hegemony – a goal they presupposed in the 1950s and had largely abandoned by the 1990s – than about maintaining the expectation that minorities should be moderate and civil, as opposed to fundamentalist or 'tribalist.'[39]

According to such liberals, all citizens should agree that religious commitment is a private matter and accept the ground-rules of a public sphere that made decisions within a framework of Enlightenment reason, as opposed to appealing to many forms of religious revelation and tradition. There was limited friction between such ground-rules and the longstanding liberal practice of using Enlightenment yardsticks to test what parts of its own traditions to keep. Moreover, diversity posed a smaller threat to the status quo if religious values were defined as private and kept off the table of public negotiation. Thus, critics charged that liberals were not really promoting a level playing field for consensus building, but rather a field tilted to their own advantage. According to such critics, liberals were pressuring minorities not to rock the boat and to accept a hegemonic system that retained a Protestant flavor.

This picture becomes murkier if we add the NCR to the mix, since its leaders treated diversity more as a nightmare than as something to take in stride. They rarely supported minority rights unless they could benefit from claiming to be a persecuted minority, and they literally perceived much of the nation's religious diversity as demonic. For example, a popular evangelical novel portrayed New Age channeling as satanic possession, and a Pentecostal minister in Guatemala stated that 'the army does not massacre Indians; it massacres demons, and the Indians are demon possessed, they are communists.'[40] NCR leaders commonly compared feminists with Nazis, for example by comparing gender-inclusive liturgies to pro-Nazi theologies of the 1930s or treating abortion as genocide comparable with the Holocaust.

Given such attitudes, the NCR's goal was less to foster dialogue toward consensus in a neutral public space and more to build hegemony – which often led non-Christians to worry less about bias in the liberal Christians approach than about working with such liberals to build alliances against the NCR. Nevertheless, the situation was complex. The liberal playing field was tilted as much against fundamentalists who appealed to Biblical literalism as it was against Muslims or Wiccans. This led the NCR to complain about bias in working assumptions about the arguments and evidence that could be used in public debates (disputes about creationism are a classic example). After the 1920s, liberals had dismissed fundamentalists as a prime example of people who disqualified themselves from seats at a table of public deliberation. By the 1980s at the latest, evangelicals were loudly demanding seats at this table. Often the result was confusion as the NCR complained about bias in ground-rules that were designed to keep everyone's 'table manners' *unbiased*. Moreover, after gaining seats in the name of equal rights, the NCR often used their seats to promote policies that denied equal rights to their opponents.

Although such ambiguities often took center stage in the culture war, the main outlines of the situation remained clear. The NCR's underlying goal was to combat the notion that it was only one minority at the table – or, in other words, that its disestablishment was a settled matter. If Muslims desired a law based on the Qur'an, the liberal ground-rules expected them either to offer a rationale for this law that could be widely accepted, or to be content to follow the Qur'an on a private voluntary basis. However, if the NCR desired a law based on the Bible, it often had enough votes to pass the law over liberal objections. Alternatively, if the NCR lacked such votes or a judge struck down one of its laws on First Amendment grounds, it mobilized to gain more votes by presenting itself as a persecuted victim of liberal bias.

Early in the new century, such struggles showed no sign of fading: neither side had enough power to defeat the other and powerful interests found it useful to prolong their strife. Culture warriors built entire careers on battling people on the opposing side of the war. Often they mobilized support through provocative quotations about their enemies, such as Pat Robertson's claim – first used in one of his fundraising letters, and later in efforts to raise money to fight him – that feminism is 'a socialist anti-family political movement that encourages women to leave their husbands, kill their children, practice witchcraft, destroy capitalism, and become lesbians.'[41] Importantly, Republicans perfected techniques of channelling the frustration of working-class voters away from economic elites (read: the 'old class') toward a 'new class' of government bureaucrats and cultural elites – a group that Republicans tried to portray as overwhelmingly liberal and secular, although it is obvious that bureaucrats, pundits, and celebrities can equally well be conservative. Thomas Frank described the dynamic: 'Vote to stop abortion; receive a rollback in capital gains taxes. Vote to make our country strong again; receive deindustrialization. Vote to screw those politically correct college professors; receive energy deregulation ... Vote to strike a blow against elitism; receive a social order in which wealth is more concentrated than ever before in our lifetime.'[42] Although critics like Frank argued that corporate priorities weakened the society and blighted the futures of working people, it remained unclear how much such critics could dent the hegemony of conservative populist discourse. The more that critics attacked the right and demanded respect for diversity, the more conservatives fed off the energy of their critiques to portray themselves as persecuted defenders of beleaguered moral traditions – a virtuous remnant struggling to survive a liberal onslaught. In this context, the authoritarian aspect of conservative theology – its stress on obedience to divine power and authority – strongly reinforced a hegemonic discourse.

Notes

1 Eugenie Scott, *Evolution Versus Creationism* (Berkeley: University of California Press, 2005); H. Allen Orr, 'Devolution: intelligent design versus Darwin,' *New Yorker* 5/30/05, 40–52; Margaret Talbot, 'Darwin in the dock: intelligent design goes to school,' *New Yorker* 12/5/05, 66–79.

2 George Marsden, 'The case of the excluded middle: creation versus evolution in America,' in Bellah and Greenspahn, *Uncivil Religion*, 132–55. Some of the key theistic evolutionists process theologians who extend theories about divine immanence in dialogue with the metaphysics of Alfred North Whitehead, postmodern science, pragmatism, and Buddhism. See John Cobb, Jr., *Postmodernism and Public Policy* (Albany: SUNY Press, 2002).

3 Data from Gallup Polls cited by National Center for Science Education, accessed at

http://www.ncseweb.org/resources/news/2004/US/724_public_view_of_creationism_and_11_19_2004.asp/.

4 Kaplan, *With God On Their Side*, 91–128. On global warming see Elizabeth Kolbert's three-part article, 'The Climate of Man,' *New Yorker* 4/25/05, 5/2/2005, and 5/9/05.

5 Harding, *Book of Jerry Falwell*, 223–4, 227; she alludes to Clifford Geertz, *Interpretation of Cultures* (New York: Basic Books, 1973), 6.

6 Janet Jakobsen and Ann Pellegrini, *Love the Sin: Sexual Regulation and the Limits of Religious Tolerance* (New York: New York University Press, 2003); Kathy Rudy, *Sex and the Church: Gender, Homosexuality, and the Transformation of Christian Ethics* (Boston: Beacon, 1999); Tanya Erzen, *Straight to Jesus: Sexual and Christian Conversions in the Ex-Gay Movement* (Berkeley: University of California Press, 2006).

7 Statement by British Quakers summarized in Tom Driver, 'On taking sex seriously,' *C&C*, 10/14/63, 176. Some paragraphs in this section are adapted from Hulsether, *Building a Protestant Left*, 175–80.

8 James McGraw, 'Scandal of peculiarity,' *C&C*, 4/16/73, 63–8. The Metropolitan Community Church was founded by Troy Perry in the 1970s and grew into the top denomination for GLBT people who want an evangelical worship style. For more on gay evangelicals see Mel White, *Stranger at the Gate* (New York: Penguin, 1995). Theologically liberal GLBT people often gravitate to gay-friendly niches in mainline denominations; the United Church of Christ is especially important because its local congregations have autonomy. For more on this issue see Hendershot, *Shaking the World for Jesus*, 114–42.

9 Norman Pittenger, 'Homosexuality and the Christian tradition,' *C&C*, 8/5/74, 178–81; Nelson, 'Homosexuality and the Church,' in *Ethics in the Present Tense: Significant Writings from Christianity and Crisis Magazine*, Leon Howell and Vivian Lindermayer, eds (New York: Association Press, 1991), 168–82.

10 Carter Heyward, 'Coming out: a journey without maps,' in Howell and Lindermayer, *Ethics in the Present Tense*, 182–7.

11 John Cobb, 'Is the Church ready to legislate on sex?,' *C&C*, 5/14/84, 183.

12 Editors, 'Debate on homosexuality,' *C&C*, 5/30/77, 116; Louie Crew, 'Barry and me, and the angels,' *C&C*, 3/2/93, 52–3.

13 Moore, *Selling God*, 256, 262; Vine Deloria, Jr., 'Bush's Indian Policy,' lecture at Carleton College, ca. 1989, videotape in author's possession; Shirley MacLaine, 'Excerpt from *Dancing in the Light*,' in Laderman and León, *Religion and American Cultures*, 918–25; Laderman, 'Shamanism in the New Age,' in McDannell, *Religions of the United States in Practice*, 268–83.

14 Frances Fitzgerald, *Cities on a Hill: A Journey Through Contemporary American Cultures* (New York: Simon and Schuster, 1986), 247–302; Paramahansa Yogananda, *Autobiography of a Yogi* (Los Angeles: Self-Realization Fellowship, 1998).

15 Moore, *Selling God*, 249, 256.

16 Patrica Brown, 'Megachurches as minitowns,' *New York Times* 5/9/02; National Public Radio, *All Things Considered* 7/18/2005; Ammerman, *Pillars of Faith*, p. 107. Jeff Sharlet profiles an NCR megachurch in 'Soldiers of Christ,' *Harper's* (May 2005). The Buddhist Churches of America, discussed below, have around 20,000 members in sixty churches according to Steve Prothero, 'Buddhism in America,' in Laderman and León, *Religion and American Cultures*, 50.

17 For the thongs see *http://landoverbaptist.org*; pendants discussed in 'VH-I celebrity

religion,' videotape in author's possession, no date, ca. 2005.

18 Stephen Powers, Stanley Rothman, and David Rothman, *Hollywood's America: Social and Political Themes in Motion Pictures* (Boulder: Westview Press, 1996).

19 According to Walsh, *Sin and Censorship*, 330, one watchdog group has oaths similar to the Legion's, plus a rating system that urged 'extreme caution' in watching *Schindler's List* (1994) because of nudity and obscenity and condemned *Mrs. Doubtfire* (1994) because the Bible states that men should not wear women's clothes. A critique often cited by the NCR – although too tendentious to have scholarly value – is Michael Medved, *Hollywood vs. America: Popular Culture and the War on Traditional Values* (San Francisco: HarperCollins, 1992).

20 Talib Kweli, *The Beautiful Struggle* (Rawkus Records, 2004).

21 Not all converts are white. Soka Gakkai International, a branch of Nichiren Buddhism, is among the most racially diverse of US religions, with many Japanese-American, African-American, and Latino/a members. It is also the largest US Buddhist group due to energetic missionary activities. Soka Gakkai stresses humanistic and this-worldly benefits from chanting the *Lotus Sutra*. See Richard Hughes Seager, 'Buddhist chanting in Soka Gakkai International,' in McDannell, *Religions of the United States in Practice*, 112–20.

22 In addition to citations in Chapter 5, see Charles Prebish and Kenneth Tanaka, eds, *Faces of Buddhism in America* (Berkeley: University of California Press, 1998); Prebish and Martin Baumann, eds, *Westward Dharma: Buddhism Beyond Asia* (Berkeley: University of California Press, 2002). I am grateful to my colleagues Rachelle Scott and especially Miriam Levering for much of my understanding of Buddhism reflected in this section.

23 We could mention Chinese as an earlier group, since they came to California in large numbers after 1850, bringing a religion influenced by Buddhism, Taoism, and Confucianism. However, most Chinese were single men and the 1882 Chinese Exclusion Act cut off immigration; thus the Japanese became the largest US Asian group. See David Yoo, 'Religious History of Japanese Americans in California,' *Religions in Asian America*, Pyong Gap Min and Jun Ha Kim, eds (Walnut Creek: Altamira Press, 2002), 121–42.

24 Recently the Tibetan Buddhism of the Dalai Lama and the politicized 'engaged Buddhism' of people such as the Vietnamese monk Thich Nhat Hanh have gained on Zen as the Buddhism of choice for white seekers, but it is hard to imagine their popularity without the foundation built by Zen.

25 Jack Kerouac, *The Dharma Bums* (1958: New York: Penguin, 1976); Miriam Levering, 'Jack Kerouac in Berkeley: Reading *The Dharma Bums* as the work of a Buddhist writer,' *Pacific World: Journal of the Institute of Buddhist Studies* no. 6 (2004), 7–26.

26 Gary Synder, 'Smokey the Bear sutra,' accessed online at *http://www.marigold.com/rt88/bear.html*.

27 Miriam Levering and Grace Jill Schireson, 'Women and Zen Buddhisms,' in *Encyclopedia of Women and Religion in North America*, Rosemary Skinner Keller and Rosemary Ruether, eds (Bloomington: Indiana University Press, 2006), 639–45. See also Marianne Dresser, ed., *Buddhist Women on the Edge: Contemporary Perspectives from the Western Frontier* (Berkeley: North Atlantic Books, 1996).

28 Quoted in Helen Tworkov, *Zen in America: Five Teachers and the Search for an American Buddhism* (New York: Kodansha, 1994), 151.

29 Robert Orsi, 'The religious boundaries of an in-between people: street *feste* and the problem of the dark-skinned other in Italian Harlem, 1920–1990,' *American*

Quarterly 44 (1992), 313–47.

30 Deborah Caldwell, 'How Islam-bashing got cool', *Religious Studies News* vol. 18, no. 4 (2003), 13, 27.

31 On gender discourses in Islam see Tate, *Little X*, Judith Tucker, *Gender and Islamic History* (Washington: American Historical Association, 1993); and Leila Ahmed, 'The women of Islam,' *Transition* vol. 9, no. 3 (2000), 78–97.

32 In addition to sources already cited see Bruce Lawrence, *New Faiths, Old Fears: Muslims and Other Asian Immigrants in American Religious Life* (New York: Columbia University Press, 2002); Khaled Abou el Fadl, *Islam and the Challenge of Democracy* (Princeton: Princeton University Press, 2004); and Steven Barboza, *American Jihad: Islam after Malcolm X* (New York: Doubleday, 1994).

33 Robert Allen Warrior, 'Dancing with wastes,' *C&C* 7/15/91, 216. A key statement on this issue is Wendy Rose, 'The great pretenders: further reflections on white-shamanism,' in Jaimes, *State of Native America*, 403–21.

34 In addition to sources already cited, see James Treat, ed., *Native and Christian? Indigenous Voices on Religious Identity in the United States and Canada* (New York: Routledge, 1995). Note that this section deals primarily with people north of Mexico; thus it brackets the major issue of Latin American mestizo culture.

35 We might also imagine someone who is both an urban dweller and wilderness camper. Using this analogy, and remembering the difficulty of disentangling native religions from whole ways of life, we can appreciate how the meaning of native tradition is changing. Certain ceremonies have grown more important, others are waning, and the overall picture (especially for urban Indians) sometimes tends toward privatization.

36 Vine Deloria, Jr., *For This Land: Writings on Religion and America*, James Treat, ed. (New York: Routledge, 1999). This is the best context in which to approach John Neihardt, *Black Elk Speaks* (Lincoln: University of Nebraska Press, 2004) a famous book adapted from the oral testimony of a Lakota holy man by a white poet. Black Elk fused his personal vision (received in Lakota language and cosmology), Sun Dancing, the pan-tribal religion of Ghost Dancing, and long-time work as a Catholic catechist. He infused this combination with a calling to struggle against conquest and help his people thrive. AIM activists, New Agers, and Catholic priests all claim that his book supports them; see Clyde Holler, ed., *The Black Elk Reader* (Syracuse: Syracuse University Press, 2000) and Paul Steinmetz, *Pipe, Bible, and Peyote Among the Oglala Lakota* (Knoxville: University of Tennessee Press, 1990).

37 Christopher Ronwanien:te Jocks, 'Spirituality for sale: sacred knowledge in the consumer age,' *American Indian Quarterly* vol. 20, no. 3/4 (1996), 415–31.

38 Zoltan Grossman, 'Cowboy and Indian alliances in the northern plains,' *Agricultural History* vol. 77, no. 2 (2003), 355–89.

39 For more discussion see the Conclusion.

40 Diamond, *Roads to Dominion*, 238; Frank Peretti, *This Present Darkness* (Wheaton: Crossway, 1986).

41 Cited in 'Roundtable discussion: backlash,' *Journal of Feminist Studies in Religion* vol. 10, no. 1 (1994), 91.

42 Thomas Frank, *What's the Matter With Kansas?* (New York: Henry Holt, 2004), 7. See also Barbara Ehrenreich, *Fear of Falling: the Inner Life of the Middle Class* (New York: Pantheon, 1989).

Conclusion: Consensus, Pluralism, and Hegemony in US Religion

Now that we have explored some of the key names and themes in US religion, let us step back to consider some overall patterns in their interaction. It would be possible to use this book (especially its chapters that introduce key players) simply as an inventory of people to know about for further study. Each group we have discussed is important on its own terms, and our maps of US culture will be incomplete unless we grasp how religion informs everyday life and wider political processes. Still, to stop at this point – with a sense that being aware of many religions is important for its own sake – is not fully satisfying. From the beginning we have stressed how religions have many dimensions and can be mapped differently from place to place. We have promoted awareness of the strengths and weaknesses of various lenses that we can use to analyze them. Thus, questions arise as our tour draws to a close: are there patterns in how our players relate to each other, larger reasons for mapping their interactions, or especially useful ways to approach them?

A second possible way to use this book (especially its more detailed case studies) is as a model for focusing on specific issues – for example, class, gender, consumerism, or race – and exploring how a range of religious people interact with such issues. Since it would take a lifetime to relate a full list of issues to a complete set of religious players, we selected a few inquiries to pursue during our mid-day breaks and evening stopovers. Hopefully readers are now in a better position to extrapolate from these cases and make informed choices among the many topics worth further exploration. Different readers will choose to expand upon different issues – but, once again, can we say anything in closing to contextualize and orient such choices?

Beyond these two ways of looking forward, we can also take stock of cases we have already explored and reflect on how they fit together. Three frameworks for such reflection are common both among religious people and scholars who study them. By clarifying the strengths and weaknesses of these frames, we can move a long way toward grasping the underlying logic of ongoing debates. If we bear these frames in mind and learn to translate among their ways of seeing, we can walk away from this study with three rough-and-ready tools to help us thrive in debates that we will encounter in future travels.[1]

The first approach is a consensus model. It responds to the diversity of US culture – as well as related concerns about secularization and individualism – by worrying about a loss of purpose for the society as a whole. One of its background assumptions is that healthy societies need moral cohesiveness on basic values. Consensus scholars are often informed by sociological theory in the tradition of Emile Durkheim; they may also appeal to natural law, the Bible, or the Qur'an.[2] However they buttress their case, such scholars argue that trying to build a society without common values is like building a house on sand. In a worst-case scenario, a lack of moral consensus could create a vacuum that a tyrant could fill or start the US down a road of sectarian strife similar to processes that tore apart the former Yugoslavia. Some scholars fear that such scenarios are already unfolding, with secular relativism playing the role of the sandy foundation, liberal bureaucrats in the role of the vacuum-filling tyrant, and racial and/or sexual sub-cultures in the role of fomenting sectarian strife. Others merely fear that such scenarios could develop in the future, and that meanwhile the nation is weakening.

Conservative evangelicals are the most vocal advocates of this model, but it also has supporters among Catholics and the Protestant establishment.[3] We can distinguish between conservative and moderate versions. Conservatives tend to present the US as a Christian nation. They do so with various levels of stridency, ranging from bald proposals for replacing the Constitution with a theocracy based on Biblical law to subtle arguments that start from a premise that societies need common values and proceed to a conclusion that the only viable candidate for such values is Christianity. Catholics stress natural law while Protestants stress a covenant with God reaching back to the Puritans. Both propose to safeguard appropriate minority rights – although, of course, one might ask what they mean by 'appropriate.' However nuanced, their goal is to revitalize a Christian (or 'Judaeo-Christian') consensus that they perceive to have been slipping away at least since the 1960s, and in some respects since the nineteenth century. Thus, their maps of US religion pay much attention to – and in the process often exaggerate – Christian aspects of the Deism that underpins the Constitution, historic precedents for laws establishing religion, and ways that Protestants established a cultural core to which other groups assimilated. Advocates of this model perceive no necessary conflict between consensus and religious freedom. On the contrary, they see themselves safeguarding democracy from tyranny or chaos; they feel that groups outside the consensus they promote should thank them for their vigilance and toleration.

Moderate versions of this consensus model seek to strengthen a sense of the common good against individualism that they see running rampant on both the right and left. Their classic proposal is to strengthen civil religion – that is, a shared commitment to the harmonious mingling of God and country, or (more precisely) to shared values underpinning religion and democracy at their best. Such civil religion builds partly on traditions like singing 'God Bless America' and celebrating Thanksgiving, and partly on the quasi-deification of heroes like George Washington, documents like the Constitution, pilgrimage sites like Mount Rushmore, and symbols like the flag. Although this approach assumes an overlap between patriotism and Christianity, it rejects overt 'Christian nation' rhetoric and invites non-Christians to share in the overlap – for example, through Buddhists sponsoring Boy Scout troops or rabbis praying at interfaith Thanksgiving services. Its heroes are Deists like Jefferson and its nostalgia is not for Protestant hegemony in the nineteenth century, but for 1950s liberal consensus and 1960s civil rights coalitions. Both moderate and conservative consensus models share the goal of strengthening common values and a fear of excessive individualism and pluralism.[4]

The second broad model is pluralist. It stresses respecting diversity as opposed to building consensus – or, more precisely, the form of consensus it promotes is a relatively thin agreement to live and let live in religious matters and to celebrate diversity. This model begins less from fear that the center will not hold, and more from fear that people will suffer discrimination based on cultural difference. Its goal is a social framework that is neutral enough to allow creative differences to be fully expressed. Although the NCR paints this approach as amoral and relativistic – and although certain pluralists may even encourage this perception – there is a longstanding tradition of defending this approach on explicitly theological grounds, as a polity well matched to spiritual humility. That is, theistic defenders of this model assume that God speaks to different people in different ways and that every form of religion (including their own) is imperfect. All should stand on equal ground, subject to critique from the perspective of divine transcendence.[5]

Despite starting from different root concerns, moderate versions of consensus and pluralist approaches overlap. Both defend forms of liberal civil religion – thicker and more substantive versions for the consensus-minded and thinner versions stressing religious freedom for pluralists – as a framework within which diverse sub-cultures can interact harmoniously, with enough shared values and agreement on ground-rules to provide a healthy degree of social cohesiveness. If everyone agrees on minimal rules of the game, civil religion can function as an open public space for all religions – a level playing field on which all comers can hammer out agreements on basic issues.[6]

As we have seen, determining what constitutes a level playing field is easier said than done, as is deciding which players are legitimate or which referees are fair. People who feel that a liberal field is tilted against them – and who (unlike the NCR) harbor little hope of taking over as referees – often embrace more radical versions of the pluralist model that exist in tension with civil religion. Such people are concerned to assert and celebrate the distinctive strengths of groups from beyond the mainstream that have been neglected or disdained in the past. Rather than working for social harmony, their priority is empowering alternative communities to disrupt and renegotiate forms of harmony that exclude or devalue them. Their underlying framework is not Durkheimian sociology, but theories of postmodernity and cultural difference that attack Enlightenment universals as illusory.[7]

A third approach, returning us full circle to our Introduction, is to analyze cases where religion, culture, and politics come together in terms of the hegemonic and counter-hegemonic goals that are in play.[8] A hegemony model can encompass the other two frames and clarify their strengths and weaknesses. We can easily recast calls for consensus as attempts to build forms of cultural hegemony. We have noted that hegemony is not necessarily a bad thing, but that underdogs who are disadvantaged by particular forms of hegemony may wish to consider alternative approaches. To what extent is it a given that US society requires a common morality based on the Bible? Might the society be stronger if no one pushed for this, because less energy would be wasted on unnecessary conflict? Would it be better – especially for minorities but also for majorities – to live in a land where a live-and-let-live approach is hegemonic? Conversely, does a society that valorizes postmodern pluralism reflect the hegemony of consumerism and dog-eat-dog corporate values? Insofar as this is the core problem in some contexts, the top priority may not be to celebrate diversity, but rather to strengthen counter-hegemonic movements that critique corporate values in the name of the common good – whether they advance this critique using religious values of justice and compassion, Enlightenment values of equal rights and citizenship, or some combination of the two. The issue becomes not a straight up or down vote for common values, but a debate about what forms of shared morality should be priorities and how diverse groups can work together toward such priorities.

Adopting pluralist approaches (for example, including women, blacks, and Buddhists in our maps) can uproot consensus models that mask the internal complexities and multiple levels of conflict in US religion. In this regard, pluralist models may be counter-hegemonic, and their way of framing issues may be crucial for people who need to establish minimal levels of recognition and equal opportunity. However, a lack of cultural recognition is not always the form of hegemony that underdogs are most worried about. Feminists may be pleased that they won the right to vote and to sit at tables of power, and they may be quick to fight anyone who tries to roll back these rights on religious grounds – but their top concern may be that decisions at this table are made on the principle of 'one dollar, one vote' rather than 'one person, one vote,' and that the specific woman at the table is Condoleezza Rice. African-Americans may be pleased that slave spirituals and black women's quilts receive equal respect alongside white male theologies in textbooks that celebrate a pluralist mosaic – yet still dissatisfied if the relations between blacks and whites are primarily conceived as harmonious and pluralistic rather than as violent and oppressive. They may be more concerned about how ideologies of color-blindness and multiculturalism distract from institutional racism. In short, a pluralistic approach may itself function as a form of hegemony to mask other forms of power imbalance.

Therefore – although there is often much value in consensus and pluralist models – at times it is better to focus directly on the hegemonies and counter-hegemonies involved in specific cases of lived religion, as opposed to beginning from concerns with building consensus or celebrating diversity. Especially in cases where suffering or oppression is acute, the task is to address the top priority problem. For example, suppose that people are being tortured or raped. It might be useful in the long run to build a moral consensus about the barbarity of torture, shared by both torturers and victims. It might be useful to explore and translate between divergent understandings of what constitutes sexual consent in different cultures. In the long run, it is even conceivable that rape and torture victims might want to reflect – informed by theologies that stress how both oppressors and oppressed are equal in God's eyes – about whether they share common ground with their victimizers or whether they made mistakes that played some part in their suffering (some people consider this theologically profound; others see it as an example of hegemony at its most disturbing). However, at least in the short run – and possibly in the long run as well – these approaches are perverse. The priority problem is to focus on the violence and how to stop it. By extension, there are many places on the US religious landscape where the priority is to focus on acute oppression and on how religion can help underdogs survive and overcome it. Although it is not always easy to discern what forms of hegemony are emergencies of this kind – recall our executive who feels victimized because he is left-handed – this is often a compelling way to understand what religions do.

Analyses of hegemony only provide a framework for thinking, not a substitute for it. The task becomes learning to think wisely – in concrete cases – about both harmonious pluralism and intractable conflict, both diversity and power imbalance. When does it make sense to stress equal recognition for all groups? When it is better to distinguish between larger and smaller groups or divergent visions of the future? Which forms of hegemony are trivial and which are foundational? Insofar as we have assumed that there is not just one cut-and-dried route through the US religious landscape, nor just one set of landmarks on any given route, nor one single kind of map to guide a trip, we have also assumed that there are no simple answers to such questions. As our tour comes to a close and we take our leave, readers will have to think for themselves about such matters. Hopefully we have learned enough about key religious players and their interactions to do so in ways that are at least better informed, and perhaps even wiser.

Notes

1 This three-way distinction represents a set of ideal types; it does not fully reflect the nuance of every scholar. Rather than opening a discussion of scholars whose work cuts across more than one of these types, this section is a synthetic reflection on books already cited. For additional exploration see William Swatos and James Wellman, eds, *The Power of Religious Publics: Staking Claims in American Society* (Westport: Greenwood Press, 1999), Mary Douglas and Steven Tipton, eds, *Religion in America: Spirituality in a Secular Age* (Boston: Beacon Press, 1983), Tweed, *Re-Telling US Religious History*, Heclo and McClay, *Religion Returns to the Public Square*, and Kenneth Aman, ed., *Border Regions of Faith* (Maryknoll: Orbis, 1987).

2 On sociological theory underlying this section see Anthony Giddens, *Capitalism and Modern Social Theory: an Analysis of the Writing of Marx, Durkheim, and Max Weber* (New York: Cambridge University Press, 1971); Brian Morris, *Anthropological Studies of Religion* (Cambridge: Cambridge University Press, 1987), Casanova, *Public Religions in the Modern World*, Hulsether, 'Religion and culture,' in Hinnells, *Routledge Companion to the Study of Religion*, 489–508, and Nancy Fraser, *Justice Interruptus: Critical Reflections on the "Postsocialist" Condition'* (New York: Routledge, 1997).

3 Good examples include Neuhaus and Cromartie, *Piety and Politics*; see also citations above on neo-conservatives and evangelicals.

4 Russell Richey and Donald Jones, eds, *American Civil Religion* (New York: Harper and Row, 1974); Robert Bellah et al., *Habits of the Heart: Individualism and Commitment in American Life* (Berkeley: University of California, 1985), Bellah, 'Is there a common American culture?,' in Swatos and Wellman, *Power of Religious Publics*, 53–68; Charles Reynolds and Ralph Norman, eds, *Community in America: the Challenge of Habits of the Heart* (Berkeley: University of California Press, 1988).

5 Hutchison, *Religious Pluralism in America*; Moore, *Godless Constitution*.

6 Martin Marty, *The One and the Many: America's Struggle for the Common Good* (Cambridge, MA: Harvard University Press, 1997).

7 Fraser, *Justice Interruptus*; John Rajchman, ed., *The Identity in Question* (New York: Routledge, 1995); Marjorie Garber and Rebecca Walkowitz, eds, *One Nation Under God?: Religion and American Culture* (New York: Routledge, 1999); C. Richard King, ed., *Postcolonial America* (Urbana: University of Illinois Press, 2000).

8 Many texts cited above reflect this approach; examples that use hegemony theory explicitly include Rhys Williams, 'Public religion and hegemony: contesting the language of the common good,' in Swatos and Wellman, *Power of Religious Publics*, 169–86; West, *Democracy Matters*, Hulsether, *Building a Protestant Left*, and Rebecca Chopp, 'Christianity, democracy, and feminist theology,' in *Christianity and Democracy in Global Context*, John Witte, Jr., ed. (Boulder: Westview Press, 1993), 111–29.

Index